A Slender Thread

ESCAPING DISASTER IN THE HIMALAYA

Stephen Venables

arrow books

Published in the United Kingdom in 2001 by
Arrow Books

13

Copyright © Stephen Venables 2000

The right of Stephen Venables to be identified as the author
of this work has been asserted by Stephen Venables in accordance with
the Copyright, Designs and Patents Act, 1988

First published in the United Kingdom in 2000 by Hutchinson

The Random House Group Limited
20 Vauxhall Bridge Road, London SW1V 2SA

www.randomhouse.co.uk

Addresses for companies within The Random House Group Limited can be found at:
www.randomhouse.co.uk/offices.htm

The Random House Group Limited Reg. No. 954009

A CIP catalogue record for this book
is available from the British Library

Typeset in Stempel Garamond by MATS, Southend-on-Sea, Essex

ISBN 9780099279068

The Random House Group Limited supports The Forest Stewardship
Council® (FSC®), the leading international forest-certification organisation.
Our books carrying the FSC label are printed on FSC®-certified paper.
FSC is the only forest-certification scheme supported by the leading
environmental organisations, including Greenpeace. Our
paper procurement policy can be found at
www.randomhouse.co.uk/environment

MIX
Paper from
responsible sources
FSC® C016897

Printed and bound in Great Britain by Clays Ltd, St Ives plc

for Rosie, Ollie and Edmond

Contents

Contents

Illustrations

First Section

Building the top camp on Panch Chuli V. *SV*
Sustad brews afternoon tea. *SV*
Telkot and the top camp at sunrise. *SV*
Climbing the rock pillar on Panch Chuli V. *CB*
Traversing the ice ridge above the pillar. *SV*
Venables leading back from the summit. *VS*
Abseiling through the blizzard on Panch Chuli V. *SV*
Sustad iced up. *SV*
Saunders administers first aid to Venables. *DR*
Venables forces a smile at the start of the lower. *VS*
Venables being lowered from the bloody point of impact. *DR*
Venables resting on rope during lower, tended by Saunders. *CB*
Renshaw and Saunders dragging Venables across the glacier. *CB*
The camp where the three climbers waited four days. *SV*
Renshaw and Venables waiting in the tent. *SV*
Sustad re-uses the fateful piton. *CB*
The helicopter pick-up. *DR*
Looking down at the icefalls from the helicopter. *SV*
Venables safely back at Munsiary with the pilots. *HK*
Venables with an emotional Bonington. *HK*
Bonington and Kapadia debrief Venables in Munsiary. *CB*

Illustrations in text

page 201 The West Summit of Monte Sarmiento. *SV*

The photographers/copyright owners are:

Chris Bonington *CB*
Harish Kapadia *HK*
Graham Little *GL*
Dick Renshaw *DR*
Victor Saunders *VS*
Stephen Venables *SV*

Maps

Author's Note

There were many threads to the Panch Chuli expedition and each of us could have written a completely different version of the same events. My account is deliberately subjective and if it seems to underplay the achievements and contributions of some of my fellow expedition members, that is not because I do not value them; I just had to keep the plot simple, focusing on my own personal experience.

Recalling the accident several years after the event has posed surprisingly few problems. Factual diary notes honed the detail of my own vivid memories of the expedition. Victor Saunders's own account, in *No Place to Fall*, corroborated much of that detail, while Dick Renshaw and Stephen Sustad discussed some of the fine points over the telephone. Where I have described events that I did not actually witness, I have based my version on others' accounts in publications such as the *Himalayan Journal*. Daily emails from Harish Kapadia also helped, as did a long interview with Chris Bonington over an excellent breakfast at the Institute of Directors. The precise timings of helicopter movements came from a detailed log supplied by the Indian Air Force (along with a very reasonable bill which was forwarded to our insurers).

Tom Longstaff's letter to W. H. Murray and the latter's thoughts on the Khumbu Icefall are quoted from an article in the 1981 *Alpine Journal*.

I would like to thank all my expedition companions for allowing me frequent joggings of their memory, particularly Chris Bonington, who checked pertinent passages in the manuscript, and Harish Kapadia, who provided the very latest Indian place-name spellings, insisting that they would all have been correct in the first place, had it not been for the mistakes of the British Raj.

I am also very grateful to Chris Bonington, Harish Kapadia, Graham Little, Dick Renshaw and Victor Saunders for lending photographs – particularly their grittily professional coverage of the accident and rescue. Nearly all their pictures came from the Chris Bonington Photo Library, managed by the ever-helpful and efficient Frances Daltrey.

Anthony and Charlotte Rowe provided a blissfully peaceful haven for me to write the book and usually sent me home with fresh vegetables or luxuriant bunches of peonies from their garden. My wife Rosie gave me masses of confidence-boosting encouragement, as did my editor, Anthony Whittome, with whom it was a pleasure to work. I would also like to thank the designer, Roger Walker.

I would like finally to thank all the people without whose compassion, skill, good humour and determination I would never have been here to write the book at all: my fellow expedition members including the splendid support team, the people of Munsiary, the staff of Bareilly military hospital, Geeta Kapadia, Romesh Battacharjee, Sudhir Sahi and Motwan Kohli; above all, those two brave pilots, Squadron Leader P. Jaiswal and Flight-Lieutenant P. K. Sharma, who risked their lives to bring me down from Panch Chuli.

Stephen Venables
November 1999

A Slender Thread

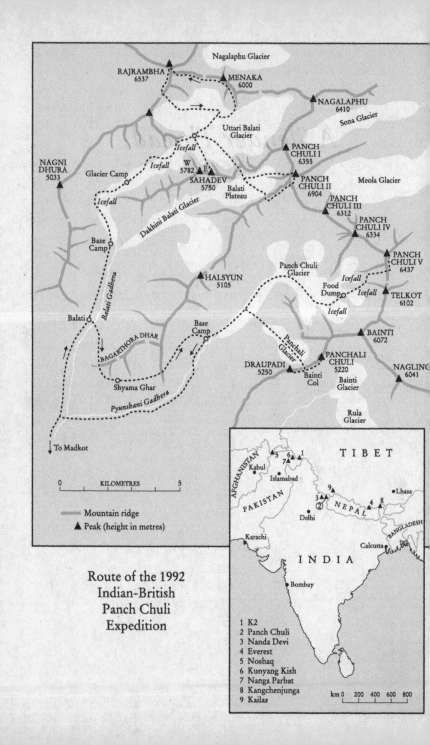

Nagalaphu Glacier

RAJRAMBHA
6537

MENAKA
6000

NAGALAPHU
6410

Sona Glacier

Uttari Balati
Glacier

PANCH
CHULI I
6355

Meola Glacier

NAGNI
DHURA
5033

Glacier Camp

Icefall

Icefall

W
5782

E

SAHADEV
5750

Balati
Plateau

PANCH
CHULI II
6904

PANCH
CHULI III
6312

Icefall

Base
Camp

Dakhini Balati Glacier

Balati Gadhera

HALSYUN
5105

Panch Chuli
Glacier

PANCH
CHULI IV
6334

PANCH
CHULI V
6437

Food
Dump

Icefall

Icefall

TELKOT
6102

Icefall

Balati

BAGAKTHORA DHAR

Base
Camp

*Panchali
Glacier*

BAINTI
6072

Shyama Ghar

Pyunshani Gadhera

DRAUPADI
5250

PANCHALI
CHULI
5220

Bainti
Col

Bainti
Glacier

NAGLING
6041

Rula
Glacier

↓ To Madkot

0   KILOMETRES   5

— Mountain ridge
▲ Peak (height in metres)

Route of the 1992
Indian-British
Panch Chuli
Expedition

AFGHANISTAN

Kabul

Islamabad

PAKISTAN

TIBET

5
6
7
1

9

3
②
NEPAL

4
8

• Lhasa

Delhi

Karachi

BANGLADESH

Calcutta

I N D I A

• Bombay

1 K2
2 Panch Chuli
3 Nanda Devi
4 Everest
5 Noshaq
6 Kunyang Kish
7 Nanga Parbat
8 Kangchenjunga
9 Kailas

km 0   200 400 600 800

Prologue

It was a damp arthritic sort of cold that seeped insidiously into weary bones. I stamped my feet and clapped sodden mittens, more out of boredom than for any hope of relief. I just wanted this long, long night to be over. Even the thunder sounded weary, rumbling far out over the plains, thousands of metres below, where the sultry land waited impatiently for the Monsoon.

Soon, in just a few days, we would be down there, on the hot plains. Harish was already back at Munsiary, organizing our transport home. The village lights, twinkling yellow against the black hillside thirty miles away, seemed infinitely attractive but our immediate goal was a closer glow of torchlight just a hundred metres below, where Bonington was waiting in a little tent perched on the edge of the mountain. By now he would have the stove going, melting snow for the first of many mugs of hot sweet tea.

We had left him almost twenty-four hours earlier and during that time our only body fuel had been a bar of chocolate and a shared water bottle. But at the tent, as well as tea, there was still some solid food. We would be able to eat a meal and perhaps there would be time for a couple of hours' sleep before continuing the descent. It would be nice to sleep longer, but today was the day we had promised to return to Base Camp, so we would have to press on down the tortuous maze of icefalls up which we had woven our improbable trail three days earlier.

We had only reached this unexplored glacier basin in the final week of the expedition, almost as an afterthought. There had been no time for a leisurely reconnaissance, but we had managed to find a way through to the jagged rim of the basin and on from there to the previously untouched summit of Panch Chuli V. The bold spontaneous gesture had paid off and the reward was to return home with a deep, contented sense of wholeness – of a journey completed.

We had reached the 21,400-foot summit at three o'clock in the afternoon. Twelve hours had now passed, and soon it would be light again. By then we should be back at the tent, for we reckoned there were two more abseils to complete. Dick had gone first on this penultimate abseil and was out of sight, beneath an overhang, nearly fifty metres lower down. Sustad was on his way down to join him, a diminishing flicker of torchlight suspended in the black void. Victor was waiting beside me, tied into the same steel peg that anchored the abseil ropes. Our torches were switched off to save the batteries, and I could make out only a dark outline hunched, like me, in a shivering self-embrace, shuffling his legs to stimulate circulation and relieve the pressure on feet that had borne his weight continuously for twenty-four hours. I moaned softly to myself. Occasionally I let out a self-indulgent, outraged howl. This long wait while the others descended the ropes seemed almost unbearable. If only I could fast-forward an hour – no, probably two hours by the time everything was sorted out – to the tent, the luxury of lying horizontal, the sweet wetness of that tea on my dry mouth, and the delicious warmth of the sleeping bag. Soon, very soon, all that would be mine, and this terrible shivering would be over. I just needed to be patient and to remind myself that a night's discomfort was a small price to pay for success.

Victor was silent and remote. Throughout the climb he had seemed quite sceptical about the whole project, but I hoped that perhaps now he would start to share some of my satisfaction. 'I'm glad that we made the effort,' I mumbled stiffly through frozen lips, 'that we actually climbed the mountain.'

He turned towards me. Even on this cloudy, starless night there was a faint gleam of residual light on the familiar gold-rimmed spectacles, hinting at the inscrutable black eyes behind. 'We're not down yet.'

Shortly after this terse reply, there was a shout from far below as Sustad reached Dick and instructed Victor to follow. He set off down the ropes and I was left to shiver alone.

It is a slow, laborious process abseiling on complex mountain terrain in the dark and I had to wait about fifteen minutes. When my turn came it was a joy to be moving at last, but every step had to be slow and meticulous. First gather the two stiff wet ropes just below their frozen joining knot and feed them into the friction brake on my harness. Check, double check and then unclip my sling from the anchor, committing myself to the ropes. Then, as agreed with the others, remove the back-up anchors. On this long series of abseils we could only afford to leave one piece of equipment at each anchor. Once three people had tested the main anchor, the back-ups could be safely removed.

Alone in a pool of torchlight, isolated as an astronaut in space, focused on the inert, abstract detail of metal and granite, I fiddled two alloy wedges out of the rock, leaving just one steel peg hammered tight in the lip of a contorted fissure. I eased myself down, bringing my weight on to the doubled ropes, stretching tight the red nylon loop that connected them to the eye of the peg.

Every action was instinctive and familiar, repeated countlessly during twenty years' mountaineering, yet I still felt nervous every time I had to abseil. In the normal process of climbing uphill the ropes are there just as a safeguard, handled by a trusted companion while you climb the mountain with your hands and feet; descending by abseil you dangle on a line, committing your life totally to the ropes. You are utterly dependent on their point of attachment. Once more I checked the whole system, and paused to stare at the single steel eye protruding from the rock, before starting to lower myself backwards down the mountain. The ropes ran at a slight diagonal over the rim of a ledge and I told myself to crouch low, trying to avoid any outward pull on the anchor. I had to shuffle awkwardly in the dark, using hands and knees to get over the edge, but then I could move more easily, leaning out over the void, legs braced across a chimney as I walked myself backwards down the precipice.

The others were waiting nearly a full ropelength below –

probably forty-five metres. One hundred and fifty feet. Craning down over my shoulder I could see the dim reflection of torchlight on snow, spilling from beneath the overhang where they were hidden. In the dark, with all perspective erased, it looked such a long way down. Between me and the island of light dim patterns of black on grey hinted at the lumpen rocky crags, seamed by smears of snow, all tilted at seventy degrees. The cliff plunged down past the others into a black void, with the glacier basin invisible another thousand feet lower down.

I directed my headtorch beam back to my immediate surroundings, focusing on my legs, braced horizontally across the rock chimney; concentrated on the steady, controlled backwards-upside-down walk; ignored the space beneath my hanging body. At first I hardly noticed the sudden acceleration. The shift from measured walk to airborne flight. The head and shoulders falling backwards, leaving legs to flail behind. Even when the terrible, violent noise started, it seemed to take me a while to understand that this was the sound of my own body bouncing off rocks. Time, in a horrible, clichéd joke, really did stand still – or at least distort beyond all normal comprehension – so that it was only in a retrospective replay of the sequence that I heard the trivial, jocular ping of a steel peg ripping from the rock above me, felt the sudden, awful, backwards lurch into space, and realized that I was falling to my death.

4

Chapter One

THERE WAS SOMETHING inevitable about the Panch Chuli expedition. After years of repeated visits to the world's greatest range of mountains, Himalayan climbing had almost become a bad habit for me. Even if I never foresaw the brutal plunge through the dark night, I think that there was a sense of unease, even doom, when I set off for India. And yet I needed – even wanted – to go to Panch Chuli. But why the need? How did I ever get into that position?

There is no simple answer to these things. If you could begin to explain in one sentence why you climb mountains, the whole activity would be pointless. So much of the reward is retrospective and yet the memories are usually of precise moments – moments when one lived utterly, totally in the present. Picking at random through a treasure-store of those moments, I could start with a summer morning, sitting alone, aged twelve, on the Welsh summit of Rhinog Fach. My grandparents were waiting below, beside the cobalt pool of Llyn Hwel. Between us lay the steep slope of crags and boulders which I had just climbed, intoxicated by the hot peaty smell of heather, the moist ferns, the dazzle of quartz crystals on warm, rough tactile rock and the sheer physical, gymnastic exhilaration of balancing through this tilted landscape. Now I sat on the flat summit, savouring the summer heat, tempered by the faintest, nostril-tweaking cool of the clear air. There was a feeling of total belonging, of oneness with the mountain, with the distant blue curve of Cardigan Bay and the serene outlines of the Snowdonia summits beyond. And with the kestrel that hung in the sky, just a few yards in front of me, apparently oblivious of my presence. The kestrel was unexpected yet seemed to make the moment perfect and complete.

It was the same fourteen years later, stopping to rest beside the Hispar Glacier in northern Pakistan, returning from an unsuccessful but deeply satisfying attempt to climb one of the world's highest mountains, Kunyang Kish. For weeks we had met no other human beings. Now for the first time we could see the flat roofs and terraced fields of Hispar village, the ripe barley haloed in the evening light. Ahead of the others, I sat down for a moment to take it all in – the slanting sunlight, the extraordinary crenellated summits that still seemed sublime after all our weeks of toil, the wasteland of rubble-strewn glacier beside which some goats rooted peacefully in a green sanctuary of willow and rose bushes. There was a faint roar from the river at the distant glacier snout and the occasional clatter of rocks collapsing from ice pinnacles; then, emerging from the background noise, something I had not heard for weeks – the sound of music. It took a moment to find its source in the still form of a shepherd from the village, sitting on a rock playing his flute. The clear treble melody was serene but with an underlying elegiac sadness that fitted my mood perfectly.

I think that there was something of that same undertone – and also a sense of uncomprehending awe – for me as a child on a winter night in Switzerland, on holiday in the Engadine valley, taking the outside staircase to join one of my brothers in the downstairs flat where we slept. The Inn river was frozen silent, hidden in a deep gorge beside the chalet and lost in the wide sweep of the valley. Thirty miles away the river bent round a sharp corner on its journey to Innsbruck, but to a child's eyes the valley seemed to stop dead, walled in by an immense mountain, the bottom part forested black, the upper slopes gleaming white. There was something comforting about its unchanging, familiar presence, the uncompromising whiteness of snow, the infinity of stars above and the palpable silence which seemed to concentrate past, present and future in that one moment.

Snow, with its gleaming, glittering, reflective powers of

transformation – and its destructive potential – has always fascinated and delighted me. The 'great freeze' of 1963 was hell if you were poor and lived in an unheated urban squat. If you were a lucky middle-class child watching Surrey's muddy winter countryside transformed into a glittering wonderland, it was a glorious treat, with frequent sledging expeditions to the normally mundane Box Hill. As the slope got icier, a local elder of the Alpine Club, Suzi Jeans, admitted to going out after dark to practise her ice-axe technique. A distinguished international concert organist and widow of the physicist, Sir James Jeans, she was always, deferentially, 'Lady Jeans' to us. One afternoon we accompanied her on a ski trek through tangled woods of yew and beech around Box Hill, which, as far as we were concerned, could have been the arctic forests of the Yukon. Our guide obviously made a deep impression, for one of our favourite family toys, a much-abused woolly dog on wheels, became known – and still is known to this day – as Lady Jeans.

It was at the end of that year that we visited the Alps on the first of several annual ski holidays. The second year my brother and I were allowed up the big cable car to Piz Corvatsch and I saw my first real, glaciated mountains in the Bernina massif. On a summer visit when I was thirteen I was treated to a day's rock-climbing course with a Pontresina guide. The other, adult, novices all seemed rather clumsy, and I felt a little disappointed, after completing a single pitch up a hundred-foot cliff, wearing a rope for the first time in my life, to be told that that was the end of the day's course. I had assumed that we would be continuing up bigger, steeper cliffs to the distant summit.

My next official taste of rock-climbing was in 1970, when I was sixteen, staying with Parisian friends near Fontainebleau. First we spent a week at their Paris apartment. I loved the city and was thrilled by the galleries – by the rich flamboyance of Poussin, David and Delacroix and the glorious Impressionist feast of the Jeu de Paume – but I was also glad after a week to escape from the cultural glut of the stifling city to the cool forest and discover its magical monolithic sandstone boulders that seemed to be sculpted perfectly for the delight of Parisian climbers. At the end of our stay my brother Mark and I joined the rest of our family in the Auvergne, while our friends the Potiers headed south for the Alps. I remember watching Jean-Pierre packing ice axes, crampons, headtorches and all the other toys redolent of alpine adventure, and wishing that I was going too.

There was nothing obsessive about my yearning, just a mental note that this was something I would like to do. At school most of my spare time was taken up with music and art, which were a wonderful escape from the awfulness of adolescent communal life. I had absolutely no talent for ball games and, although I represented the school once or twice in cross-country running, I usually came in last. In the mountains it was different. I was quite a bold, competent skier and, from my tiny experience so far, I seemed to have some talent for rock-climbing. Moving through steep terrain felt natural and it was a much needed source of physical expression. At home I had to make do with trees, but seaside holidays, from the age of seven – and, later, visits to the hills of Wales and Scotland – whetted an appetite for exploring the bare geological bones of the landscape. I loved to puzzle out moves, testing balance and friction, occasionally working myself into a blind sweat of fear as I made an irreversible move on some boulder, fifteen feet above a nasty landing, struggling until I could revel in the catharsis of escape as I committed trembling fingers to the finishing holds.

Those little victories over fear were all part of the game. They were also part of a bigger cultural heritage – of identifying childishly with the heroes of exploration. I read Edward Wilson's Antarctic diaries and Ernest Shackleton's *South*. When I was eight or nine, I followed the boy hero of James Ramsay Ullman's *Banner in the Sky* on his fictional first ascent of the Matterhorn. On a more realistic note, I consumed Francis Younghusband's *Epic of Everest*, lapped up the Gallic hyperbole of Gaston Rebuffat's *Snow and Rock,* pored lovingly over Pierre Tairraz's accompanying alpine photos, and followed Eric Shipton's laconic odyssey through the unexplored mountains of Africa, India, Tibet and Patagonia. But the book that made the biggest impression was Kurt Diemberger's translated autobiography *Summits and Secrets*, which appeared in England in 1971, when I was seventeen. It was a dangerous, seductive blend of Germanic fanaticism and Mediterranean *joie de vivre*, bursting with life-affirming enthusiasm and the romance of adventure.

A few months later I went up to Oxford and joined the University Mountaineering Club, which seemed to consist mainly of dour, earthbound scientists from the north of England. I was of course equally gauche, probably more so, and I did after a while discover that beneath the brittle, chip-butty-eating crust of my fellow club members, there lurked aspirations every bit as romantic as mine – not to mention some formidable intellects. I also learned that many of them were much stronger and more dedicated climbers than I.

Some of them became good friends and twenty-five years later they remain better climbers than I. Others died young. In my third summer, four days before starting the marathon of final exams, I decided to clear my mind with a weekend in the Lake District, persuading myself that it would pay dividends in my Wordsworth essay. I climbed that weekend with a second-year man from Christ Church called Paul Beney. He was a brilliant climber but I managed almost to rise to his level, moving with a new, fluid confidence and enjoying the best weekend's rock-climbing of my life. On the Saturday there were six of us who raced over Throstle Garth and the Great Moss, to climb on the magnificent architectural ramparts of Esk Buttress. Only two of us are still alive. Paul fell to his death a few weeks later, when an abseil anchor failed on the Aiguille de Peigne. John Weatherseed died in a separate accident, on the same day, a few miles away on Mont Blanc. Steve Parr disappeared about ten years later, exploring alone in the mountains of Nepal. Andy Brazier, always a very cautious climber, drifted gradually away from the mountains and took up marathon running; out training one day, aged thirty-three, he collapsed and died from a heart attack.

I was in Chamonix, resting in the valley after a climb, on the afternoon Paul and John died. We heard about Paul within an hour or two of the accident and I remember painfully my stunned, dazed, inadequate attempts to say something – to rise above the mundane – as I went through the motions of cooking our evening meal, hunched miserably in the polythene shelter that served as a kitchen on the squalid campsite. We did not hear about John's death until a week later. He and another Oxford climber had fallen down the Brenva Face of Mont Blanc with Dave Luscombe, who had been my partner on my first alpine season two years earlier.

Of course I was tempted to pack it all in and go home. Perhaps it was a deep-seated protestant ethic that made me stay the course – a feeling that I should see the thing through. I had always known that people might die. I myself had come close to dying the previous year, in a stupid accident in the Avon Gorge. But I had decided then that the rewards outweighed the risks, and that I would try in future to be more careful. Now, with my face rubbed so brutally in those risks, I had to make the decision again, telling myself that it was worth reviving the dreams that had brought me here in the first place.

I had grand plans for that summer of 1975, but without a similarly motivated climbing partner the reality fell short of the dream. Nevertheless I did some good climbs and right at the end of the season got to know Lindsay Griffin, an ex-Oxford physicist who had become a virtual full-time mountaineer. At last I had found someone more experienced, who seemed to share my aspirations and who was prepared to take me under his genial wing.

The following year I did my first alpine winter climbing with Lindsay. Later, during the hot summer of 1976, working as a stage hand at Glyndebourne Festival Opera and incarcerated for hours every day under artificial light, I was thrilled to get a letter from the Griffin. I think we were setting up for the second act of *Figaro*. I loitered behind the Contessa's boudoir, pretending to be busy fixing a stage brace while I read and re-read the magic words, 'somewhere in the Himalaya . . . perhaps the Hindu Kush . . . an expedition next summer.' So in 1977 I didn't go back to Glyndebourne and the vague possibility of a career in opera. Instead I caught a bus to Afghanistan.

While Griffin and I travelled overland, the other three expedition members flew out to meet us in Kabul. From there we drove up the Russian-built highway to the wild northern province of Badakshan, and on to the Wakhan Corridor, the buffer zone created a hundred years earlier by Lord Curzon to separate the empires of Britain, Russia and China. We climbed high into the luminous autumn blue sky of Central Asia. For the first time in my life I climbed completely new routes, where no humans had ever been before. The finest was on a peak called Kohe Sahkt which gave countless precious 'moments'. Perhaps the most contented was the first bivouac, ensconced comfortably with Griffin and Roger Everett in a spacious chimney, warm in my sleeping bag, cooking the evening meal on our little gas stove, pleasantly tired from the day's exertion, delighted by the beautiful rock pitch I had just led and full of happy anticipation of more to come in the morning. At that particular moment, looking out toward Chitral through the open window of our chimney, I knew there was nowhere else in the world I wanted to be.

Kohe Sahkt's summit was four thousand feet higher than I had ever been before. Out of curiosity, we then tried a much higher peak – a huge mountain called Noshaq, whose main summit is 7,492 metres above sea level. Our attempt petered out at 6,800 metres (about 22,400 feet), crushed by the stultifying effects of altitude. Equipment was part of the problem – we just didn't manage to keep warm or melt enough snow for fluid – but that was just part of a bigger failure of strategy. We didn't know how to pace ourselves and look after ourselves. We hadn't developed the psychological tricks for overcoming weakness and lethargy and I was thoroughly depressed by my failure to motivate myself.

The wonderful thing about high altitude climbing is that you get better at it. Three years later, in 1980, I reached 7,000 metres again, this time on a peak in Pakistan called Kunyang Kish. It is a giant of a mountain – the 22nd highest in the world – with a summit 7,852 metres above sea level – almost 26,000 feet. For five weeks I toiled with Phil Bartlett and Dave Wilkinson to try and complete a new route to the summit. Amongst the 'moments' on Kunyang Kish there were instances of sheer bloody awfulness. The most painful was waking up in the middle of the night as a blizzard flung snow through the entrance of what was intended to be a temporary overnight shelter. It was a nightmare – struggling out of sleeping bags, forcing feet into double boots and putting on windproofs. Ice-cold spindrift blasted our faces as we dug for two hours with our ice axes, enlarging the cave interior, then narrowing the doorway to keep out the maelstrom. For six days we were marooned in that cave at 7,000 metres, unable to go up or down, eking out food supplies until there was nothing left for a summit attempt and we had to descend.

A week later we climbed back up for a second attempt, only to be hit by another storm. Once each night we had to clear the snow-choked entrance of the cave to ensure ventilation. When my turn came I was gripped by claustrophobic terror. I had to force myself to burrow headfirst into the icy powder, fighting my way through until I could gasp at the thin air outside, where the wind was still lashing the mountain and only one or two stars appeared fitfully between scudding clouds.

Those instances of animal hardship and fear, remembered in isolation, seem utterly horrible. Yet, as part of a greater struggle – of realizing the dream of a soaring line up a magnificent mountain, living and moving in the grandest vertical landscape imaginable – they were acceptable, even exhilarating. Despite our failure to reach the summit, the prolonged attempt on Kunyang Kish – where three of us gave everything we had, stretching ourselves to the mental and physical limit – was intensely rewarding. On Noshaq the failure had been a passive, dispirited thing; here it was a glorious failure, where I felt in control and knew that, with a bit more luck, nothing would have stopped me reaching the summit. I could play this high altitude game and I wanted to do it again.

And so the habit started. Throughout the eighties I kept returning to the Himalaya, as well as seeking other adventures in Africa, Peru, Bolivia and the sub-Antarctic island of South Georgia. At first I supported the habit with school-teaching.

Then I left the school where I was working in York, hoping to become a full-time professional mountaineer, but actually becoming a carpenter, with meagre extra earnings from the occasional lecture or article. However, in 1985 I managed at last to get an advance for my first book *Painted Mountains*, basing it in part on a particularly memorable expedition earlier that year to the Indo-Pakistani war zone on the Siachen Glacier in northern Kashmir.

If I had not accidentally dropped a rucksack full of essential bivouac equipment from a precarious ridge at 7,000 metres, Victor Saunders and I would probably have reached the summit of Rimo I – one of the highest unclimbed peaks in the world. Instead we retreated with our tails between our legs, for me to lick my wounds while Victor treated everyone else at Base Camp to spirited re-enactments of my deranged, howling anguish in the moments immediately after the fall. However, on the climb itself, during our days of pre-lapsarian bliss, edging ever higher along the knife-edge in the sky, he had been the perfect companion – skilful, intelligent and totally committed. It had been one of the best climbs of my life, with the background rumble of Indian and Pakistani artillery adding an exotic touch.

Because we were visiting a sensitive security area we had to be part of a joint Indo-British team, under the leadership of a Bombay cloth dealer called Harish Kapadia. Without Harish we would never have got to the mountain and in any case the journey would never have been such fun. He approached everything with reckless, head-on enthusiasm – the frantic packing in Bombay, the long journey north, accompanied by crates of his beloved Alfonso mangoes, the endless wrangles with officialdom, the interlude at Srinagar with Shikara rides on the Dal Lake and visits to the Mogul gardens, marathon feasts in Leh while he sparred again with officials, the drive over the highest road pass in the world, across to the Nubra valley and finally our Terong valley, where we split into groups to roam around an entire unexplored glacier basin and make many first ascents to compensate for my fiasco on Rimo I.

Rather like the great English explorers, Bill Tilman and Eric

Shipton, Harish loved to unravel geographical puzzles – to follow a valley, or cross a pass to see round the next corner. Even if at the end of the twentieth century the field had been narrowed to crossing the t's and dotting the i's, there was still the same joy of discovery. With Harish there was also a very Indian identification with the religions, cultures and myths of his beloved Himalaya and, thank goodness, a touch of sybaritic indulgence that would probably have appalled Shipton and Tilman. You never went hungry on a Kapadia expedition.

I enjoyed the 'Indo-British Siachen Expedition' so much that I determined to plan another joint venture. Harish proved a tireless and rather bullying correspondent and the airmails zipped relentlessly back and forth between Bombay and Islington, where I was now lodging in Victor's house. We decided on a 1988 joint expedition to a massif called Panch Chuli – the five Chulis – in Kumaun, close to India's border with western Nepal. I had always wanted to visit this part of the Himalaya, attracted by the promise of deep forest gorges and exquisite alpine meadows, immortalized in the writings of Tom Longstaff, Frank Smythe, Eric Shipton and Raymond Greene. Unlike the famous summits of Kamet, Nanda Devi, Dunagiri or Changabang, the Panch Chuli massif, rising further east, above the great chasm of the Goriganga river, had hardly been touched. Harish was particularly keen to lay to rest an Indian expedition's claim to have climbed three of the main peaks in just over a day in 1964. The claim was transparently false, several summits were still unclimbed and there was good work to be done.

Our plans for 1988 fizzled out. On the British side we dithered. Then I was invited to join an American expedition to the Kangshung Face of Everest. A new route on the biggest face of the world's highest mountain was too good a chance to turn down, and I sent an apologetic letter to Harish. On the way to Everest, I stayed with him and his wife Geeta in Bombay and was pleased to see that my fickleness had not damaged our friendship. Four months later, two stone lighter and hobbling on crutches, with three-and-a-half frostbitten toes rotting in the Monsoon heat, I returned to Bombay, on the way home from the most powerful experience of my life. We had succeeded on our spectacular new route and I had reached the summit of Everest without supplementary oxygen, surviving a bivouac in the open at 28,000 feet on the way down. Geeta nursed me for a day then packed me off on the plane back to England with a celebratory case of mangoes, first sending a telegram to Harish, who was somewhere in the Himalaya. A congratulatory telegram came winging back and soon we were discussing more future ventures. We settled on another unclimbed peak in northern Kashmir for 1991, but then again I had to drop out, for by now my life had changed completely.

When my girlfriend Rosie saw me off at Heathrow on my departure for Everest in 1988, our relationship was quite stormy. I was for once in my life focused very single-mindedly on my ambitions and had at last managed to make a living out of writing and lecturing, almost taking pride in my selfish determination not to let anyone get in the way. The previous summer and autumn I had been away for four months in Pakistan and Tibet; now, after a brief interlude, I was off again for another four months. Rosie's feelings for me were understandably ambivalent, especially as she believed, as she told me afterwards, that I 'was going to snuff it' on Everest.

I managed not to snuff it and, on the basis of my fifteen minutes' fame, began to earn some bigger lecture fees, achieving some kind of security. I bought a car for the first time in fourteen years and made plans to get a mortgage on a house. To some extent Everest calmed the demon of ambition and for a while I was in no hurry to push myself hard on a mountain. Rosie felt that I had become a nicer person, and suspected that high altitude brain damage might have something to do with it.

When I next set off on an expedition, this time to South Georgia at the end of 1989, the departure felt harder, as we were now living together in a small terrace house on the edge of Bath. Returning in the spring of 1990 I was glad that I had over a year to go before the next expedition – to Kashmir with Harish. Then, that autumn, we discovered that Rosie was pregnant. The baby was due in June 1991 – the exact time of the expedition – and it would be impossible for me to join Harish. Once again I cancelled. Meanwhile, however, the old Panch Chuli project had been revived for 1992, this time with a completely new leader.

I was in the bar at Plas y Brenin, the national mountaineering centre, when the idea was first mentioned by Britain's undisputed doyen of the mountain world, Chris Bonington. Twenty years older than me, he had done his first rock climbs in Wales before I was born. I was only eight when he shot to fame with the first British ascent of the Eiger North Face in 1962. Subsequent broadcasting spectaculars such as the Old Man of Hoy consolidated his unrivalled position in the national consciousness, but, growing up without a television and rarely looking at newspapers, I remained completely ignorant of his existence. It was only in 1971, when I read a library copy of his recently published *Annapurna South Face*, that I finally became aware of Britain's most famous mountaineer. The Annapurna climb the previous year had been a breakthrough in Himalayan mountaineering, tackling the kind of giant steep wall that would have been unthinkable a few years earlier. For Bonington, as expedition leader, it brought renewed fame and glory which was further enhanced in 1975 with success on the South-West Face of Everest.

Public acclaim did not always equate to popularity with his peers. For a long time it was commonplace in the climbing world to deride Bonington as a ruthless publicity-seeker, whose perceived commercialism transgressed the amateur ethos of mountaineering. That sneering was a typically British jealousy of success, fuelled by ignorant prejudice. Bonington's commercial clout in fact had its precedents, most notably in the careers of Edward Whymper, the Victorian lithographer who so assiduously publicized his first ascent of the Matterhorn, and Frank Smythe, a Himalayan climber whose books and lectures had a huge following in the 1930s. While many of his contemporaries in the sixties and seventies scowled and mumbled into their beards, Bonington engaged the public with unembarrassed enthusiasm, committed as he was to making a living from his chosen pastime. There was a myth that, actually, he was not a particularly good climber, but you only had to look at his record to see how often he was at the sharp end of the rope, out in front, leading some of the hardest climbs of his day. Whilst he was the first to admit that some of his contemporaries, such as Joe Brown or Martin Boysen, had the technical edge on steep rock, as a forceful all-rounder he had few equals. Most remarkable was his ability to sustain that enthusiasm over the decades, so that when I first met him in the mid-eighties he was still tackling some of the most prestigious and elusive summits in the Himalaya.

The occasional meetings became more frequent after 1990 when Bonington became President of the British Mountaineering Council and asked me to be one of his vice presidents. At first there seemed to be a certain wariness. Rosie said that we were like a couple of male dogs sniffing each other's bottoms. Although I could not remotely match his experience, dedication and huge popular following, and posed no threat to his position, there was nevertheless a hint of caution – the grand old man of British mountaineering anxious, perhaps, not to have younger men snapping at his heels. On my side, habitual reserve – and probably envy of his sustained single-mindedness – made me quite prickly.

Be that as it may, I warmed to Bonington's uncomplicated friendliness. I was also grateful for his frequent generous words of encouragement, dating back to my first book four years earlier. And I felt inevitably flattered in 1991, when he suddenly announced in the Plas y Brenin bar, 'I'm hoping to do a trip with Harish next year. He's been asking me to lead a joint expedition for ages and he's suggested some peaks called Panch Chuli. It would be really good if you could join the team.'

So, instead of leading my own expedition to Panch Chuli, I found myself joining an expedition to exactly the same objective, led by Chris Bonington. I tried not to feel bitter and twisted, telling myself that a Bonington expedition was an essential in the career of any serious mountaineer and that it would probably be a great experience. After all, twenty years earlier it would have been the most thrilling, unimaginable privilege. I accepted the invitation gratefully, then Panch Chuli was filed away under 'future plans' as I got on with other more important things, such as attending the birth of my first son, Oliver.

It was a gruesome ordeal which made Everest without oxygen seem a doddle. Rosie suffered terribly and Ollie was very weak for the first few days. But then her pain healed and the strange new person in our lives began to smile and laugh and fill us with delight. Having cancelled that summer's trip with Harish, I had planned a consolation climb in Nepal, in the autumn; but when the time came to leave, four months after Ollie's birth, I was surprised at how hard a wrench it proved. Despite the idyllic trek through Nepal's foothills and the intense absorption of a new route up the spectacular peak of Kusum Kanguru, eighteen miles south of Everest, I felt frequent twinges of homesickness.

The expedition finished in late November. As we were walking back down through the jungle of the Kusum Khola, all yellow, orange and crimson with an autumnal hint of melancholy in the pale luminous sky, one of my companions, Dick Renshaw, who was also on the forthcoming Panch Chuli expedition, commented, 'We're going to have to come back again in just six months. Are you going to feel like it?'

I wasn't sure, but I had an uneasy feeling that when spring came, I might not want to drag myself back to the Himalaya, even for the glorious verdant beauty of Kumaun and its glittering Panch Chuli summits.

By chance, a few days after returning home, Chris Bonington was lecturing in Bath and stayed the night at our house, rocking the foundations with his notorious, apocalyptic snoring. The snore lived up to the legend and I made a note to pitch my tent at a safe distance on Panch Chuli. We talked briefly about the expedition, Chris quizzing me on whether I was really committed. I gave a hesitant 'yes' with the proviso that I could only go if it were completely funded. After Christmas we had a full expedition meeting at the Badger Hill, on the edge of the Lake District, where Chris has lived with Wendy and his two sons for over twenty years. There would be six of us from Britain on the expedition – Chris, me, Victor Saunders, Dick Renshaw, Stephen Sustad and Graham Little.

I had never met Graham before but had read about some of his expeditions, which usually involved travelling prodigious distances on foot, often in very remote country, carrying very heavy loads. The most recent had been to the snowy volcanoes of the Atacama Desert in northern Chile. Nearer to home he had been pioneering new rock climbs on some of the remoter Hebridean islands. As a marketing executive with the Ordnance Survey, he was probably the closest any of us came to a normal, bourgeois, middle-class existence. Which wasn't very close.

Graham is tall, powerful, very fit and seemed on a first meeting to have a straightforward manner completely at odds with, say, Victor Saunders, who is mercurial, quixotic, inscrutable and can be endlessly infuriating to those of us who like to know where we stand. His moods swing from secretive silence to manic bonhomie; conversation is precise and witty one minute, perversely elliptical the next. Once, setting off up the motorway from London, Rosie made the mistake of letting him explain why the sky is blue; by the time we reached the Lake District, six hours later, he was still talking but she was none the wiser. In the mountains he could be obsessively competitive, indulging in niggling games of one-upmanship; but, as I discovered on Rimo I, during our first Kapadia expedition in 1985, Victor could also be a kind, intelligent, generous companion. He coped patiently with all my foibles and later, as my landlord in Islington, he and his wife Maggie proved heroically tolerant of my frequent bursts of temper.

As a mountaineer, Victor had few equals in Britain and, even if he did once admit to taking Machiavelli for essential expedition reading, his great virtue was that he was never boring. He liked to share his eclectic enthusiasms, whether it was atmospheric physics, the novels of Thomas Pynchon or the churches of Nicholas Hawksmoor. His own architectural career, working for a big London council, was coming to an end in 1992, as he took the bold step of abandoning his monthly salary to become a freelance mountain guide.

Stephen Sustad, like both Renshaw and I, had spent quite a chunk of his life working as a carpenter, but had now graduated to sophisticated furniture-making. I had met him briefly in Tibet in 1987, sharing the same squalid Chinese concrete hotel in a drab border post called Nyalam. I had just failed on the world's thirteenth highest mountain, Shishapangma, and he had failed on the North-East Ridge of Everest, beaten back by the same icy storm that had swept through the Himalaya that October. Long before that I had read about his formidable exploits at extreme altitude with the British guru of Himalayan climbing, Doug Scott. Of all these exploits, the most remarkable was an attempted traverse of the world's fifth highest mountain, Makalu.

In 1984 Scott, Sustad and the French film-maker, Jean Affanassieff, spent five days forging their way up the gigantic South-East Ridge. On the twisting upper section they took a short cut, leaving the ridge and traversing down into the world's highest hanging valley, where they had to plough through knee-deep powder to get on to the final headwall of Makalu. Just two or three hundred feet short of the summit, they stumbled on the frozen body of a Czech climber, Karel Schubert, still sitting upright, where he had fallen asleep eight years earlier, never to wake up. The sight of that dead body, compounding worries about the weather, seemed to panic Affanassieff, who suddenly refused to complete the final section to the summit and insisted on retreating the way they had come up. So, instead of traversing the summit and descending the easier North-West Ridge, Scott and Sustad were forced to retreat into the hanging valley, then climb a thousand feet back *up* on to the South-East Ridge, which took another two days to descend.

Several times, wading back out of the hanging valley, starved of oxygen, 26,000 feet above sea level, with all the food finished and no gas left to melt snow for water, Sustad wondered if they were going to collapse and die, but somehow he managed to do his share of the superhuman trailbreaking and return safely. Reading the accounts of that epic struggle I assumed that, like Doug, Sustad must be a thirteen-stone hulk, but when I met him three years later he turned out to be a skinny specimen, proving yet again that these things are mainly in the mind.

Sustad grew up in Seattle, where his father was a schoolteacher. In the mid-eighties he settled in Britain, where he has lived ever since. At the time of the Panch Chuli expedition in 1992 he had just split up with his wife Rose and was living in Oswestry, where he rented a workshop. With his long hair and John Lennon spectacles, he looked like an understudy for Doug Scott's 1970s persona. He loved English beer and spent much of his spare time in Oswestry's Boar's Head, or Whore's Bed as he called it. Amiable and laconic, he gave no hint of the long hours he often put in at the workshop, nor of the kind of determination that had got him through so many Himalayan climbs.

Of all the team, Renshaw had the most experience of putting up with me. Thoughtful and taciturn, he is an ideal expedition companion and we had already been on four trips together, most recently on Kusum Kanguru, which had revived an old partnership after eight years of going our own ways. As a young man Dick had been totally, obsessively committed to mountaineering, pushing himself to extremes with his fellow Manchester student, Joe Tasker. In 1975, the year Chris Bonington led an all-star team to success on the South-West Face of Everest, Renshaw and Tasker drove an old van out to India to make what was then considered a presumptuously bold two-man ascent of the South-West Ridge of Dunagiri, not far from the Panch Chuli range.

After Dunagiri, Tasker and Renshaw went their own ways, but in 1980 they joined forces again, with Peter Boardman, to attempt K2. Two years later the three of them attempted the unclimbed North-East Ridge of Everest with Chris Bonington. It was here, climbing one of the hardest pitches ever done at that altitude, above 8,000 metres, that Renshaw suddenly felt one side of his body turn numb. He recovered, but down at Base Camp a mild stroke was diagnosed, forcing him to leave the expedition. A few days after he got home, the news came through that Boardman and Tasker had disappeared on their final attempt and were dead.

Rethinking his life after the disaster, Renshaw decided, on the doctors' advice, not to attempt the world's highest mountains again. In future he would stick to lower peaks; he would also devote more time to other interests, particularly his developing passion for sculpture. On the way home from Everest he had brought some specimen hardwood blocks in Hong Kong. A year later, in 1983, when I was with him on Kishtwar-Shivling, he spent hours at Base Camp whittling away with his gouges and chisels. Over the next few years his carvings became steadily more sophisticated. By the time of the Panch Chuli expedition he had sold several pieces and had just cast his first bronze. He was also starting to work in stone and was getting his first gallery commissions.

This was the team – a sculptor, an architect-turned-mountain-guide, a cabinet maker, a map salesman, and a jobbing mountain writer – that assembled in January 1992 at the Bonington office, to hammer out an expedition prospectus and delegate jobs. We all had high hopes of Chris's money-raising clout and he promised to work his magic with *The Times* and Kodak. Then he told us to hurry up and finish all our business so that we could go out to play at Castle Crag in Thirlmere. We parted at dusk after an exhilarating climb. Later that winter news came from Harish that Godrej, India's third largest manufacturing company, had agreed to cover the entire expedition costs in India. Air India gave us a generous extra baggage allowance and the ever-supportive Mount Everest Foundation and Sports Council produced grants. With just £2,000 left to find, I approached a Bath company, Future Publishing, who agreed to sponsor us in return for a feature in their new magazine *Photo Plus*.

Meeting the publisher and editor over a pub lunch, relishing the sweet thrill of a deal successfully clinched, I began at last to feel enthusiastic about the expedition. The money was raised, the flights were booked and the whole bandobast had been set in motion; I had made the decision to go and could now immerse myself in the practical details. But there was still a niggling ambivalence. I was unhappy about the size of our group – five Indians and six British climbers – and the vague multiplicity of objectives. There were two different valleys leading into the Panch Chuli massif, with several objectives in each. Harish was determined that we should make the highest pyramid, Panch

Chuli II, our prime objective, even though it had been climbed before. I was more tempted by other, unclimbed summits, but there was no specific plan to attempt them. And there was the Victor factor – Saunders's penchant for manipulative gamesmanship. At least, that was the way I saw it, thinking back nostalgically to the straightforward, open, co-operative spirit of my American companions on Everest.

In that slightly paranoid, ambivalent mood, I began to dread the moment of departure. It had been a mild winter and spring came early in 1992. By early April the tulips were already unfurling in the tiny garden which had become my obsession. One day Rosie and I strapped Ollie in the back of the car and drove down to Scott's nurseries in Dorset to indulge in some new shrubs, stopping on the way to visit Margery Fish's famous garden at East Lambrook. Another week, like hundreds of thousands before us, we went over to Kent to gawp at the genius of Great Dixter and Sissinghurst. On Easter Monday, we risked the crowds and drove north to Hidcote. Ollie was thrilled by the bold vista of the famous Hornbeam Walk and its huge expanse of smooth grass. Laughing, giggling, crawling at high speed, then standing up for the first time, with a steadying hand on a fence, he played to the crowd with exuberant, joyful confidence.

England was at its most beautiful and I was going to miss my son's first birthday. Why did I have to lead this schizophrenic existence? Why forsake a warm, loving home for uncertainty and discomfort? Why the age-old dichotomy between farmer and nomad, settler and wanderer? Why the desperate need for contrast? I had been through it all so many times before, but this time the doubts seemed more insistent. The only way to cope was to concentrate on the practical details of last-minute preparation and to remind myself that once I was in the mountains the doubts would fade away.

Deeper fears, unspoken, were stirred by a telephone call one Sunday evening in March. Andy Fanshawe, one of the country's best-known young mountaineers, had just died on Lochnagar. High winds, a moment's careless imbalance and a sudden battering fall. Random annihilation. It almost seemed a bad omen when I was asked to take over the book he had started – an ambitious illustrated history of modern Himalayan climbing. His widow, Caroline, came down to Bath to hand over all the notes and correspondence. We talked about the magical spring day, a year earlier, when we had all climbed on Scafell, returning at dusk to the cottage in the Eden valley for a huge fondue. It seemed hard to believe that all we had now were the memories of Andy's energy and huge, life-affirming enthusiasms. Caroline was very poised, coping bravely with her loss, but I couldn't help contrasting her sudden isolation with our cosy domesticity, as Ollie delighted everyone with his most engaging smile.

The flight was on 6 May, four days after my 38th birthday. One of the *Photo Plus* staff had promised to drive me to Heathrow to get a team photo for the magazine. I completed all my packing the night before and rose at six o'clock for a final potter round the garden in the dewy white light of a perfect spring morning. Everything was bursting with promise – crimson brilliance forcing open the green sepals of the paeonies, irises swelling, the muted purple of Ceanothus exploding into a shower of lapis lazuli, and the roses ... if only I could wait another week for the the rich, heady scent of *Souvenir de Malmaison, Louise Odier, Souvenir de Mme Alfred Carrière* ... if only I didn't have to go through with this perverse self-exile to a bleak, all-male environment.

I had a quick breakfast on my own then went back upstairs to our bedroom where Rosie was feeding Ollie. When he had finished his bottle, I played with him, chasing him round and round the bed, loving his gurgling shrieks of laughter. Then there was a knock on the door and we all went downstairs. I helped Rick carry three heavy rucksacks out to the car, came back for a last hug and a kiss, then walked back up the path to the waiting car, turning round for a last wave to the open doorway where two faces watched and smiled bravely.

Chapter Two

HARISH AND HIS team were waiting at Bombay airport when we arrived at three o'clock in the morning. Victor threw himself at our old friends from the 1985 expedition, hugging, gesticulating, laughing in manic jubilation. Harish extricated himself and turned to me. 'Ah, here is Steve-sahib, the proper reserved Englishman.'

Sleepy and disoriented, I followed the crowd out into the hot night air, where we were loaded into cars and driven to the Kapadia family home at Vijay Apartments. The sparrows and bulbuls had started their dawn chatter by the time we arrived. Over breakfast Harish bombarded us with gossip and plans, which had to take into account a local strike – a Bandh – by the extremist political movement Shiv Sena. A newspaper reference to the baton-happy police 'mildly lathi-charging the crowd' soon had Victor in disdainful stitches. Monesh Devjani, the youngest member of the team and new to Islington liberalism, smiled politely. Bhupesh Ashar, also a new face to us, took Sustad and Renshaw back to the airport to spend the day in heroic negotiations, extricating the expedition baggage from the steaming customs go-down. The rest of us retired to the Cricket Club, deemed an appropriate billet for Kapadia's English guests, where there was just time for two hours' sleep before we had to drive out for lunch at the model factory complex of our sponsor Godrej.

Mr Godrej enthused nostalgically about his sojourns at Davos, Crans Montana and other fashionable alpine resorts. Like several other senior figures in Bombay's parsee mafia, he had a weakness for mountains, was a tireless supporter of the Himalayan Club, and had agreed generously to bankroll the Panch Chuli expedition. After lunch I gave a talk to some of the company executives, by way of a warm-up for the main press conference in the evening, where Chris presided in a roof-top garden, responding patiently to all the old chestnuts such as 'How many times have you climbed Everest?' 'Is it true that you are leading a big litter clean-up on Everest?' 'How have you coped with losing so many friends in the mountains?' 'What are your thoughts about the Himalayan environment?' And so on.

Another day we did a double-bill lecture for the Himalayan Club. Talking to knowledgeable friends and well-wishers was a pleasure – and for me a nostalgic one – indulging in a public replay of Everest memories, recalling an expedition which had begun right here, in Bombay, four years earlier. Inevitably, though, there were inward comparisons between my hopeful excitement then and uneasy ambivalence now. There was an uncanny *déja vu* going with Geeta to a silversmith to buy protective Ganesh pendants for all the team. I still had the elephant god she had bought me four years earlier. I had worn it to the top of Everest and Kusum Kanguru and now I had it round my neck again, on the same faded red string, blessed by a Tibetan Ringpoche in Kathmandu.

'Thank you, Geeta. I'll stick with the old one for Panch Chuli. I'll send this one to Ollie for his first birthday – it's next month.'

'*Achha*,' she acknowledged reluctantly, 'but maybe you should take two for extra protection!'

'Too much weight. This is meant to be a lightweight 'alpine-style' expedition.'

Back at the Kapadia flat, as she had done in 1988, she performed a Hindu 'pujah' – a blessing ceremony – for our safety in the mountains. It is impossible to ignore religion in India and particularly in the Himalaya – the 'Abode of Snow' where almost every peak has some religious, mythological significance and the whole landscape seems inescapably numinous. The mountains of Kumaun, source of Ganga – the Ganges – have for millennia been the goal of Hindu pilgrims, holier even than the lowland site of Kashi, or Benares as it is now known. The ancient Sanskrit text of the Skanda Purana has come down to us in various translations, but I particularly like this version of the section on Himalaya, or Himachal:

> He who thinks of Himachal, though he should not behold him, is greater than he who performs all worship in Kashi. And he who thinks of Himachal shall have pardon for his sins, and all things that die on Himachal and all things that in dying think of his snows are freed from sin. In a hundred ages of the gods I could not tell thee of the glories of Himachal, where Shiva lived and where the Ganges falls from the foot of Vishnu like the slender thread of the Lotus flower.

The famous British mountaineer of the thirties, Frank Smythe, quotes a slightly different version, concluding 'As the dew is dried up by the morning sun, so are the sins of mankind by the sight of Himachal.' The notion that the very sight – even just *thinking* – of the Himalaya should have such redemptive power made rather a mockery of our predatory conquest. Still, there was always the consolation that if we were, in Rosie's words, to 'snuff it' in the Himalaya, pardon would be guaranteed. But did that depend on the manner in which we approached the mountains? Was reverence and the subduing of ego a prerequisite of redemption – in which case did the very act of mountain-climbing condemn us to damnation?

Although expedition conversation, certainly on British expeditions, tends to shy away from anything so inherently personal as religion, even the most thick-skinned climber cannot help but feel something of what those sages were getting at. Whether mountain landscape is proof of divine power, or a substitute for a non-existent deity, the emotions it inspires – a sense of what, for want of a better word, we lump under the vague umbrella 'spiritual' – amount to much the same thing. Within the Panch Chuli team we had quite an ecumenical range. On the British side four of us, nominally at least, were Anglican; Graham Little, who would be arriving later and meeting us in Delhi, was Catholic; Stephen Sustad came from a family of

Scandinavian Lutherans and was usually referred to by Victor simply as the Lutheran. On the Indian team, Harish Kapadia was a Gujarati Hindu, Bhupesh Ashar a Hindu Bhatia and Monesh Devjani a Sindhi whose family emigrated after Partition from what is now Pakistan; Vijay Kothari was a Jain and Muslim Contractor's first name spoke for itself.

Seeing him on the 1992 team list, Bonington had remarked, 'Contractor – that's an unusual name. Still, no different from Baker or Butcher, I suppose. But is his first name really Muslim?'

'Yes ... Christian,' replied Victor – quick, clever and either endearing or infuriating, depending on your mood at the time.

Muslim's family actually came from the Bohra caste – at the least fundamental end of the Islamic spectrum – and, like the Kapadias, spoke Gujarati as the family language. Victor and I both remembered his gentle irony with affection from the 1985 expedition.

After three days in Bombay, we headed north, seen off from the railway station by a huge crowd of family, friends and helpers. Sealed in our air-conditioned carriage, I stared out of darkened windows at the palm tree silhouettes, swamps, creeks and shimmering salt pans, as we left the city behind and the tannoy announced 'You are welcomed aboard the Rajdhani Express. During the journey of 1,380 kilometres to Delhi, we shall be passing through six states.'

How different from the grimy sweat of my early shoestring expeditions! What glorious luxury to arrive in Delhi, refreshed after a good night's sleep, to be whisked off (with Graham Little, who met us at the station) to another air-conditioned lunch, followed by afternoon tea and a shower at the house of Geeta's cousin Sarita, then ferried to the India International Centre for the final speeches, ceremonies, drinks and lavish buffet.

From there things got a little tougher. There was no avoiding the night chaos of the Great Indian Trunk Road, but I slept intermittently through the bumping, hooting bedlam. Late the following morning, after a steady climb from the plains, our minibus reached the cool sanctuary of Ranikhet, where we stayed at the Dak Bungalow – one of the hundreds of simple lodges built throughout the Himalaya by the Raj forestry department.

Since leaving Delhi we had been in India's largest state, Uttar Pradesh, formerly known as United Provinces during the Raj. It encompasses astonishing variety, from the industrial and agricultural heartland of the great northern plains to subsistence agriculture and nomadic shepherding at the very limits of habitable land. The northeastern corner of UP, wedged up between Tibet and Nepal, is called Kumaun. Originally covering a wider area than its present boundaries, it was ruled by the Nepalese Gurkhas. In their successful bid to wrest control from Nepal in the war of 1815, the British enlisted the support of the Maharajas of Teri Garhwal, Gauri Garhwal and other statelets around the headwaters of the Ganges. In recognition of their support, the area west of Nanda Devi became known as Garhwal and today Kumaun refers only to the eastern area between Nanda Devi and the present Nepalese frontier.

Whether one calls it Kumaun, Garhwal or both, the whole mountain region north of Ranikhet is amongst the loveliest in the Himalaya and it was exciting to think that so many famous Europeans had set out in the past from this very same Dak Bungalow. One of the first was G. W. Traill, the first Deputy Commissioner of Kumaun, whose 1830 crossing of the Himalayan axis is still known as 'Traill's Pass'. He was followed by Richard Strachey in 1848, and the three Schlaginweit brothers, Adolf, Hermann and Robert in the 1850s. Much of their work was completed before the arrival of the formal topographical survey, which originated with Sir George Everest's monumental Grand Trigonometrical Survey. Every visitor to Kumaun was struck by its highest mountain – Nanda Devi, the twin-peaked 'Mother Goddess' which dominates the entire region.

Towards the end of the nineteenth century, European mountaineers began to think in terms of actually attempting to climb Himalayan summits, translating their alpine skills into the thin air of extreme altitude. In the eastern Himalaya, both Tibet and Nepal were closed to foreigners, whilst the austere desert country of the Karakoram, in northwestern Kashmir, was so remote from the Indian plains that only the most determined expeditions ventured that far. Kumaun by contrast was easily accessible and, in those days of unpolluted air, dazzlingly visible from the hill-stations of Dehra Dun, Nainital and Ranikhet. Perhaps there was also an element of comforting familiarity – take away the smells of hot chili and oriental incense, and those pine forests, flowery meadows and smoke-blackened timber houses could almost be in Switzerland.

The first mountaineering expeditions gravitated inevitably towards Nanda Devi. In 1883 W. W. Graham and two Swiss alpine guides attempted unsuccessfully to find a route through the barrier of mountains which encircles the goddess. The riddle of the 'Nanda Devi Sanctuary' was to puzzle seven more parties before it was finally unravelled in 1934. Amongst their number were some of the most famous names in mountaineering history, including the physicians Alexander Kellas and Tom Longstaff, the missionary Howard Somervell and the ebullient Gurkha officer General Charles Bruce, all of who were later to make their mark on another holy mountain further east – Chomolungma, or Everest as it had been named by the Survey of India. In fact it was by way of consolation, after the intransigent bureaucrats at the India Office refused permission for a projected reconnaissance of Everest in 1907, that Longstaff, Bruce and the experienced alpinist A. L. Mumm turned instead to the high curtain of peaks surrounding Nanda Devi. In the manner typical of the era, each brought his personal retainers: Mumm was accompanied by the Zermatt guide Moritz Inderbinen, Longstaff by the Brocherels of Courmayeur, while Bruce brought nine Gurkhas from his regiment, including a trained plane-table surveyor. The assembled team did not manage to penetrate the inner sanctuary, but they got very close and, in the course of a glorious odyssey of exploration, succeeded in reaching the summit of Trisul, which at 7,128 metres was the highest mountain ever scaled at that time.

The Everest reconnaissance had to wait until 1921, when the colonial masters in Delhi finally agreed to make the necessary overtures to Tibet. The first fullscale attempt in 1922 was led by Charles Bruce (whose nephew Geoffrey established a new world altitude record of over 27,000 feet, during the expedition – his first ever climb) and Tom Longstaff, who came as expedition doctor. Longstaff was not enchanted by the rocky brute towering over the stony wastes of Tibet, writing that 'it has no athlete's grace of form but the brutal mass of the all-in wrestler.' One senses a nostalgic longing for the more picturesque charms of Kumaun – not only for the region itself, but also for the whole philosophy of his early expeditions, when the Himalayan experience had been so fresh and new. Nearly fifty years later, writing as a retired general practitioner from his home in Wester Ross to another Scottish explorer of Kumaun, he enthused: 'There is no more lovely place in all Himachal. You have seen the best – and now understand what I mean by "living in the present": just forget all before-and-after and soak the moment into you so that it will never come out. Just travel is the thing. Number your red-letter days by camps not summits (no *time* there) ... Enjoy – and for always, as you can thro' concentration.'

That dismissal of summits, from a man who had established a new altitude record in 1907, might seem disingenuous, but for him the delight of travel really was 'the thing' and his approach to the Himalaya was echoed by his immediate successors in the thirties. The pattern was similar. Frank Smythe, perhaps the outstanding British mountaineer of the decade, led an expedition in 1931 to make the first ascent of Kamet. Now the highest scaled summit stood at 7,756 metres. With Smythe on the summit were Dr Raymond Greene, brother of the novelist Graham, and two coffee-planters who had met in Kenya – Eric Shipton and Bill Tilman. All four would subsequently do time on Everest's bleak North Face. Shipton took part in no less than four Everest expeditions before the Second World War halted the Tibetan campaign. However, for all the dogged bravery of their Everest attempts (Smythe got to within 300 metres of the summit in 1933, without oxygen, and Shipton was not far behind), their really interesting journeys were the ones they made away from Everest.

Everyone on the Kamet expedition was enchanted by the beauty of Kumaun and, in those spacious, leisured days, was happy to return slowly to the plains, crossing passes and exploring as they went. Shipton and Tilman in particular recognized that this was to be the future focus of their lives. Back in Africa the following year they teamed up for a trip to Uganda's Ruwenzori mountains. Soon after that they both wound up their plantations. Tilman rode a bicycle across the entire continent, surviving mainly on bananas, to catch a steamer home from the west coast; Shipton sailed for Bombay to join the 1933 Everest expedition. In 1934 they teamed up again, this time to do their own Himalayan expedition, on their own terms.

Those terms were bold and imaginative. They cut food and equipment to the bare minimum. Where ever possible, approaching though the inhabited lower valleys of the Himalaya, they bought local supplies, sticking to a very simple diet. With minimal baggage they could be flexible, only having to hire a handful of local porters when absolutely necessary. The rest of the time they were accompanied by three Sherpas – the natural mountaineers from Nepal who were becoming synonymous with Himalayan exploration. All three, Pasang Bhotia, Kusang Namgay and Angtharkay, had been with Shipton on Everest the previous year.

This was the team that in 1934 finally reached the elusive Nanda Devi Sanctuary, after forcing a spectacular route up the walls of the Rishi Gorge – the only point in the entire surrounding wall where the ridge drops below 5,000 metres and where the entire glacial basin is drained by a single torrent. Where most modern expeditions would be proud with just that achievement, this team went much further, leaving the Sanctuary by a very difficult new pass over the wall, then returning several weeks later, after the Monsoon, to complete their survey work. During the interim they explored another part of the Kumaun Himalaya, descending on one occasion into an uninhabited valley where they ran out of food and had to survive off wild bamboo shoots.

In 1935 Shipton and Tilman got the chance to try their

First view of the Panch Chuli massif from Munsiary, at dawn. Panch Chuli II is the highest peak. To its right are Panch Chuli III, IV & V, Telkot and Bainti.

Wind-blown snow blasts off Rajrambha, the right hand peak, 4,000 metres above the Balati valley, on the second day of the walk-in.

Left: The team at base camp. Back row l to r: Wing Cmdr. Anil Srivastava, Muslim Contractor, Dick Renshaw, Chris Bonington, Harish Kapadia, Stephen Venables, Graham Little. Front row l to r: Vijay Kothari, Bhupesh Ashar, Stephen Sustad, Victor Saunders, Monesh Devjani.

Right: Advance Base Camp beneath Sahadev.

Below: Venables preparing local salad at Glacier Camp. Sustad, protected from the sun, tends the stove.

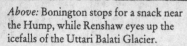

Above: Bonington stops for a snack near the Hump, while Renshaw eyes up the icefalls of the Uttari Balati Glacier.

Right: Looking down the Balati valley from the Hump.

A stunning view opens up for the Panch Chuli II team, looking over Rajrambha to Nanda Devi, the Mother Goddess of the Kumaun Himalaya.

The reverse view towards Panch Chuli II as Saunders nears the summit of Menaka, on Day 2 of the Menaka-Rajrambha traverse.

Left: Saunders and Sustad about to reach the bivouac on Day 2. The following day the team climbed right up to the tiny notch in the final pillar just below the cloud.

Below: Stopping at the notch to get organized for the night.

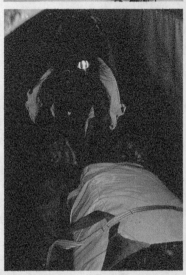

Above: Half an hour later, Renshaw, Saunders and Sustad ght with the tent poles, being careful not to drop any.

ight: Saunders preparing to set off on another pre-dawn art.

Sustad nears the end of the three mile traverse on Day 5. Panch Chuli II dominates the background, with the peaks of western Nepal in the far distance.

Left: The crossing to the Pyunshani valley starts with a day of steep jungle bashing to cross a high ridge.

Below: Traversing beyond the ridge Kapadia, Dhansinh and Revatram wonder where to go next.

Descending back into the jungle, Bonington offers his views (far left) before everyone stops for a rest (above) and Kapadia staves off hunger with wild salad (below, far left). On the third day, Contractor arrives happily at the head of the valley.

Right: At last - a glimpse of the Panch Chuli Glacier with untrodden peaks rising above it.

Below: After a long hard day the team relaxes in the new Pyunshani base camp. Bonington and Kapadia discuss return dates while Saunders and Sustad sort out rations for the final climb.

Right: The following afternoon, at the head of the glacier, the British team stares up the chaotic icefalls guarding Panch Chuli V.

lightweight methods on an Everest 'reconnaissance expedition'. They did not get very high on Everest itself, but the expedition did make first ascents of twenty-six lower Tibetan peaks. In 1936 Shipton was asked to return yet again to Everest with a more traditional fullscale assault led by Hugh Ruttledge. Tilman, meanwhile, returned to Kumaun to lead an Anglo-American expedition back up the Rishi Gorge, this time to attempt an actual ascent of Nanda Devi.

Looking back now, at the end of the century, one gets a sense that the 1936 Nanda Devi expedition was the highlight of a golden age of exploration – an unusually contented, cordial pairing of American innocence with British experience. The young Americans, on their first Himalayan encounter, deferred to the judgement of Tilman, the gruff veteran of the First World War trenches. True, there was some grumbling halfway up the Rishi Gorge when a porter strike forced Tilman to leave behind many of the supplies. As Ad Carter recalled forty years later, 'Tilman announced that only strictly nutritious food would now be carried to Base Camp. That meant that everything edible was left behind.' But the grumbling was lighthearted and everyone soon shared in the excitement of pushing the route up Nanda Devi's south ridge.

In purely mountaineering terms it was a fantastic achievement, all done with the most basic equipment and none of the fixed ropes which have become so common on the world's highest mountains nowadays. But what really distinguished the team was their gentlemanly camaraderie. The telegram announcing their success mentioned no names – just 'two reached the summit'. The Harvard physiologist, Charlie Houston, was to have been in the summit team but became ill with food poisoning at the top camp, so Tilman took his place alongside Noel Odell, the English geologist who had witnessed Mallory and Irvine disappearing into the clouds near the summit of Everest, ten years earlier, in 1924.

The 7,816-metre main summit of Nanda Devi was to remain the highest peak reached by man until Annapurna, the first of the 'eight-thousanders', was climbed in 1950. For Tilman, noted generally for his poor performance at altitude, it was a personal triumph, yet his account is typically modest, substituting wit for any unseemly betrayal of emotion, diverting attention away from himself with gentle digs at his scientist companion:

> Odell had brought a thermometer, and no doubt sighed for the hypsometer. From it we found that the air temperature was 20 degrees F, but in the absence of wind we could bask gratefully in the friendly rays of our late enemy the sun. It was difficult to realize that we were actually standing on top of the same peak which we had viewed two months ago from Ranikhet, and which had then appeared incredibly remote and inaccessible, and it gave us a curious feeling of exaltation to know that we were above every peak within hundreds of miles on either hand. Dhauligiri, 1,000 ft higher, and two hundred miles away in Nepal, was our nearest rival. I believe we so far forgot ourselves as to shake hands on it.

Even Tilman, though, then manages to forget himself a little further and allow himself, at this crowning moment of his mountaineering career, a brief splurge of purple prose:

> After three-quarters of an hour on that superb summit, a brief forty-five minutes into which was crowded the worth of many hours of glorious life, we dragged ourselves reluctantly away, taking with us a memory that can never fade and leaving behind 'thoughts beyond the reaches of our souls.'

It had taken all morning to reach the summit from their top camp; afternoon cloud obscured their view east across the Sanctuary wall and the Goriganga valley, so they probably did not see the Panch Chuli massif. At this stage, only one mountaineer, Hugh Ruttledge, had investigated the peaks, exploring the Sona Glacier on their eastern side, in 1929. Then the Panch Chuli were virtually ignored by foreigners, until after the Second World War. During the war itself, two Austrian internees escaped a British prison camp and made their way through Kumaun to Tibet, eventually reaching the holy, forbidden city of Lhasa. One of them, Peter Aufschnaiter, produced some astonishingly detailed maps but never really publicized his achievements. The other, Heinrich Harrer, had already made history in the Alps and would later become even more famous through his Tibetan exploits.

Like many ambitious mountaineers, Harrer dreamed of climbing in the Himalaya. In the thirties, that dream was realized by only a handful of lucky or very determined climbers. Shipton and Tilman had shown what could be done on a shoestring budget. However, in real terms, their expeditions still cost a lot more then than they would now. In any case, they both had private incomes to help them on their way. Most expeditions were still hugely expensive, national affairs to the highest peaks in the world, with the British enjoying a monopoly on Everest, while the Americans attempted K2, the French and Swiss explored Hidden Peak and the Germanic alpinists made several grand, heroic attempts, first on Kangchenjunga in Sikkim, then on Nanga Parbat in Kashmir. Harrer wanted desperately to make a name for himself and get invited on the 1939 Nanga Parbat expedition, so he decided in 1938 to tackle the most notorious 'last great problem' in the Alps – the huge and dangerous North Face of the Eiger.

Following the route of earlier attempts, from which only one party had returned alive, Harrer and his companion Fritz Kasparek made slow, patient progress. It seems amazing today to think that Harrer took no crampons for the extensive icefields on the wall, relying just on old-fashioned nailed boots, in the mistaken belief that this was primarily a rock-climb. About halfway up the wall the Austrians were overtaken by two Germans, racing up the icefields in the latest twelve-point crampons. Anderl Heckmair, through his friendship with the film-maker Leni Riefenstahl, had been introduced to Hitler. Patronage by the Nazi party had given him and his partner Wiggerl Vörg access to national training facilities and the best equipment available. Heckmair was in any case a highly talented climber. And a generous one – agreeing to Vörg's suggestion to team up with the less accomplished Austrians, even though that would slow him up on a wall where, in those days, there was no chance of rescue if bad weather closed in.

Bad weather did close in. Spindrift avalanches poured down the wall and the bivouacs were cramped, shivering trials of endurance. Yet Heckmair had the technical skill and intuition to fight his way up the maze of gullies and cracks at the top of the face, knowing that the only way out was over the top.

The Führer was thrilled by the Eiger success. The symbolic German–Austrian partnership on the wall was a serendipitous propaganda tool, coming just after the *Anschlüss*, and he fêted the four young heroes before ecstatic crowds. In Britain the editor of the *Alpine Journal* ranted at the depravity of suicidal Fascists perverting the true course of alpinism and many years passed before the British climbing establishment recognized the Eiger ascent for what it was – a brilliant piece of route-finding by a very brave and talented team. Heckmair's brief flirtation with the Nazi party machine had in fact been a reluctant affair, and it was Heinrich Harrer, the ambitious Austrian, who was a Party Member and a member of the SS. He *did* get his place on the 1939 Nanga Parbat expedition and found himself in British India when Britain declared itself at war with Germany and her allies, that September. With his adventurous spirit, it was hardly surprising that Harrer should persuade his friend Aufschnaiter to escape across the Himalaya, rather than spend the whole war cooped up in a dreary internment camp.

Harrer later made a huge name for himself with his best-selling *Seven Years in Tibet*. It is an extraordinary adventure tale and one of the few western accounts of life in Lhasa during the final years before the Chinese invasion. Its universal appeal inevitably eclipsed his mountaineering exploits, and people tend to forget that after leaving Tibet in 1950 he continued to make some notable first ascents, including Mount Deborah, in Alaska, and the elusive Carstenz Pyramid in Papua New Guinea. He also returned to the country of his internment – now the independent state of India – in 1951 to make the first determined attempt on Panch Chuli. Although he did not manage to reach the summit of the highest peak, he did get most of the way there, pioneering the western approach from the Goriganga valley which we were soon to follow ourselves.

Interest in the five Chulis seemed to be hotting up, for the previous year, 1950, a Scottish expedition had attempted the eastern side of the mountain. The leader, Bill Murray, had written a famous book on his Scottish mountaineering exploits whilst incarcerated in a German prisoner-of-war camp. Now, five years after the end of the war, he wrote another book recounting his first Himalayan expedition. Recalling his first view of the Himalaya from Ranikhet he described 'a great continent of the heavens, wholly apart from Earth' and he called the Panch Chuli 'the most beautiful peaks in the world'. His team reached the massif only at the end of a long ambitious journey of exploration, too late to make a determined attempt on the summit. But something of the Buddhist's renunciation of desire and ambition seems to have rubbed off during the pilgrimage as he concludes philosophically:

The final peak of the Panch Chuli stood right before our eyes – a shining chisel blade of ice. So thin were its upper edges that over a stretch of a thousand feet we could see the sun shining through. The entire basin was of undulating snow, ringed by satellite peaks, whose long skirts were splayed out fan-like and fell silkily to the basin's floor. At the outer rim perched our tiny tent, a pin-point on the brink of the first great fall, where the Sona Glacier plunged to the Darmaganga, now ten thousand feet below among the clouds. Beyond its bottomless gorge the ranked snow-ranges of an unknown mountain land, all topped by towering cumuli, receded into the everlasting blue that roofs Tibet.

Truly that *was* the Abode of the Gods and the Five Brothers, worth much sacrifice of the flesh. It is worth reflecting that we should never have seen or entered this sanctuary of the Panch Chuli, never have had the experience at all, had the summit not drawn us up to beat us.

After Bill Murray's and Heinrich Harrer's attempts on Panch

Chuli, there were no more foreign visits to this part of Kumaun. Like many other Himalayan regions of India it was put out of bounds. Attempts on the Chulis became the preserve of home-grown teams and it was an Indian expedition that finally climbed the main peak in 1973. Arriving in 1992, we were the first foreigners to attempt the mountain for forty-two years. It seemed ironic that in 1950 Murray's expedition had been given permission to cross an invisible bureaucratic hurdle called the 'Inner Line' and visit the Darma valley to the east of Panch Chuli, whereas now, even with our famous Indian leader, we were not allowed to cross the line and had to stick to the western approach. In fact we were nearly blocked even from that. Harish chuckled with glee telling us about the endless negotiations with the Indian Mountaineering Foundation in Delhi, when they realized that the magic line ran exactly along the summits of the Chulis. Even if we approached from the west, once we stood on any summit we would have had one foot over the line. The IMF officials got into a terrible bother, so Harish told them to wait a couple of days. 'Then I telephoned all important generals, Captain Kohli ... all these chaps in ministries ... all the important fellows. Two days later IMF said, "no problem with Panch Chuli."'

The Inner Line, like so many of India's bureaucratic encumbrances, was a British creation, but the modern obsession with the line stems from the sixties, when large sections of India's northern frontier, including an area the size of Wales in Ladakh, were taken over by Chinese troops. Much of the Himalayan watershed became a militarized zone and traditional traffic over the Himalayan passes suddenly came to an end. It was sad to think that the villages in the upper Goriganga valley were now all deserted because there was no longer the trade with Tibet to sustain them. Back in 1950, before the Chinese had consolidated their occupation of Tibet, Bill Murray's party had met huge flocks of goats, laden with twenty-pound paniers, carrying wool, salt, grain and spices over the watershed. Now the passes were deserted.

It wasn't only politics that had changed. In 1950 they had

started walking soon after leaving Ranikhet, with pack animals and porters carrying their baggage through the forest. Now much of the forest has succumbed to the pressures of a national population that has nearly trebled since Independence. The whistle and tongue-clicking of the muleteer has been smothered by the tortured grind of diesel engines. Emission controls are a distant Western luxury and the air hangs thick and heavy in the crowded bazaars. Stopping during the drive from Ranikhet at sweltering tea houses, trying to reaccustom myself to sweet cloying milky 'chai', I dreamed of cool salads and longed to be with Ollie and Rosie. After a fourteen-hour drive we crossed the final pass and reached our destination – Munsiary. Cloud obscured the summits during a day devoted to that most unavoidable expedition chore, once referred to by a Himalayan hotelier as 'the packaging and repackaging of equipments', and it was only at dawn the following day that we finally saw the Panch Chuli massif.

The Panch Chuli massif from Munsiary. From left to right, the main peaks are Panch Chuli II, Panch Chuli III, Panch Chuli IV, Panch Chuli V and Bainti.

It was a wonderful vision to lift jaded spirits. Five summits, dark purple in a pale violet sky. Landscape reduced to its essentials. Two-dimensional silhouettes, quintessentially mountain. Archetypal pyramid forms, each with its own personal nuances, but the highest also the simplest, uncluttered, serene. No hint of crevasses, ugly landslides or nasty brittle ice slopes to spoil the numinous image.

Chuli means hearth, fireside, resting place, and it was at these five hearths that the five royal Pandava warrior brothers of the ancient kingdom of Hastinapura stopped for their last earthly rest – their final bivouac – before ascending to heaven. My attempts to familiarize myself with Hindu mythology never got very far and I always felt that in a hundred ages of the gods I would never even begin to unravel the plots and myriad subplots of the Mahabharata. Harish – and to a greater extent Geeta – often took the trouble to explain, and although I was a poor learner, any journey with them was all the richer for their interest in the legends and beliefs that underpin their mountain landscape.

It also took me a while to grasp the mundane labelling of the peaks. Somewhere along the line the numbering and the nomenclature seems to have become confused, because the furthest right silhouette was actually called Bainti. Panch Chuli V was second from right and the highest pyramid, at the left end of the chain, was Panch Chuli II. I never quite worked out what Number 1 was, but it seems to have been a rather insignificant lump further left still. Perhaps it all made more sense from the Darma valley, on the far, eastern, side of the range.

Be that as it may, there was no mistaking the stately, classic pyramid of Panch Chuli II, dominating the whole range, rising to almost 7,000 metres above sea level, immediately opposite but separated from us by the great divide of the Goriganga river, whose bed here is just 1,240 metres above sea level – an elevation of nearly 6,000 metres in fifteen miles. It was a magnificent peak and perhaps this was the hearth of the most illustrious Pandava – Arjuna, the mighty archer. As daylight brought three-dimensional form to the landscape, we could make out our valley, climbing steeply from the Goriganga into the Panch Chuli massif. We could just discern the fork where one branch led to the right of Panch Chuli II towards the untouched peaks of III, IV and V, while the left branch curved round the back of the highest pyramid. I was most tempted by the right branch, but Harish had committed us to the left-hand valley which offered a known route to the highest summit. He was adamant that, even though three Indian expeditions had reached the summit before, it should be our main objective.

It was easy to see why. In a country where serious mountaineering has tended to be the preserve of the military and paramilitary, particularly the India Tibet Border Police, it would be a fine gesture for this civilian expedition to climb such a prestigious summit. Panch Chuli II was the main act but, given the size of the team, there would also be scope for sideshows on other peaks. There were several good secondary objectives up the left-hand valley and, to keep me sweet, Harish also held out the carrot of the right-hand valley as a possibility for the end of the expedition.

Chapter Three

ON THE MORNING of 15 May, just five days after setting off from Bombay, we left Munsiary on the final short journey to the roadhead, lumbering down in clouds of dust to the searing bed of the Goriganga where we were dumped in a fly-blown village called Madkot. While Harish negotiated with a contractor to hire a hundred porters for the three-day walk-in, the rest of us retired to the local café for ubiquitous rice and dal and Victor challenged Bonington to chess. Negotiations continued late into the afternoon, so in the end Harish stayed behind with Bhupesh and Monesh, telling the rest of us to set off on a steep climb to the cooler village of Ringo.

By the time we arrived, the camp staff had already commandeered an empty house where they were preparing a huge stew of fresh vegetables and, at last, weak lemon tea instead of the usual hardboiled milky stuff. Revatram, the cook, was a tall handsome man with infinite kind patience, who would keep us in good health throughout the expedition. Pasang Bodh, the sirdar, or head man, had worked for several Kapadia expeditions, but also had his own guiding business and was an experienced mountaineer in his own right. He looked dapper in a pink hat decorated with red sequins. The pill box shape was typical of Manali, in Himachal Pradesh. Both Pasang and Prakash Chand lived in Manali, but looked thoroughly Tibetan like many of the 'Bhotias' who have settled in Indian regions south of the Himalayan watershed. Some of the ten camp followers who would be helping for the duration of the expedition were from Kumaun and two of those were familiar from the 1985 Rimo expedition.

Harsinh Mangalsinh (known as Senior) and Harsinh Balaksinh (Junior) both came from the same village of Harkot in the Saryu valley. Harish had met them in the early eighties when they joined him to help with a youth expedition he was leading. They had become loyal retainers, working on nearly all his subsequent expeditions, including our 1985 trip. It was flattering to be recognized and remembered. Good to reminisce, with Muslim translating, about the wild river crossings in the Terong valley, the ropeways over the cliffs where the Kumaunis had done their first reluctant rock-climbing, the naff sahibs cadging bidi cigarettes off an astonished Harsinh Junior . . . Harsinh Senior's face, now more lined, grinned in recollection and his narrowed oval eyes still had the same kind twinkle.

That night rain beat on the bamboo roof and beyond the verandah the trees glistened purple. The whole valley was lit by gigantic flashes and the thunder exploded over the mountains. Despite the downpour, Graham chose to sleep outside, driven away by Bonington's thunder-challenging snores, and we found him drying out in a field the next morning as we headed off through Ringo village in the fresh washed light of a perfect Himalayan morning, cheered on by the laughter of children who had probably never seen Europeans before.

Ochre and whitewash houses with masterfully carved deodar windows. Terraces of barley and maize. Walls woven with wild flowers. Children playing on earthen verandahs. A woman fetching water in a faultlessly elegant brass jar. Ten days after leaving home, I was at last getting into the rhythm of things, allowing myself to relax and enjoy the meander through the village, then the steady climb through the forest – first the rich darkness of rhododendron then, on the second day, the fresh spring lime-green foliage of majestic hardwoods, underplanted with luxuriant arching clumps of bamboo. Emerging from the dappled shade into a sunny clearing, I found Harish, Muslim and Bhupesh resting beside a stream. 'Well, Mr Venables , are you glad to be in Kumaun? You know I have never seen such unspoilt virgin forest. *Everywhere* in Kumaun, they are over-grazing, cutting timber, making new pastures, but this is untouched.'

We did in fact pass some woodcutters and at the camp that night, in a glade of stately planes and deodar cedars, we were suddenly startled by a huge flock of goats stampeding through the undergrowth, but it seemed that so far, in this particular valley, local villagers had achieved a sustainable balance with their glorious forest inheritance. The ground was strewn with naturally dead, untouched, timber and the hundred local porters, whom Harish had now cajoled up the valley, sat in groups round fires, huddled in homespun woollen blankets, some of them spinning more yarn as they sat there, others chatting, singing, cooking and playing cards.

On the third, final day of our walk-in, Victor and I went into horticultural rapture, rushing through the undergrowth in a manic spree of amateur botanising. 'Look – it's jasmine – this one with the little pointed leaves and, yes, see these things with the blue-grey leaves, a bit like columbine, they're *Thalictrums* –'

'*Thalictra*, surely.'

'Well yes, I don't know what's happened to plurals, but the botanists seem to talk about *ums* these days. No standards. Now here's a – a, er . . . oh, come on brain – *Piptanthus*, that's it, yes, *Piptanthus nepalensis* . . . a bit like laburnum. We've got one at home. The seeds came from Anne Russell, daughter of George Finch – you know, the Everest man. Or we did have one until the bloody dog from next door ripped it up. Rosie had a big row with the owner and he came round in his policeman's uniform.'

'Did he mildly lathi-charge you?'

'What? Yes . . . umm . . . no . . . What are you talking about? Now look at these wonderful prickly leaves. Must be some kind of *Mahonia*, except I think they now call this one a *Berberis* – they keep changing their genera.'

There was a final thicket of Cotoneaster and then we emerged from deep forest into more open country with our first view of two malignant glaciers, black with slaty rubble, ploughing their way down through the upper belt of Himalayan birch. Straight ahead was the Dakhini Balati Glacier, which would be the logical western approach to Panch Chuli II if it were not so horribly steep and fractured, seeming to tumble vertically out of the sky. Balati means hard, fierce, difficult. Just to the left of the Dakhini (South) Balati, snaking round the back at a slightly gentler angle was the Uttari (North) Balati Glacier – the improbable route pioneered by Frank Thomas, Heinrich Harrer and three Sherpa companions in 1951 and repeated by the Indian expeditions of 1964, 1972 and 1973. This was to be our route too and now the hard work was about to start.

Planning is a fine thing in the Himalaya as long as you don't expect to adhere to it too rigidly. Harish had hoped to make Base Camp in a meadow some way up the side of the glacier but the will of the people – in the form of a hundred Kumauni porters – dictated that it should actually be down in the valley, in a sandy clearing where the river belched forth from the glacier's gritty tongue. At just 3,200 metres above sea level, it was one of the lowest glacier tongues in the whole Himalaya and an unusually low base camp site; the summit of Panch Chuli II was still 3,700 metres above us.

In the hope that the porters might change their minds, some of the party went ahead to the old 1973 Base Camp site and in the morning Chris and I climbed up for an hour or two to find Dick and Graham on a grassy knoll, where they had spent the night in bivouac bags. They were busy with breakfast and Dick, squatting beside a wood fire in his old working clothes, his chin stubbled dark and bits of grass in his hair, looked like a creation by Thomas Hardy.

While we drank smoky tea, Muslim came past with some of the porters, bringing up the bulk of the luggage to be dumped part-way up the glacier in a compromise deal. The dump was at the point where the glacier made a right-angle bend and we could now see into its main east–west flow, although this glacier did not so much flow as lurch in three great cataracts, squeezed between unyielding rock walls. Heinrich Harrer had written no detailed account of the 1951 reconnaissance and subsequent Indian teams – even the successful expedition of 1973 – had been equally vague about the route. Twenty-two years on, we wondered where exactly to go. At least the first part was straightforward. Looking up into the corridor, it was obvious that we could bypass the first icefall, by traversing over a big hump on the retaining hillside. Beyond the Hump it was easy to walk out on to the glacier ice, weaving for half a mile or so, between some fairly innocuous crevasses to a broad flat area, where 'Glacier Camp' was pitched on the ice.

I could not begin to describe all our complicated movements over the next ten days. I don't think there was a single occasion when every member of the expedition was gathered in the same place. People came and went, ferrying tents, food, stoves, fuel and climbing gear in a generally uphill direction. At first we tended to sleep at Base Camp, then we gradually settled into Glacier Camp. I used to love going down to the dump to collect a load, each day finding less snow on the Hump, and some new plant emerging. One magnificent herbaceous specimen with golden umbels turned out to be *Megacarpea polyandra*. It tasted a bit like chicory and we always collected a sheaf of its crisp young leaves for our lunchtime salad, mixing it with wild garlic leaves, tuna fish and mayonnaise.

The British contingent generally ate lunch separately, but then joined a communal meal in the evening. The team dynamics were complicated and it was still uncertain how we were going to employ our excessive numbers on the mountain above. Whilst Harish was determined to move his entire bandobast of supporting staff up the mountain, stage by stage, we were keen at some point to cut loose and go 'alpine-style'. For the time being though we had to concentrate on getting everything to 'Advance Base'.

Renshaw and I went up early one morning to choose a site, setting off in the dark to dash nervously up the horrible rotten gully which bypassed the second icefall, then across the next level to bypass the third icefall, climbing an interminable snow gully, past an old frayed rope left by the Indian Army twenty years earlier. Dick reached the top first, a silhouetted figure, knee-deep in a swirling torrent of spindrift, haloed by slanting shafts of sunlight, with, at last, the summit pyramid of Panch Chuli II visible behind. After the claustrophobic confines of Glacier Camp, it was wonderful to feel the landscape open up, with new gleaming vistas compensating for the dirty melting snow and rubble below. The upper glacier basin covered a huge area and its only exit was the narrow gorge which we had just climbed. Later I read Harrer's theory that this concentrated squeezing of such a huge volume of ice accounted for the unusually low tongue of the Uttari Balati – an interesting argument, except that the glaciers on the other side descend equally far into the Darma valley.

We found a suitable campsite, sheltered by a rock outcrop, dumped our loads, then headed back down. The next day it rained heavily and everyone remained at Glacier Camp. In the wan light of evening we emerged from our tents to stand around in the snow and eat supper. Harish's ebullient banter lifted spirits. Sustad, the long-haired carpenter from Oswestry, talked wood with Bhupesh, employed in the Bombay timber trade. Bonington reminisced about his friend Arne Naess, the Norwegian shipping magnate married to Diana Ross, which shifted us laterally to showbiz and the Bombay film business. That got us on to Salman Rushdie and someone mentioned the bulbous-nosed pickle taster in *Midnight's Children*. 'Achha!' Harish produced a huge jar and shouted, 'Hey, Steve-sahib, come and have some of your favourite Bombay pickles.' I had no desire to have my mucous membranes seared numb so feigned deafness, busying myself with a camera by my tent. There was some sniggering from Victor and a reference to the battered old trilby hat, pulled on over a hood, sheltering my thin stubbled face.

'Hey, Freddy, come over here.' I ignored them.

'Freddy!'

'Who's Freddy?' I looked up, bored.

'Freddy Kruger.'

'Freddy Who?'

'Don't pretend you don't know,' Victor chided. Sustad, steeped in Hollywood culture, added incredulously, 'Where've you been? You must know about Freddy Kruger – *Nightmare on Elm Street*.'

'Ah, yes, that rings a bell. *Nightmare on Elm Street*. Some kind of horror film, isn't it. So Freddy –'

'Yes, yes,' they all groaned.

A few weeks later I saw the photos of me in the hat and they did look quite sinister. Anyway, the name stuck, and, to avoid any confusion with the other Stephen, Sustad, I became known for the rest of the expedition as Freddy, which was a lot better than my extraordinarily inappropriate schoolboy label of Terry, referring to the footballer.

The following day most of the team did a load-carry to Advance Base and back. Bonington, at fifty-eight much older than most of us, still moved like a young man but, by his own admission, he found load-carrying harder work these days; so the following morning Victor suggested, 'Why don't you go up and stay at Advance Base to rest and acclimatize. Graham can stay up there too, and that'll still leave four of us to ferry loads.'

Renshaw, Sustad and I concurred with varying degrees of enthusiasm. Bonington, with typical effusiveness, burst out, 'That's really kind. Thank you. I must say, this is a nice team. You're so much easier than that lot I had to deal with back in the seventies.'

'That lot' on the ground-breaking new face climbs on Annapurna and Everest had been a hard-bitten, individualistic bunch and it had required a difficult blend of firm leadership and consensus politics for Bonington to hold them all together. Now, with Everest safely behind him and his position as a public figure unassailable, he was an altogether mellower person. But there was still a streak of opportunistic ambition. You could see how this man had got where he had got, and I couldn't resist a moment's grudging admiration when we came back up to Advance Base three days later to discover that, instead of waiting politely and resting while we toiled in the icefalls, Bonington and Little had stolen a march on us, grabbing the first ascent of the most attractive peak above Advance Base. The only consolation was that they had gone mistakenly to the slightly lower of its two summits. Harish suggested calling the peak Sahadev, after one of the Pandava brothers, which seemed curiously confusing. If it had two summits, why didn't we name one Sahadev and the other Nakula, after his twin brother? However, it seemed unwise to try to interfere with Hindu nomenclature, a subject close to Harish's heart.

It was now 27 May, three weeks since we had left Britain. Apart from Harish's fellow cloth dealer, the gentle Jain, Vijay Kothari, all the expedition members were established with food and supplies at Advance Base. It was a glorious spot perched on the edge of the wide upper basin of the glacier, ringed by high peaks. The lumbering caravan still had to shift another level, to the final plateau beneath Panch Chuli II. In the meantime, the British foursome hoped to emulate the old master and snatch a training peak or two.

On 28 May, for the fifth day in a row, we rose reluctantly for the 3.00 a.m. 'alpine start' – a perverse masochism developed by the earlier alpine pioneers to beat the midday perils of melting snow, collapsing snow-bridges, avalanching ice towers and crucifying heat. In the Himalaya, closer to the equator and operating at higher altitudes with less protective atmosphere, the heat is particularly oppressive. During the spring pre-Monsoon season in Kumaun, regular afternoon cloudbursts were also added to the list of incentives to start and finish early.

That morning, by way of further acclimatization, we tackled a small peak close to Advance Base, soloing up a straightforward snow face. I felt weak and breathless and, as the other three drew steadily ahead, I became more and more depressed. Slumped over my ice axe, panting, gasping, aching . . . I wondered, not for the first time, what on earth I was doing here. Sustad, the long-haired superman, was forging ahead. Renshaw was his usual fit self. Even the wheezing, asthmatic Saunders was keeping up. They disappeared and when I eventually reached the crest of the ridge, they were already coming back down towards me.

'You bastards – why didn't you wait?'

'Too warm,' Sustad shouted bluntly. 'The snow's getting soft. We've got to go down.'

'You could have waited just five minutes, to let me join you on the summit.'

'We didn't even go –'

'Selfish bastards – why are you always in such –'

'Freddy, look at me. We didn't go to the summit. It was too far.'
'What? Ah . . . well . . . I see. So it's not that bump there. Well,
er . . . are we going down now?' I looked suitably apologetic and
followed silently back to Advance Base, trying to sublimate ego
in the serene beauty of our surroundings and persuade myself
that this was where I really wanted to be, not sitting in the garden
with Rosie, sharing a bottle of wine.

Back at camp, Bonington and Little were preparing to set off
for another climb on the far side of the glacier. They made an
unpropitious departure after lunch, just as the clouds lowered.
Half an hour later ball-bearings smashed from the sky and the
tents were whipped by a vicious wind. Bonington's untended
dome took off, bowling at high speed across the snowfield
towards the lip of the huge icefall. By pure chance, Prakash and
Pasang were just arriving from Glacier Camp and managed to
field the tent in the nick of time.

Thunder rumbled through most of the night but by morning
the storm had blown over and we emptied out the errant tent, to
spend a couple of hours sifting through a jumble of clothes,
books, computer batteries, used tea bags and Olympus lenses all
sticky with spilt orange powder. The owner returned with
Graham at lunchtime. Both men looked tired and jaded after a
miserable bivouac and a nasty encounter with a huge crevasse.
'And', Bonington added, 'when it got light we realized we were
on the wrong bloody mountain.'

It snowed again that afternoon and most of the next day.
Renshaw and I brooded in our tent. Every so often Victor and
the Lutheran would join us for tea, coffee or a meal.
Conversation circled around possible objectives. We were four
characters in search of a mountain, not quite sure which way to
turn. I still felt unmotivated but at least had some lukewarm
enthusiasm for Sahadev, whose highest point had eluded
Bonington and Little. There was a magnificent steep ridge on the
far side of the peak, studded with monolithic granite towers that
could refire my imagination.

Sustad also seemed quite keen on Sahadev, but Victor was
sitting on the fence. The alternative choice was Rajrambha, a

higher peak at the head of the glacier. Its South Face had been mooted back in England, but now, after our experience of late May heat on Kumaun snow slopes, we were less keen on ploughing straight up the face. I think it was Renshaw's sketch which finally pushed us towards an altogether more enticing plan. Now that sculpture was the real passion of his life, when he was separated from his mallet and chisels he consoled himself with pencil and charcoal. Looking up at Rajrambha he drew a minimalist outline of its South Ridge, dropping in great steps to the broad curve of a saddle, which then swept up to the summit of Menaka, before plunging down again to the glacier basin.

Here at last was a vision to excite and unite us while waiting for the final shift up to Panch Chuli II – a great ridge traverse which Victor compared to the famous Peuterey Ridge on Mont Blanc. The summit of Mont Blanc is 4,807 metres above sea level; here we would *start* from an Advance Base of 4,840 metres. The actual ridge was about three miles long and would probably take three or four days, perhaps longer as we would have to stop most days soon after noon to shelter from the afternoon snowfall. But, being on a ridge, there would be no problem with spindrift avalanches and there would almost certainly be sites for our two dome tents.

Harish was delighted by our plan. 'You realize that Menaka has never been climbed. So Britishers will kill two birds with one stone – first ascent of Menaka and new route on Rajrambha.'

'So, how did they climb Rajrambha on the first ascent?'

'ITBP came from the far side in 1975.' Our walking Himalayan textbook had the movements of the India Tibet Border Police off by heart. 'No one has ever attempted it from this side.' He went to explain that Rajrambha was the most beautiful of the Apsaras – guardian fairies who protect the Devas from interfering mortals; Menaka was another Apsara – some kind of junior fairy, I think. I promised to tiptoe reverently along our ridge. Sustad, ever practical, said never mind about fairies – we would just see how far we could get and turn back if we ran out of food or enthusiasm or climbable snow conditions.

As the weather seemed to be improving that afternoon, we packed for an early pre-dawn departure. I was still not totally sold on the idea of the great ridge traverse, but I was glad that we had at least made a decision. And, after all the fractured vacillation, I was glad that we were committed to working as a team of four. Apart from the practical advantages of sharing the weight of climbing equipment, it would be more sociable than splitting into pairs and with four of us there would be a comforting sense of security.

I was touched that evening when Monesh, the youngest expedition member, came round to shake hands, wishing each of us in turn good luck for the adventure ahead. The formal but heartfelt gesture added a touch of ritual, rare these days in British climbing circles, where we tend to hide behind a gauche, brittle cynicism. Comforted by his good wishes, I retired to our tent to continue checking through my personal gear for the climb, then snuggled deep into my sleeping bag, finally getting to sleep an hour before the midnight alarm clock roused us for departure.

Chapter Four

IT WAS A disgruntled quartet that set off across the glacier at 2.15 a.m. Victor's stomach was grumbling from the effects of two full pans of coffee. After an hour's plodding across the frozen snow the grumbling became vocal, so I took a turn in the lead, trying to find the best route through a maze of half-seen crevasses. Then the slope steepened and I despaired at my weakness, ploughing up knee-deep powder to the start of the buttress which would get us on to Menaka.

Daylight improved my mood and when we stopped to put on suncream it was good to rest for a moment and look across the basin to Panch Chuli II and Sahadev – serene, white forms floating above the hazy blue depths of India's great northern plain. Focusing on the closer detail of the glacier, we suddenly noticed four black dots crawling through the white immensity on the far side of the basin – Muslim, Bhupesh, Pasang and Prakash, starting the recce to the upper Balati Plateau. On our mountain, we too climbed into the blazing heat of the day, Sustad leading us over a vertical ice step just before it melted irredeemably. Above that there were rocky slopes leading to a great ice dome where we stopped gratefully at midday to dig ledges for the two tents. Afternoon cloud subdued the heat and I settled down with a couple of paracetamol to kill a nagging headache.

On the second day I began to enjoy myself. Once again the four of us roped together, with Renshaw and I taking first turn in the lead at 4.30 a.m., breaking trail to the 6,000-metre summit of Menaka. It was good to reach an unclimbed summit, but the real excitement lay ahead, where the ridge dropped in an elegant parabola before sweeping up in three giant steps to the distant summit of Rajrambha. The grand vision was inspiring but when it came to the immediate mundane detail of some horribly brittle ice, I was glad to let Sustad take the lead down on to the connecting saddle to Rajrambha, where we stopped early to camp.

The third day of June was our third day on the climb. It was also the twenty-eighth day since leaving home. I thought about the two faces watching from the doorway on that bright morning four weeks earlier, but instead of wrenching my stomach the memory was now merely nostalgic. At last I was managing to live in the present, happy with our simple nomadic existence, moving day by day along a white ribbon in the sky.

It was actually a piebald ribbon and today we hoped to traverse several black rocky sections and reach the top of a prominent black pinnacle on the final step in the ridge. We had a long way to go, so we left very early, at 2.15, climbing by the light of headtorches. Victor led masterfully, ploughing through cold powder snow and scrambling over rock steps that felt awkward in the black night. Despite the numb feet and the cold sweat I enjoyed the night climbing, revelling again in the surreal thrill of trespassing high above the earth, where no one had ever been before. Dawn was pinkish grey with distant muted shapes appearing over the Nepalese border to the east, then sharpening to a whiter clarity. To the north we could see far into what must be Tibet, where peaks rose above the high passes now closed to Indian traders. One of those peaks must be Gurla Mandhata. And Kailas must be there too, the holiest mountain of all, rising close to the source of the Indus, Brahmaputra and Sutlej rivers – the geographical epicentre of Hinduism and Buddhism.

At the first real steepening of our ridge Sustad took over, leading meticulously and carefully through rock bands smeared with blue ice. At one belay I watched him arranging the anchor and was struck by the precision of someone who learned his technique on the gigantic vertical walls of Yosemite's El Capitan, where awesome exposure concentrates the mind wonderfully. Here the rock was not granite but some kind of shale and Sustad was hammering a steel knifeblade piton into a thin bedding plane between layers of solidified black mud, laid down in some ocean long before the Indian subcontinent drifted into Tibet 50 million years ago and was thrust several miles up into the sky to form the greatest mountain range on earth. That, as far as I could gather from geologists, was the gist of it, except that it was not only uplift that made the mountains: it was the subsequent erosion of that uplifted material that created the sublime forms we now know. As with a sculpture, it is the removal of material – in this case by wind, ice and the scouring action of the great Himalayan rivers – that makes the finished form possible. Without the Darmaganga and Goriganga rivers, there would be no Rajrambha.

Victor took over again, moving with slick efficiency, Renshaw did a stint and then I had a turn in front, glad to be leading again. Back in Europe, leading a rock-climb at the limit of my ability, every move would be fixed in my memory. The pleasure of working out a sequence of moves, then finally succeeding, with body and mind working in synchrony, can be exquisitely satisfying: as satisfying as mastering some musical phrase and discovering its perfection – delighting in the absolute rightness of the shape of the thing unfolding. On Rajrambha, 6,000 metres above sea level, with a 15 kg rucksack on my back, it was a more a case of sight-reading or improvising – less subtle and more concerned with the bigger shape of things, but still pleasing in its own rough and ready way.

We had an efficient system where, generally, we would all be moving together with the rope clipped into several anchors at any one time, in case of a fall. On steeper sections we would usually stop to 'pitch' it, one at a time, but on this steep chimney bay, with nowhere convenient to stop, I kept moving, shouting to the others to follow, confident in my ability to complete the next section safely. When we all paused finally to sort out gear, there was a touch of acid in Sustad's laconic Seattle drawl: 'Exceptional lead. Do you always move together on ground that hard?' I stuttered an excuse and headed off again, through more shale bands to the top of the pinnacle, where a short horizontal crest led to the niche we had earmarked for overnight accommodation.

The main anchor was a gratifyingly technical arrangement of alloy wedges held in tension by connecting slings. 'Nuts in opposition,' I announced with triumphant, naïve enthusiasm. Someone sniggered over 'Freddy's nuts in opposition', and I sat on a rock, taking photographs and making encouraging noises while the others hacked away at the narrow crest, sending great blocks of snow crust tumbling into the veiled depths. The afternoon blizzard arrived early today and wind clutched at the precious tent fabric as they struggled on their tiny stance to erect the two domes and secure them to the ropes. By the time we were all inside, the flakes were falling with a soft heavy thud. Opening the door to pass a half-smoked roll-up through to the sharers in the other tent, Dick found fluffy powder piled on the connecting ledge. He scooped up a panful and added it to the hanging gas stove. As the afternoon faded to dusk, we worked through the usual comforting routine of tea, soup, fruit drinks and coffee, accompanying biscuits and cheese, noodles and the other subsistence rations we relied on to replace the day's calorie loss. This distillation of life to its purest animal essentials of food, shelter and sleep, enhanced by the utterly tangible, physical sensation of a day's hard work completed, was immensely satisfying.

Less satisfying was the 2 a.m. wake-up call the following morning. On Everest I had always been the one to take the lead in the cold anxious hours before dawn. Now, sharing a tent with Renshaw again, I deferred to his habitual monastic discipline, wallowing idly in my sleeping bag while he organized breakfast.

Wind had battered the tents all night and at dawn there seemed to be no let-up. Shouting backwards and forwards between the two sealed tents, we decided to wait for the sun's warmth before venturing outside. We finally made a late start at 6.30, with Victor leading us round to the left, in a characteristically devious manoeuvre to avoid the steep black crest of the final step. By late morning, several hundred feet higher, we re-emerged on to the crest of the ridge at a levelling before the final summit step. Clustered round a pile of titanic shale blocks, we ate some lunch and discussed tactics. During our four days on the ridge, we had become an effective team and consensus had served us well, but on this final step we were split down the middle on how to play the summit. Should we stop here and leave it for the morning or try to race over the top and bivouac on the far side, starting our descent before food and gas rations dwindled any lower?

For some reason the gung-ho faction prevailed and after lunch we continued. I harboured thoughts of 'told you so' as the afternoon blizzard swept in with unusual vehemence. I was doing a stint in front, spurred on by conflicting shouts of advice, Renshaw urging me to stay well to the left, Victor telling me to go further right, closer to the crest of the cornice. 'Don't worry,' he insisted, 'we can hold you if it breaks, and you'll be able to move much faster on the soft snow.'

He was actually quite right. Sticking to textbook rules, traversing low down on the windward side of the crest, forced one to crabcrawl precariously on steep brittle ice. But up near the crest, where the snow was flung east by the wind into wickedly beautiful, overhanging whirls, the terrain was softer and more level. The idea was to stick immediately left of the probable fracture line of the great overhangs. Secured by the others from a solid belay it was a perfectly reasonable option, but by now I could hardly tell where I was at all – sleety snow was icing up my glasses and reducing the world to a confused grey blur.

The others had vanished in the swirling cloud. Ice particles stung my face. Spindrift swept over the mountain's icy skin, obscuring detail, destroying perspective. Then the air began to buzz around my head. I had first experienced that dread sound on my very first alpine climb, twenty years earlier with Jean-Pierre. A couple of years later, benighted in the Bregaglia Alps, I had huddled in terror during a whole night of thunder and lightning, but it had never struck our mountain. Now here it was again. The air was charged with million-volt menace and we were perched close to the summit of Rajrambha.

The air was still buzzing when first Renshaw and then Sustad joined me. There was no chance of bivouacking on the tilted ice where we stood, so they suggested that I carry on immediately to investigate the crest. I unclipped from the anchor and inched up warily. Peering through the murk, I suddenly made out the diffuse outline of a cornice hanging over space. My heart lurched as I registered the proximity of the fragile edge. In the same moment there was a yellow flash and a terrible sound, like ripping paper amplified a million times, tearing across the crest just a few feet above my head.

'Take in the rope!' I reversed frantically, jabbing ice axes in a diagonal slither, as the other two hauled me back to comparative safety. While Victor approached, unseen, from the cloud below, the three of us huddled on our ice perch, helpless as the lightning struck again, pumping millions of volts into the ridge above our heads. My heart juddered but luckily not through the convulsions of electrocution. For some merciful reason all the energy dissipated on the crest above, although some secondary current did seem to flow down the ridge, for out of the murk below we heard a little voice going 'Aargh!' then 'Ouch!' then 'Owh – shit that hurt.' When Victor finally joined us, he pointed to the bundle of alloy tent poles, projecting from his rucksack, like an antenna above his left shoulder, and complained, 'It was really painful – horrible – like a cattle prod.' There was a pause while the dark eyes darted back and forth, questing a sympathetic look, then a muttered, 'Why are you all laughing?'

The lightning had moved on and, apart from Victor's mild zapping, we were unharmed. However, the blizzard still raged, so we agreed to go back down to the level section of the ridge and find a bivouac site there. I went first, followed by Sustad. His hair was a wild tangle of hoar frost and his spectacles lenses were opaque, like the sea-scoured glass pebbles you find on the beach. Completely unfazed, competent as ever, he exclaimed, 'I'm rather enjoying this.'

Down on the level section, I belayed Victor, while he put his theories into practice, exploring the very tip of the fragile cornice. From above we had spotted some extravagantly convoluted structures on the east flank of the crest and Victor now investigated these, stamping around on a subsidiary formation which he hoped might provide a platform for the tents. There was a loud bang and the rope came tight as Victor dangled in space, watching a ton of collapsed cornice rumble down into the Darma valley. Then more 'ouch' noises as he realized he had pulled a muscle in his back. Then eager noises as, from his unique dangling viewpoint on the east side of the ridge, he spotted a great fluted pillar underpinning a cornice further along the crest – the one feasible spot for our overnight accommodation. Two hours later we were all safe and snug in our sleeping bags, enjoying a well-earned supper.

At dawn on the fifth day, I traversed the brittle ice slope for the third time. This time it was for real and we continued along the final ridge to the summit of the guardian fairy. At the scene of the previous afternoon's lightning flash, the others belayed from well below the crest, spurring me on to move quickly, walking the plank, close to the fracture line. I enjoyed a few easy steps before there was a crumpled bang. My feet shot away beneath me and for a glorious instant I flew through the air, before stopping with a gentle bounce on the elastic rope. Hanging there for a brief moment of relaxation, watching the cornice tumbling far beneath me in a sparkle of atomized fragments, it occurred to me that I might rather enjoy bungee jumping.

On the other side of the ridge, Renshaw commented, 'Freddy's fallen through the cornice' – a curiously superfluous statement from a man of so few words. Then Sustad and Victor helped him pull me back on to the crest to complete my pitch. Ten minutes later, securing the others as they came up to join me, I had time to look back at our achievement. Sustad and Renshaw were heroic statues, silhouetted on a brilliant, sparkling white, Rococo fantasy. Behind them the detail faded, but the overall shape of our ribbon in the sky could be traced in an elegant curve, dropping far below to the saddle, then back up over the summit of Menaka, two miles away. Towering behind Menaka, putting the whole thing in context, the serene pyramid of Panch Chuli II dominated the entire range.

Stephen Sustad, silhouetted on the left, is just approaching the point where the cornice broke.

At 6.45 a.m. we stood on Rajrambha's domed summit. For the first time we could see across the immense gorge of the Goriganga to the highest mountain wholly in India – Nanda Devi. From here the two summits of the Mother Goddess were profiled in line, appearing almost as a single gleaming spire, and we could only just make out the further Main Summit, with Tilman's and Odell's line on the left. Almost obscuring it was the nearer East Summit. On his very first Himalayan expedition in 1905, two years before Trisul, Longstaff had attempted the East Summit of Nanda Devi from a col on the Sanctuary wall. The summit was finally climbed by a Polish expedition in 1939, and repeated in 1951 during a bold French attempt to traverse the precarious, jagged ridge linking the two summits. On the support party, Tenzing Norgay, the Sherpa who was to make history on Everest two years later, reached the East Summit with Lionel Dubost, then climbed all the way back to the summit a second time in a vain bid to search for the traverse party, but he found no sign of Roger Duplat and Gilbert Vignes, who had been seen setting off from the distant Main Summit eight days earlier. They were never seen again.

Hidden behind the great spire's protective wall lay the elusive cirque of the Sanctuary. In 1934 Tilman and Shipton had found it teeming with wildlife. Later, the fragile ecosystem began to suffer as more humans intruded. It was here, in the mid sixties, that a secret American expedition, sponsored by the CIA, had placed a nuclear spying device, intended to pick up Chinese movements north of the Himalayan frontier. For the climbers involved it was a wonderful opportunity to climb Nanda Devi, at a time when virtually the whole of the Himalaya was officially closed to foreigners. Unfortunately the device was subsequently lost in an avalanche and, with much embarrassment, the CIA had to dispatch a second expedition to locate it. They never did and to this day there are fears that one of the holiest sources of Mother Ganga was contaminated by radioactive material. The whole business was kept hushed up until 1978, when an American magazine spilled the beans, causing both the CIA and the Indian government more acute embarrassment. Climbing expeditions to the Nanda Devi Sanctuary were suddenly banned 'for environmental reasons'. It is possible that the nuclear device had caused environmental damage; but far more obvious were the effects on the ecosystem from less sensational causes – the wood-burning porters accompanying mountaineering expeditions and the local shepherds bringing their flocks up the path that now openly adorned the Rishi Gorge. Whatever the genuine reason – and political embarrassment seems the most plausible – the area still remains closed to all but a select group of Indian military expeditions sent in for periodic 'environmental assessments'.

Before news broke of the CIA debacle, there was a brief spell, in the mid seventies, when several foreign and local civilian teams were allowed to roam in the Sanctuary. One of them was Harish's attempt on Devtoli in 1974. It was on this expedition that he broke his hip, falling into a crevasse. It took six days to stretcher him down the comparatively gentle ground to Base Camp; then a helicopter arrived, sparing him the horror of a stretcher journey down the precipitous Rishi Gorge. Back in Bombay the doctors told him that he would not walk for two years. Naturally rebellious and determined, Harish used yoga to speed the healing process and within a year had made his first mountain trek on crutches.

The mountains on the Sanctuary wall also held memories for Renshaw. Even at this distance we could make out the slanting line of Dunagiri's South-West Ridge, which he had climbed with Joe Tasker in 1975, setting the world a new standard of what two climbers could achieve in a simple 'alpine-style' push, without any supporters ferrying supplies to prepared camps. Dunagiri was not achieved without cost. New to the Himalaya, the two men became dangerously over-extended and during an afternoon blizzard on the descent, struggling deliriously with iced ropes, Renshaw got the tips of his fingers badly frostbitten. By the time they completed the descent, both men were pathetically weak, hallucinating, and teetering on the edge of survival. Seventeen years on, a mellower Renshaw seemed happy to forego that kind of catharsis. Our five-day journey up Rajrambha, despite the electric storm, had been strangely relaxed and I felt that we had enjoyed a healthy margin of safety. We had stayed in control.

We held on to that control during the descent. Sustad started off first, leading us down the West Ridge, to a col where we turned left and headed down a steep snow face back into the glacier basin beneath Rajrambha. Reversing ropelength by ropelength, safeguarding ourselves with a metal anchor plate, encouragingly called a 'deadman', we moved quickly and efficiently. How lucky, I thought, to be with this team of some of the most competent, experienced Himalayan climbers in the world. Despite the obscuring afternoon cloud, a serendipitous blend of intuition, skill and luck seemed to get us down the one smooth slope between gaping bergschrunds on to the glacier. Hoping for a clearing, we pitched one of the tents and settled inside to share the last of the coffee. Spirits were high and when the cloud failed to clear we carried on anyway, relying on pooled observations from our days on the ridge. Victor, the one professional mountain guide (as he kept reminding us), seemed to have memorized the lie of the land particularly well. Chatting, laughing, enjoying the light-hearted end-of-term mood, relishing the novelty of flat ground, but still talking each other carefully round dangerous 'slots', we emerged beneath the cloud to find that we were precisely on route. In the final hour of twilight we trudged back almost to the point where we had set foot on Menaka, five days earlier, then, in a broad sweeping curve round a crevasse field, we made our way back to Advance Base.

In our absence, the main caravan had moved on up to the Balati Plateau and was now at work on Panch Chuli II, but two of the Kumauni porters, Yograj and Khubram, were looking after the camp. Within minutes of our arrival they had produced a big pot of tea, followed by deliciously spicy spinach, paneer and rice. After supper there was more tea and, as a special celebratory treat, Renshaw, the closet hedonist, produced a packet of Gitanes cigarettes. Sprawled in the warm fug of the cook tent, I felt a glorious, contented sleepiness wash over me, and soon I retired to my own tent to relish the luxury of a long night in bed, free for the first time in five days from the need to keep on my harness and tether myself to the mountain.

Chapter Five

'I HAD FORGOTTEN HOW much it takes out of you – a big climb like that.' After twelve hours in bed, followed by a luxuriously late breakfast, Renshaw was sitting in the sun at Advance Base. I also felt tired, now that the tension was relieved. True, we had all done tougher climbs at much higher altitudes – on Everest, for instance, the real climbing had only started close to the height of Rajrambha's summit – but five days' hard work, with relentless early starts, little sleep and not much food, all at around 6,000 metres above sea level, had taken its toll. Everyone was slightly dazed and bleary. It was not an unpleasant sensation, but we were looking forward to a few days' rest and no one was in a hurry to join the others on Panch Chuli II.

Five days earlier we had seen the ant figures toiling up the long white ramp to the Balati Plateau. Now from down here at Advance Base the plateau was hidden, but we could still see the pyramid itself, rising behind. We trained a telephoto lens on the skyline, trying to find the Bombay team on the South-West Ridge, but could not see them. Then Renshaw spotted two dots on the closer West Ridge. Bonington and Little had discussed this steeper ridge – more of an ice buttress – as a possibility, and there they were. I clicked a magnifying doubler on to the 200-mm lens and had another look. One figure was stationary. Above it, another moved laboriously, inching up a slick sheet of ice, gleaming repellently in the mid-morning glare. I thought thankfully of our return to the valley.

We set off down. First the long steep snow gully. Then a rising traverse on the flank of the glacier to 'Harish's Horror' – a human ibex trail across a crumbling precipice, safeguarded with fixed ropes. Then another long steep snow slope, where the penalty for failure would be a tumble over undercut cliffs at the bottom. Tapping the elaborate steel crampons on our state-of-the-art plastic boots to remove balled-up clods of sticky wet snow, we four sahibs moved with meticulous pedantry, and were startled by a sudden shout as Yograj and Khubram appeared above, hands in pockets, lolloping down the slope, kicking nonchalantly into the lethal slush with their cheap sneakers. As they raced effortlessly past, we felt rather overdressed.

We caught up with them half an hour later, down at Glacier Camp. There we also, unexpectedly, met Vijay Kothari. During the last two weeks we had hardly seen the Jain cloth merchant, who for some reason had been relegated to the rearguard of Harish's expeditionary force. Now, when we finally met, we found him stranded at Glacier Camp with a broken ankle. Two days earlier, on the way up to Advance Base, he had slipped on the big snow slope, failed to brake with his ice axe, and rocketed 200 metres down the slope, catching an ankle on the way. It was probably only the prompt action of the sneaker-clad Kumaunis, grabbing him by the scruff of the neck at the last minute, that had stopped him hurtling over the base cliffs to far worse injuries.

Wing-Commander Anil Srivastava, our liaison officer, had gone down to Munsiary to try to organize a helicopter rescue. Now we cleared a flat site close to Glacier Camp and marked it with a prominent H. We promised to send up more supplies from Base Camp, then continued our homeward journey.

The whole valley was in metamorphosis. Snow had melted from the lower glacier, leaving bare its ugly bones. Quitting the the rubble wasteland to climb over the Hump, we entered Eden. When we arrived in May the snow had only just started retreating, allowing the first life to burst through winter's matted brown coat of dead vegetation. I had wondered about a patch of pale glaucous spears, so full of promise, and now, sure enough, they were a mass of purple Kumaun Iris flowers. And the primulas were out – the deep velvet, purple-blue of *Primula macrophylla* clustered above rosettes of robust fleshy leaves designed to survive up to 5,000 metres above sea level. Never mind that the book described them as 'widespread and promiscuous throughout the Himalaya'; I was just thrilled to see these vulgar tarts again. And all the new acquaintances. Like the creamy lily trumpets, and the miniature jewelled yellow Star of Bethlehem, and the sweet-scented dwarf *Rhododendron anthopogon* whose fragrant leaves are burned for Buddhist pujahs, and the dazzling electric blue of *Corydalis kashmeriana*, and the mysterious tentacle-leaved plants which had puzzled me on the way up and now revealed the mottled yellow-purple inflorescence of *Fritillaria roylei*.

Victor had become a born-again botanist and joined enthusiastically in my floral ecstasy, while the Lutheran looked scornful, exclaiming intermittently, 'Oh dear, I seem to have trodden on a flower.' Renshaw settled on the crest of the Hump to do a sketch and the rest of us sat down beside him to share the view down the valley. Even after eight days our eyes were hungry for green and this particular landscape had a youthful vibrancy about it. The Himalaya is one of the youngest mountain ranges on earth. It is in a constant state of flux and in recent years many of the glaciers have been shrinking drastically. The two Balati glaciers, having forced their way so far down the valley, were now in retreat, their tired grey ice shrunken far below the crest of the lateral moraines. There was a natural genius in the curve of those giant furrows – the sterile rubble of the glacial trench accentuating the brilliance either side, where the soft dip between moraine and mountainside was filled with young birch leaves shimmering amongst the bottle green of venerable conifers.

During the next four days' rest at Base Camp, I returned a couple of times to the alpine meadows of the Hump. I thought about Frank Smythe, the famous Thirties mountaineer who had spent a whole summer in a similar valley not far from here, recording his experiences in the classic *Valley of Flowers*.

Frank Smythe discovered the Bhiundhar valley almost by accident in 1931, when his team crossed the Bhiundhar Pass on the way back from making the first ascent of Kamet. The Monsoon had broken. Wind and wet snow made the crossing a misery. Then, descending through the mist into the Bhiundhar valley, Smythe's 'gaze was arrested by a little splash of blue, and beyond it were other splashes of blue, a blue so intense it seemed to light the hillside. In all my mountain wanderings I had not seen a more beautiful flower than this primula; the fine rain drops clung to its soft petals like galaxies of seed-pearls and frosted its leaves with silver. ... Next day we descended to lush meadows. Here our camp was embowered amidst flowers. ... The Bhiundhar valley was the most beautiful valley that any of us had seen.'

Back in Britain, Smythe often remembered the Bhiundhar valley, 'wandering in spirit to those flowerful pastures with their clear-running streams set against a frieze of silver birches and shining snow peaks', but his mountaineering took a more serious turn as he became embroiled in repeated attempts on the world's highest mountain. In 1933, like Edward Norton before him, he reached Man's altitude record, less than a thousand feet from the top, but the summit continued to elude repeated expeditions and Smythe, like so many of his colleagues on those pre-war sieges, became disenchanted with the whole process: 'The ascent of Everest has become a duty, perhaps a national duty, comparable with attempts to reach the poles, and is far removed from pleasurable mountaineering.' So in 1937 he decided to return to pleasure and revisit his Valley of Flowers. By now he had left London, was living in the country and had become a gardener, discovering just how many British garden plants originated in the Himalaya. At that stage, nearly all the serious plant-collecting had been in the far eastern Himalaya, particularly Sikkim, and further still, in South-East Tibet, Yunnan and Szechuan. Very little had been done in the Central Himalaya and, although much of the flora of Garhwal and Kumaun is also found further east, there is a significant number of endemic species. So Smythe decided to make plant-collecting the focus for his journey and spend an entire summer season witnessing the botanical cycle of the Bhiundhar valley.

The whole ecosystem here, in the Balati valley, was almost identical to Smythe's Bhiundhar valley. In 1951, while Heinrich

Harrer had attempted Panch Chuli, Kailas Sahni, from the Dehra Dun Forest Research Institute, had collected 400 different flowers in this very valley. I didn't count, but I did marvel at the complex symbiosis of plants jostling successfully for space, each growing in precisely the right conditions, taking turns throughout the summer to flower in the kind of continuous, effortless, rhythmic display of colour and form which gardeners struggle so hard to emulate. Even during the brief spring season we were experiencing, the richness of it all was intoxicating.

Unlike us, Smythe travelled without fellow sahibs. At Ranikhet he met four Sherpas from Darjeeling who were to be his only companions in the Valley of Flowers. He seems to have been all too happy to remove himself from a civilization which, in 1937, seemed doomed. 'In Garhwal I found no red, green or black shirts, no flags or emblems, no mechanisms, no motor cars or aeroplanes, but I did find a happy and contented people. . . . I met a true civilization, for I found contentment and happiness . . . I had never before realized until I camped in the Valley of Flowers how much happiness there is in simple living and simple things.' Memories of simple things sustained Smythe through the war and later he planned to return to the Garhwal/Kumaun region to attempt Panch Chuli. However, that project never happened. In 1949, shortly after leaving Darjeeling for Sikkim, he became very ill from a mosquito bite and died of malaria, weakened, perhaps, by his years of extreme exertion at altitude.

I could identify with Smythe's enchantment with simplicity, but, wandering in the forest and meadows of the Balati valley, I felt a restlessness. I suspect that, for all his flirtation with the oriental contemplative life, Smythe's happiness also derived from having a job of work to do. While he was in the valley he explored passes, climbed peaks, and was kept busy with his plant collections. For me, wandering around looking inexpertly at flowers was all very well for a few days, but there had to be some purpose to make sense of our mountain retreat. Without some focus, the whole thing would become insipid. I seemed, against my better judgement, to be agreeing with Kant's thesis that, 'It is by his activities and not by enjoyment that man feels he is alive.

In idleness we not only feel that life is fleeting, but we also feel lifeless.'

After four days' rest at Base Camp, enjoying twelve hours sleep every night and making the most of Revatram's cooking, the work ethic prevailed and we decided to head back up to join the main effort of Panch Chuli II, or at least to find out what had been going on.

Just below Glacier Camp we heard a shout. Vijay had already left, flown out by helicopter two days earlier, so it must be some of the main party. Soon Bonington appeared between two hummocks of ice, followed by Harish and the rest of the Bombay wallahs. They all looked triumphantly tired and we knew immediately that they had been successful. Muslim Contractor looked particularly happy. With Pasang Bodh and Monesh Devjani he had reached the summit of Panch Chuli II, whilst Harish and Bhupesh waited in support on the plateau. His success came on a ridge with a history. The first attempt on 10 June 1951 was thwarted by hard, glassy ice. Both the Sherpas accompanying Heinrich Harrer and Frank Thomas slipped, became very frightened and had to be escorted down. The following year an Indian team, led by D.D. Joshi failed to climb the rib. A P.N. Nikore attempted the route alone that year, then returned in 1953, claiming the first ascent. In the absence of any proof, his dubious claim was rejected. Then in 1964 Group Captain A.K. Choudhary led a large team from the Indian Mountaineering Foundation. They too were unsuccessful and it was only in 1973 that Mahendra Singh's ITBP team finally succeeded in reaching the summit.

Where the 1973 military expedition had fixed thousands of feet of rope and employed countless porters, the civilian Bombay-Kumauni trio had climbed in one simple push, with a camp halfway up the ridge. It was a triumph for Pasang and the Bombay civilians. Bonington and Little had shouted to the Indians as they descended from the summit, watching from their own top camp on the parallel West Ridge. That had been the day after we spotted them from Advance Base. Bonington confirmed that the ice had been hard work: 'Yes, horrible brittle stuff. And

some dicey snow as well. Then Graham got the most terrible headaches at night. I was really worried that he was getting cerebral oedema, because nothing seemed to make him better. I was very scared, until he explained that he had a bad head injury as a child. Apparently he suffers a lot from headaches. Anyway, he was fine both mornings, so we carried on. The summit view was fantastic and the other valley looks really interesting. Harish thinks we should go round there.'

'Yes,' Harish was already planning ahead. 'If you are happy to miss out Panch Chuli II, we just have time to explore Pyunshani valley, if we travel light.'

Sustad was delighted. 'Oh good – now we don't have to climb Panch Two.' After the Rajrambha odyssey we had all been rather lukewarm about the official expedition objective. At best we would have been tagging on to the efforts of others. Now that the expedition had achieved a double success on the highest summit in the range, we could concentrate on what I had always wanted to do – exploring the right-hand valley. Suddenly everything was working out perfectly.

Bonington, only just down from his first big Himalayan summit since Everest in 1985, looked weary and asked if we would fetch down Graham Little. 'He insisted on staying up at Advance Base to have another look at Sahadev and nab that other summit. He has to go back to work in a couple of days, and he just wants to have one more go at it before leaving, but I would be much happier if he came down.'

So while the victorious Panch Chuli team carried on down, we slept the night at Glacier Camp and continued early the next morning on our final slog to Advance Base where we found a meditative Little contemplating his elusive summit. I sympathized with his urge to fit in one more climb and settle the score on Sahadev's highest top, but none of us wanted to accompany him, nor to wait while he attempted the climb solo. The whole momentum had shifted to the Pyunshani valley and we wanted to move as soon as possible. Feeling a touch hypocritical, I joined the others' boring voices of reason, persuading Little not to risk a solo attempt. After some deliberation, he agreed and we packed up the remaining tents and gear to take down.

Late that afternoon, at the end of a long day, slithering down the old snow slopes below the Hump, we were caught by a storm worthy of King Lear. Thunder exploded around us. Lightning ripped purple-green light across the valley and water cascaded down the mountainside, hurling rocks, earth and uprooted trees on to the glacier. It was cataclysmic, biblical, melodramatic – a brilliant display of elemental forces. However, for us there was no ignominious banishment, no denial of shelter. The storm was a celebration of the resounding success of the expedition and our reuniting at Base Camp, where we rushed to our tents to remove drenched clothes and shiver into layers of warm, dry fleece and goose down, before joining the rest of the team in the kitchen shelter to lounge contentedly on the dry hay floor, feasting on soup, popadums, chapattis and a huge curry, with lots of tea and whisky and a tin of Sumatran cigars donated by our Dutch film-maker friend, Kees 't Hooft, who had shared many similar drenchings on past expeditions.

Bonington retired early and rose uncharacteristically late the next morning. 'There's no doubt that it takes longer to recover at my age,' he commented ruefully, 'and the thing I really hate is that your skin goes all saggy.' I wondered how many fifty-eight-year-olds could climb steep ice with a heavy rucksack, bivouacking twice on the way to a summit nearly 23,000 feet above sea level and then contemplate traversing round into an unknown, unexplored valley, with the possibility of attempting further peaks? Even at thirty-eight, I had been glad of four days to unwind after Rajrambha; Chris was only getting three.

Harish announced that our transport from Munsiary would be leaving in under two weeks. By the time we had packed up Base Camp, we would have ten days at the most to find our way into the Pyunshani valley, attempt some exploration of its untrodden glacier and make our way back to the roadhead. Already the bulk of the luggage was being sent down to Munsiary with Pasang. Vijay was now back in Bombay having his broken ankle set; Bhupesh Ashar and Graham Little were due back at work. That left just eight of us, plus five of the Kumauni porters, to travel light into the unknown valley.

Once again, we were back at the old game of 'packaging and repackaging the equipments', deciding what we really needed and sending everything else down with Pasang. Harish, Muslim and Monesh kept minimal climbing gear for a possible glacier pass. Sustad and I sorted out slightly more gear for a possible summit, but still kept things to a minimum. Food was running low, but we just about had enough, including high altitude rations for three or four days. Victor, our medical officer, decided to send the main medical chest down, to save weight, keeping just a skeletal first aid kit for emergencies.

Between packing sessions, we savoured our last hours in the Balati valley. I went for one final walk up to the Hump to photograph the fritillaries. Bonington cranked up his solar panels to power one last game of Strategic Conquest on his beloved Apple Mac. Victor, his only fellow gadget freak, joined him at the VDU, then challenged him to a final game of chess. Even the considerate Renshaw joined in the resounding cheer when Bonington won.

Home still pulled. I thought frequently about Rosie and Ollie and was excited at the prospect of seeing them within a couple of weeks. Our mail runner's visits to Munsiary had all coincided with public holidays, so we had received no mail in the last four weeks. Meanwhile, I had been sending weekly letters and now I sent a final one with Graham:

Base Camp 14.6.92
Darling Rosie
Again I have to write very quickly. Graham has suddenly announced that he is setting off for home and taking mail. I wish that I was coming too, but the difficulties of changing flights etc. might prove too much. Anyway it would be good to attempt one of the other Panch Chulis up the other valley – there is just time. I hope you got the card I sent a few days ago. We had a brilliant five-day climb on Rajrambha. Chris, Graham and the Indians climbed Panch Chuli II. So everyone is very pleased. The flowers are more wonderful every day and are some consolation for being away from you and Ollie. I can't wait to see you both – only seventeen days now. Then all the summer ahead of us. Graham is fretting to be away so I must finish. I love you very much. See you soon. Will phone from Bombay.
Lots of Love,
Stephen

Perhaps I exaggerated my reluctance to stay, for I was actually very excited by the prospects in the other valley. Rajrambha, after all my initial doubts, had proved intensely fulfilling but on its own it had not been quite enough. I wanted something else to take with me. I wanted to see a little further round the next bend, discover more of this exquisite corner of the Himalaya, and perhaps even reach one of those cooking hearths so far visited only by the Pandavas.

Harish confirmed that Panch Chulis III, IV and V had definitely not been climbed by mortals. Not for the first time he was poised to prick the sensitive skin of the Indian establishment,

Panch Chuli V

Telk

Nepal

Panch Chuli IV

Darma Valley

Looking down into the Pyunshani valley from the summit of Panch Chuli II.

not out of any sense of disloyalty – for he is fiercely patriotic – but purely from an insistence on honourable, accurate reporting. In his quest for historical accuracy, he had a stalwart ally in Jagdish Nanavati, the Grand Inquisitor of Bombay, whose analysis of spurious summit photos has rumbled many a false claim. So far the Indian Mountaineering Foundation had stood by its claim to have climbed Panch Chuli III, IV and V over two days in 1964. Even before arriving in Kumaun, we had seen enough from distant photos to know that each was a formidable peak in its own right, rising to well over 6,000 metres, with steep ridges and faces on every side. Seeing the peaks from Munsiary at the beginning of the expedition had only confirmed our disbelief. What made it doubly ludicrous was that the 1964 expedition claimed to have made its ascents from the Balati Plateau, at the head of a completely separate valley! Having now visited the plateau himself, Sherlock Kapadia had realized the origin of the misunderstanding.

Group Captain A.K. Chowdry led the 1964 expedition up through the Balati icefalls to the Balati Plateau, from where the team attempted the South-West Ridge of Panch Chuli II. Unsuccessful on the main peak, they then decided to bag three pleasant-looking bumps at the bottom end of the ridge, each rising a short way above the plateau. The moment Harish saw these bumps, twenty-eight years later, he realized that these must be the three peaks claimed by the IMF. They were approximately the same altitude as Panch II, IV and V, and just happened to be in the wrong place. They made no doubt for two pleasant days' excursion in magnificent scenery. But what did the climbers think when they looked down the southern precipice, plunging deep into a whole different glacier system, from which rose three proud, formidable peaks, comparable to Panch Chuli II, and equally worthy of the Mahabharata's divine warriors? All rather puzzling, until Harish reminded us that many mountaineers – and not just Indian ones – are notoriously poor map readers.

On 14 June, we folded up the Godrej banner that had adorned our Balati Base Camp for four weeks, and left. It was a sparkling morning and Victor, Sustad and I dawdled beside the river, stopping to admire some swallowtail butterflies basking in the hot sand, attracted by some mineral deposit. A little further on I was delayed by the crimson flower spikes of *Morina longifolia*. Down in the forest the jasmine, roses, thalictrums and lilac were all in flower. Spring was moving into summer and soon the Monsoon would arrive.

We were cutting it very fine and I wondered for a brief moment if we shouldn't all just go home. But no, the decision had been made and it was time for our ways to part. In the glade where we had camped on the way up, we stopped for a lunch of fresh fruit and tomatoes, brought up from Munsiary by the Harsinhs. Then we said goodbye to Graham and Bhupesh, who carried on down the valley with four of the Kumauni porters. Once they had gone, the rest of us shouldered our rucksacks, turned left and headed for the unknown valley.

Chapter Six

DHANSINH WAS A hunter and general odd job man from Madkot. On the approach march he had been persuaded to carry a particularly unwieldy storage barrel, for double pay. A couple of weeks later he had reappeared at Base Camp, with a lethal-looking muzzle-loader. He had failed to find any ibex or Blue Sheep and, in the absence of anything edible to shoot, he had hung around our kitchen for a while, passing the time of day with Harish. He had mentioned a past hunting trip to the Pyunshani valley, so when we decided to head that way ourselves, Harish sent a message to Madkot, summoning the hunter.

Dhansinh explained that he had not visited the valley for about ten years, but he thought that he could remember the way. He certainly started off promisingly, after Graham and Bhupesh departed, leading us down through dense scrub and across the bouldery river bed to an unobvious plank bridging the main roaring flow. It was now mid afternoon and we stopped on the far side at Phunga Gair – the Place of Flowers. It was a beautiful but midge-ridden spot, so I zipped myself up in a tent and settled down for some indulgent reading. I had the very paperback copy of *Tess of the D'Urbervilles* that I had first opened when I was fifteen, on a skiing holiday at Saas Fee. Hardy's genius had enthralled me from the first page, just as, by day, I had been mesmerized by the snow flutings of the Dom and Täschhorn, soaring with such inviolate, crystal perfection above the rutted piste. Twenty-three years on, had that sense of wonder and discovery become stale and jaded? Or was it deepened and enhanced by a slow groping towards some kind of maturity? I don't know. Perhaps Hardy's pervading melancholy now struck a deeper chord; and his sense of implacable doom may have stirred faint doubts about our own enterprise; but my main feelings were indulgent pleasure and a sense of the appropriateness of our misty surroundings to Tess's bucolic existence.

In the morning the hard work started. Rather than follow the Balati river down to its confluence with the Pyunshani, Dhansinh had brought us across the former several miles upstream, intending to take us on a short cut over the high ridge dividing the two valleys. We now had to climb very steeply through the forest. As Sustad observed, Dhansinh's technique seemed to involve heading through the densest thickets he could find, studiously ignoring clearer ground either side. No one could quite agree whether there was any sign of a path, but it all looked to me suspiciously like virgin territory.

We thrashed our way through tangled birch and rhododendron, stooped beneath the lightning-charred remains of ancient deodar cedars. We stopped frequently to rest, Sustad and I rewarding ourselves with meanly-furled roll-ups, eking out the last supplies of Golden Virginia. After four or five hours the forest thinned and we kicked steps up a muddy gulch filled with primulas and marsh marigolds, arriving finally on a broad saddle where we sat down to rest in a meadow of cream-and-blue anemones.

We lounged in the damp mist and ate a snack. I took advantage of the soft light and lack of ubiquitous sunglasses to snap some portrait shots of Bonington. Photos of famous people always sell. The grizzled beard looked distinguished and the hooded blue eyes seemed content. For a Leader of Men, he was delightfully relaxed, apparently happy to go with the flow and defer to Harish's ebullient organizing. In fact, the whole group seemed genially mellow. We had achieved a satisfying equilibrium and were glad to be sharing this final, slightly bizarre, adventure, wanderingly happily in the clouds with our mad guide.

The surreal atmosphere intensified when a man in lurid purple-checked trousers suddenly appeared from nowhere, brandishing a muzzle-loader like Dhansinh's. He was joined by two companions who came over to have a look at the first Europeans ever to wander into their territory. They told Harish that they had been up here for five days on a hunting expedition, sheltering in a cave. They had seen nothing at all and were now very bored and very hungry. Harish explained politely that our own rations were severely limited, now that we were travelling light. We wished them good luck and continued on our way.

There was still no sign of a path and Dhansinh remained obdurately vague. Dropping over the south side of the ridge, we could only see a short distance down rough grassy slopes, so we traversed, skirting along the high flank of the valley, between shifting layers of cloud. Just occasionally the cloud would drift aside and allow us to glimpse the far wall of the valley, where white-streaked gullies fell from unseen mountains, but the summits themselves remained hidden.

'Look – strawberry plants,' shouted Victor, suddenly bringing us all to a jerking halt. 'They're actually *Potentilla atrosanguina*,' I retorted smugly. 'See here – these deep red flowers. But the leaves *are* very similar – same family.'

'What's the use of strawberries you can't eat,' grumbled the Lutheran, moving us on for a while, until we upset the whole caravan again to drool over the exquisitely sinister cobra heads of some mottled *arisaemas*, nestling amongst boulders. Then the delicate alpine subtlety was smothered suddenly in rank docks and nettles, gorged on the unnatural richness of goat droppings. Vestigial remains of stone shelters confirmed that shepherds had stayed here in the past. Perhaps Dhansinh was leading us the right way after all.

With their usual efficiency, Revatram and the other Kumauni helpers erected the kitchen shelter, got the stoves going and in fifteen minutes had brewed a huge pot of restorative sweet tea. Everyone was starving and gobbled down handfuls of bhel – one of Harish's many delicious Bombay snacks. This one was made from puffed rice, puri, fried savouries, boiled potatoes and onions, served with a sweet chutney. It was like a very superior, savoury version of Rice Krispies.

We retired to our tents. I was sharing with Renshaw, who

asked for next turn with the Hardy. 'Of course,' I promised. 'Isn't Angel Clare ghastly – sanctimonious little shit.' Dick went out to do some sketching and as the day faded to a bleak twilight, I followed Tess's dawn journey to the gallows at Stonehenge, reading the last bleak page by the light of a failing torch bulb. Thank God for human companionship, I thought, as Harish's voice penetrated the mist, rousing me with a shout of, 'Chalo! Chalo! Come and have dinner.'

On the third day it was still misty. There was no sign of the Panch Chuli peaks and the blind continued to follow the blind. Every hour or so we would stop to rest and drink from our water bottles. Food was limited, so Sustad and I dampened our hunger with cigarettes, mingling the tobacco aroma with the smell of ferns, unfurling amidst colonies of blue and white anemones. Every so often Harish, Revatram and Dhansinh would stop and point into the impenetrable cloud, gesticulating wildly and firing questions at each other in a rapid mixture of Hindi and Kumauni. In the English party, the elder statesman, Bonington, stayed diplomatically aloof, while the four young-middle-ageds began to fret. Tempers began ever so slightly to fray and Sustad wisely suggested topping up the blood sugar levels. We stopped and shared out some of the precious high altitude chocolate rations. After that everyone felt better but some of us were still getting very impatient with Dhansinh.

'For God's sake, why don't you sack him?' I asked Harish. 'He's hasn't got a bloody clue where he's going.' Harish shrugged pityingly at my occidental angst. I was sick and tired of the endless up and down, as we followed every laborious lumpy re-entrant of the steep mountainside. Surely it would make sense to get down into the bed of the valley and follow that? Sustad, Victor and Renshaw agreed and we set off down the hillside, only to hear the elder statesman call after us: 'Remember that we have the porters, the tents and all the food.'

Muttering humble pie, we panted back up the slope and rejoined Dhansinh's laborious high traverse. Later that afternoon he finally agreed that we should drop into the valley bottom and we charged gleefully down into the jungle. Dhansinh headed illogically rightwards, and as far as I recall we never saw him again. We slanted left, in the general direction of the Panch Chuli peaks. I took out my kukri knife to wage war on a chaotic tangle of rhododendron trees then stopped to admire familiar tendrilled leaves and cream flowers. 'Look Victor – a *Clematis montana*. It was that Governor's wife ... what was she called ... Lady Amherst. She was the first person to bring it to Europe.'

The slope got steeper and steeper and at one point we went over a cliff, slithering hand over hand down ropes of bamboo. I was in bushwhacking heaven. Feet tripped on roots concealed beneath rustling piles of dead foliage. Faces rubbed in the delicious earthy leaf mould. Burrs clung to fleece jackets. Rucksacks caught in wiry creepers and the jungle was filled with a Babel of English, Hindi, Kumauni and Gujerati curses. I emerged first to run headlong down a final vertical meadow into the bed of the Pyunshani river. Looking back up the slope, I watched the jungle shudder and tremble, shaken by a giant, invisible, cursing caterpillar. Then, one by one, figures were disgorged from the undergrowth, to tumble down to the river.

We had made it! A few hundred yards upstream we could see the grey rubble terminal moraine of the Panch Chuli Glacier. Victor and I rushed ahead to look for a campsite and as we clambered over the riverside boulders the cloud at the head of the valley suddenly lifted to reveal a brief sunny vision of great snowy peaks – the Promised Land. 'That's Panch Chuli IV, isn't it – with a bit of a shoulder on the left? And ... yes, look just coming out further left, that must be Panch Three. Fantastic!' Then the veil dropped again, intensifying the sense of a sudden, precious revelation.

Close to the glacier we found a little clearing in the birch trees and there, clustered idyllically around a burbling stream, we pitched our tents. The Kumaunis, who had been carrying much heavier loads than we, were exhausted from the twelve-hour day, but they set to immediately, rigging the tarpaulin shelter and setting the giant kettle on a blazing fire. Once again I relished the primal contentment of the nomad finding rest and shelter, the smell of woodsmoke, the sweetness of fresh water, the well-deserved meal, the reward of arriving, at the end of a long hard day. The problem was – it was *such* a beautiful spot that I didn't want to leave. I thought, why not just stay here for three days, pottering about for a bit, before heading slowly down to find a route back to Madkot? A Short Potter in the Pyunshani? Wouldn't that do?

Apparently not. The brief unveiling of those secret summits had been enough to remind me why we were here and to ignore them would risk terrible disappointment later on. Already Sustad was busy going through all the high altitude rations, re-packing for a dawn departure. Victor and Renshaw were checking the climbing gear, paring it down to the minimum we could get away with. Bonington, hunched over a mug of tea, was in conference with Harish, who had the Indian Survey India map spread out.

'You see up here, on the side of the valley – I think that there is a pass between Panch Chuli Glacier and Bainti Glacier. I am calling it Bainti Col. This is the plan for Mus, Monesh and me. We leave main peaks for Britishers. Do you think it is possible in the time?'

Bonington looked doubtful. I assured Harish that we should just be able to climb one of the main peaks. But it was going to be a tight-run thing. It was now Tuesday, 16 June. Harish planned to be back in Munsiary by the morning of the 23rd to organize return transport to Delhi. That would mean leaving this new Base Camp on the 21st – Sunday. We had just five days to reconnoitre, climb and descend a completely unknown Himalayan peak. In fact we still didn't know which peak we were going to climb. Bonington looked torn between joining the Bombay team on their comparatively close col and attempting one of the big peaks with us. Afterwards he said that he had been wary of intruding on the four-man team that had built up such a good rapport on Rajrambha – worried about upsetting the dynamic. But then he had thought about the possibility of a magnificent unclimbed summit and had been unable to resist the temptation.

Harish promised that if the five of us had not returned by

Sunday he would leave two of the Kumaunis to man the camp and help us down to Madkot with the luggage. He would also leave some food, although there would not be very much. Already during the last three days, we had been getting quite hungry. Rations were running low and even Harish was starting to show some bone structure. 'Don't worry,' he chuckled, 'in a week's time we will have all the food we want. And on the way back we are stopping at Nainital – a beautiful place with lovely restaurants. And in Delhi we will have to have pani puris – you remember last time?'

How could I forget. You take a hollow, crispy, deep-fried puri, tap a hole in the top and fill it with curried potato, chickpeas, mung beans and sweet chutney, then dip the whole thing in mint-flavoured water (pani) and pop it in your mouth. All the while Harish would burble instructions: 'Hey, Steve-sahib, you must eat *at least* fifty puris, and you must make a big slurp when you eat them. The puri must explode in your mouth. There – Victor is doing it right. You know we are having big competitions – the record is one hundred and fifty!'

With Kapadia every journey was a gastronomic adventure. I remembered again a particularly fine chutney made from coconut, coriander, ginger, lemon and garlic ... thought about Delhi's creamy buffalo milk yoghurt ... the mangoes now ripening. ... But it would all have to wait a few days longer. In the meantime, a slight hunger was a small price for the chance to explore these unknown peaks which he had first told me about seven years earlier. I was rather glad that we had kept them for the final days of the expedition. I enjoyed the impromptu urgency of it all. I liked the idea of finishing on a high note with a swashbuckling dash to the summit, to return with a glorious prize. The prize was of course worthless to anyone else: there was nothing tangible we could take home other than our own inner contentment, but that was worth a lot.

Chapter Seven

HARISH SAW US off at dawn, sending two of the Kumaunis to help us on the first day's load-carrying. For the first four hours we followed the ablation valley along the side of the Panch Chuli Glacier, tramping through scrubby undergrowth. Every hour we stopped to rest, sucking boiled sweets to stave off hunger.

The trough of the ablation valley petered out, forcing us on to the old moraine crest. Ethereal fragments of mountain appeared amongst the shifting clouds, hanging high above the Panch Chuli Glacier. Then the moraine ran up against the mountainside and it was time to descend on to the ice. There was no reason for hunters to come this far and we knew that no mountaineers had ever penetrated this valley; we were almost certainly the first human beings to tread on the glacier. That pioneering thrill sustained me for a while, but as the hours passed and Victor, Renshaw and Sustad drew ahead, I began to grow weary. I stopped to sit on a rock, dizzy in the glare of reflected sunlight. Bonington arrived and slumped down beside me. I drew some comfort from the fact that he seemed equally tired. I handed him a mug of water and went to refill the bottle from a surface pool. We sat there for ages, slumped in silent torpor, before getting up reluctantly to continue. The two Kumaunis overtook us and I wondered how we were going to manage the next day without their help.

All the bravura of the previous evening seemed to have dissipated in the heat and at midday, when we reached the spot where the others had decided to camp, I slunk into the tent to lick my wounds and hide from the sun. A large mug of tea helped restore me and from the other tent Sustad urged us all to eat as much as we could. 'We can't carry all this up the mountain, so we might as well eat as much as we can now – better to carry it in our stomachs than on our backs. And drink – lots and lots of fluid.' We obeyed dutifully, working our way through tins of tuna and mackerel and a large pan of mashed potato.

We discussed further ways of reducing the payload, now that we were on our own. Victor and Sustad had taken Bonington under their wing in a tightly crammed two-man tent with a yellow flysheet. Renshaw and I had the other, red, tent made from a single skin of Pertex. There could be no reductions there, but we decided to leave one of the three climbing ropes, one gas cylinder and enough food for a meal on the way down. After eating and resting I began to perk up and take some notice of our surroundings. Our tents were pitched on the flat wide basin of the lower glacier, immediately beneath Panch Chuli IV, which seemed the most feasible peak to climb. Bonington was keen to avoid unnecessary complications and make that our objective. However, late in the afternoon Sustad suggested a short walk to assess other possibilities. We looked a ramshackle bunch, shambling across the ice in our saggy-bottomed long johns and loosely-laced plastic boots, at odds with the glorious cirque of peaks all around us.

'If only we had more time,' I complained. 'Just look at all these wonderful peaks. Why didn't we come here at the beginning?' The rock in this valley was some kind of granite, completely different from Rajrambha's stacked shale, and the mountains had a tactile, architectural appeal. It was a tantalizing treasure trove of untouched spires and buttresses and we were the first people ever to see them from so close. And we only had four days!

Forced to choose one single objective, I had been keen all along to go for the most southerly of the main peaks – Panch Chuli V. It was the highest unclimbed summit and in distant photos it had seemed to be the most interesting. After walking a few hundred yards from the tents we could see the peak clearly. Sustad had a pair of binoculars trained on its South Ridge, profiled against the evening sky, with a magnificent great pillar of rock just crying out to be climbed. Above it the ridge eased off, then steepened to a snowy foresummit, before rising again to the highest point of Panch Chuli V, 6,437 metres above sea level.

Even Victor, still aching from his cornice encounter on Rajrambha, was excited. 'That pillar looks wonderful . . . but what about getting to it?' For all its classic proportions, Panch Chuli V was guarded by an anarchic jumble of fractured ice. Huge, chaotic, labyrinthine icefalls spilled down in every direction, blocking off the mountain. Bonington mentioned the straightforward approach to Panch Chuli IV. I quickly started a diversionary improvisation. 'Hang on. What about this icefall on the right? I think we could get through fairly easily . . . up on to that upper smooth bit –'

'Then over to that gully . . . and up on to that dividing ridge . . .' Victor took up the strain, with prompts from Sustad. Renshaw gave the odd nod of approval. With mounting confidence we broke the problem down into its constituent parts. The South Ridge of Panch Chuli V rose out of a distant hanging valley, or cwm. The spelling is Welsh; the pronunciation is similar to the Somerset version 'combe'. The most famous cwm of all, named by George Mallory, is Everest's Western Cwm, protected by the notorious Khumbu Icefall. The icefall tumbling from our cwm looked equally dangerous, perhaps more so. However, we might be able to approach it obliquely. First we would climb my easier icefall far over to the right and traverse left above it into Victor's gully. That would get us on to a solid buttress from where we should be able to traverse left through another icefall, which looked tortuous but possible. That would get us on to a second buttress and once over that we would be in the cwm. From the snowy bed of the cwm we would slant up steep ice and rocks on to the ridge of Panch Chuli V itself. The fact that it was so elusive, guarded by such complexity, gave the whole project a delicious frisson of uncertainty besides which the more practical alternatives on Panch Four seemed insipid.

It was now Wednesday evening. On Harish's schedule we

were supposed to reach any summit on Friday, but negotiating this maze through to Panch Chuli V might take a bit longer. Nevertheless we reasoned that if we reached the top on Saturday morning we should, with a huge effort, be able to get back down to Base Camp by Sunday night. And if necessary we would just have to be a day late.

While the young-middle-aged Turks built castles in the sky, the elder statesman kept tactfully quiet. Others with his experience and clout might have tried to bully us out of it, but Bonington has always prided himself on his belief in democratic consensus. So when Sustad stated, 'It's Panch Five then, is it?' Bonington went along with the majority decision.

A thunderstorm delayed our departure the next morning and grey light was already filtering on to the glacier by the time I reached the first icefall. Zigzagging quickly along a series of ramps, overhung by giant gargoyles, I managed to find a quick route through to smoother ground. Then it was a case of simple hard plod until we reached a plateau above the icefall. And there, a few hundred yards away, was our gully. It was all working!

Now on a snow-covered glacier with the possibility of concealed crevasses, the five of us roped up. As the gully got closer we noticed a gap in the line of white snow where the bottom ten metres had melted away. 'In fact,' commented Sustad, 'it's a bloody waterfall.' Bonington issued school-masterly praise as Victor, the mountain guide, volunteered to lead the pitch, zipping himself tight in waterproofs. While he battled noisily with the icy torrent, I took the second rope and explored some ledges round the corner. I managed to stay dry, but my one-upmanship took me on to some precarious terrain and by the time I had wobbled my way into the couloir, the others had all shivered their way through the waterfall.

The sun defrosted, then broiled us, as we kicked an interminable staircase up the couloir. At the top we stopped for some lunch on the crest of the buttress, perched on an island of solidity between the surging chaos of the first two icefalls. Immediately level with our perch, the second icefall was a splintered bomb site and our only hope was to climb further up the buttress and try to get on to the ice higher up. Sustad and I tied on to one rope and went to investigate. After two steep pitches he managed to get on to the second icefall.

I shouted the good news down to the others then followed the Lutheran. 'Watch the rope here, I'm crossing the slot.' Unseen round the corner, he kept it tight while I eased myself over the gap between two up-ended railway carriages, then waded over some soggy hummocks, slithered into a trough and sidled under an immense gothic archway festooned with ice daggers.

'No place to dawdle.'

'No,' agreed Sustad, 'but it seems to get better from here. I think this is going to work.' I loved the man's quiet, unflappable competence. He would never admit to anything so vulgar as ambition, but beneath the laconic shell there seemed to be a huge reserve of determined power. For the next forty minutes he led us through the labyrinth, searching, testing, calling out warnings of fragile bridges, weaving a tenuous line through a maze of maneater crevasses. One of them involved a big leap, with the landing lower than the take-off. I wondered idly how we would tackle 'the long jump' on the return journey, but any nervousness was quelled by confidence in our strong team and its infinite capacity for improvisation.

Near the far side of the labyrinth, I took a turn in front, thrilled to emerge on to the second buttress, less thrilled by the thigh-deep soggy snow we had to climb to its crest. Every day that the warm, damp air of the Monsoon wafted closer, the snow got worse. It was exhausting and I stopped frequently to look back down on the labyrinth, tracing the sinuous line of our tracks. On the far side, three little figures were inching under the ice-daggers. 'Why don't they move faster, it's crazy.'

'I think it's Chris. He's knackered. Look how long it took him to get up that couloir.' It was only ten days since his climb on Panch Chuli II and he had never been given a chance to recover properly. I wondered how I would fare at this kind of thing in twenty years' time – wondered whether we were unfair to drag Bonington up this long, tortuous route, then dismissed the idea with a brutal 'He Chose to Come.'

I was tired too, but also exhilarated by success. From the top of the second buttress the pyramid of Panch Chuli V was suddenly right in front of our faces. And, at our feet, the elusive hanging valley – the final piece of the puzzle. Once again we were on an island between ice cataracts. A short way below us, the smooth flow of the cwm tumbled over the edge but there was just room for us to get on to the smooth surface, above the lip of the abyss. Sustad belayed me while I ploughed down into the basin, then waded over a hummock, fighting, panting, exultant, through bottomless porridge.

The surface improved in the middle of the cwm and we climbed gently to a good campsite. Looking up at the left wall on to the face of Panch Chuli V we suddenly noticed a huge ice tower – a great tilted skyscraper, hanging above the cwm. From the lower glacier it had seemed insignificant; now it suddenly seemed to dominate the mountain. Bits of its shattered masonry were scattered across the cwm, so we made a point of excavating the tent platforms well away from the ice rubble, below a large crevasse that would swallow all but the most monstrous avalanches.

Sustad and I pitched the tents ready for the others' arrival and got a brew going. I fussed around, perfecting the platform, until Sustad told me to relax and share a cigarette. I was pleased with the day's work, proud to trace the improbable weavings of our tortuous line through the minefield, all the way down the distant spot on the lower glacier, over a thousand metres lower, which we had left thirteen hours earlier. Had we taken unjustifiable risks? Did our route justify the sort of doubts Bill Murray expressed towards the end of his life, recalling the day in 1951, a year after his Panch Chuli expedition, when he, Tom Bourdillon, Ed Hillary and Eric Shipton became the first people to climb Everest's Khumbu Icefall?

I felt terrified whilst climbing it, as Shipton later confessed he did too. . . . Was this physical courage or moral cowardice? I wondered at the time, and think it was neither. Mountaineers do develop a nose for degrees of danger, and while the

Khumbu Icefall always will be dangerous, we had this instinct
that the avalanche risk was tolerable, despite first appearances.

Over the previous four years I had frequently pondered the
morality of our 1988 route on the other side of Everest, arguably
more dangerous than the Khumbu Icefall, but had come to the
same conclusion, the same hunch that it was not actually as dangerous as it might seem to outsiders – that 'the risk was tolerable'.

I certainly felt that that was the case with today's approach to
Panch Chuli V and gazed down proudly on our creation. Further
down the valley, where the glacier curved out of sight towards
Base Camp, massive clouds were piled up in a Van Ruisdael sky.
It wasn't exactly textbook climbing conditions, but the weather
seemed adequate at least. Shafts of light broke through the
cumulus and behind us our rock pillar glowed enticingly, warm
and peach coloured.

The others didn't seem quite so enthralled when they arrived.
Talking in undertones that night, Renshaw commented
gloomily, 'I just couldn't believe how slow we were through that
icefall. Chris was hardly moving. It's so unlike him – his heart
just doesn't seem to be in it. I don't know how we're going to
manage tomorrow.' In the past Dick had nearly always been the
cautious foil to my impetuousness, but he had also always been
very determined when he felt it justifiable to continue with a
climb. On the finest climb we had done together, the first ascent
of Kishtwar-Shivling in Kashmir, we had shared an equal
commitment to the climb, even when conditions became
unpleasant on the last day. Here, on Panch Chuli V, he seemed
equally resolute about pushing on and in fact it was he who was
the driving force the next morning.

Warm, damp, muggy air induced procrastination at dawn.
Negative vibes poured out of the other tent. For the first time
Bonington suggested a retreat; there were dire warnings of
putting our heads in a noose. Victor said he would be very happy
to go down. 'Arse-crawling sycophant,' I muttered. Renshaw
sighed and looked glum. We continued to pack our rucksacks
and work through the routine of preparation, trying to ignore

the waverers and show a determination to go up, not down. I managed to keep reasonably quiet and leave the circumspect Renshaw to put the summit case; coming from him it sounded so reasonable that Bonington and Victor agreed eventually to continue. Only later did I discover that Bonington's agreement stemmed from magnanimous motives: he didn't want to deprive Victor of a chance at the summit and he knew that in any case the rest of us would have been pushed to climb and descend the mountain with only one rope.

It was Friday and we had to get as close to the summit as possible that day to have any chance of meeting our return deadline. There were two options once we had passed beneath the ice tower. One was to go right to the head of the cwm then climb up to a col – a notch on the South Ridge of Panch Chuli V, immediately beneath the rock pillar. The other option was a more direct line, slanting straight up the face to emerge on the ridge above the pillar. Keen to keep the upward momentum going, I favoured the direct option and set off in the lead, up steepening snow slopes.

It was a bad decision. I had not gone far when the ice tower roared, sending down a shower of blocks far closer than I had anticipated. I had misinterpreted the fall line and it was suddenly obvious that a big avalanche might sweep right across my proposed line, wiping us out. I was about to suggest an adjustment to our plans when Bonington shouted from below:

'I really think we should go down.'

'Hang on a minute.' I turned round and stared down the slope. The five of us were spaced out along one-hundred metres of rope, with Bonington and me at opposite ends of the ropes, one of us focused ruthlessly on the summit, the other wanting to get out. He reiterated, 'I think we should go down. I just don't feel happy about being here.'

'Well why the fuck did you come here in the first place then?'

'Shut up, Freddy,' chorused the three in the middle, heads swivelling up and down the slope in amazement.

'No I won't shut up. I'm sick and tired of being held back all the –'

'Be quiet,' screamed Victor, creating a space for Bonington to launch his rebuke.

'You really are incredibly self-centred, you know. This is the last time I'm going on a mountain with you.'

'Well that's pretty rich coming –'

'Shut up!' The others tried to silence me, but I launched into another diatribe, before Victor interrupted me again. 'Just ignore him; he has to have these little tantrums – or should I say tantra?'

'Sycophant.' I was now muttering quietly to myself, letting the storm subside, while the others returned to objective discussion. In the end we agreed on a compromise: we *would* continue, but by the longer route to the col on the ridge, which was clearly a better option. And we would stop early to camp there, not committing ourselves any higher on the mountain until we saw what the weather was going to do. As we were now high on the wall of the cwm, I set off traversing the slope towards the far end of the basin, kicking angry steps in the tilted snow crust. An hour later we reached a big icefield in the far corner of the cwm and Renshaw took over, leading us directly up to the col. As there was no crevasse danger we unroped, each moving at our own speed.

The col was a cramped spot with huge drops on both sides. We were back to the Rajrambha bungee-jumping game, taking turns to stand roped on the brink and send another ton of fragile cornice whooshing into the Darma valley. Once we had established the true, firm crest of the ridge, we could start to widen it. With a carpenter, an ex-carpenter, an ex-architect and a sculptor in the team, we warmed to the task, cutting huge blocks of snow windcrust, packing them firmly across the ridge, underpinning them with lumps of rock and eventually creating a three-by-fourteen-foot ledge with just enough room to pitch the two tents end to end.

The therapy of construction calmed my anger and by the time Bonington arrived I was regretting my earlier outburst. Poised precariously above a thousand-foot drop, he threw a mittened arm around my shoulder and we both simultaneously blurted out an embarrassed 'sorry'. Then, ever the gentleman, he praised our elegant construction work and settled into night quarters. The incident in the cwm was never mentioned again.

I was touched by Bonington's magnanimity, but still keen to keep the group psyche thinking 'up', so before settling in, Victor and I took the two ropes to fix the first part of the pillar. After a short horizontal knife-edge, the ridge reared up steeply. I tried it direct, squeezing hopefully up a vertical chimney rattling with loose crockery, until Victor's voice of reason brought me down and sent me on a leftward flanking manoeuvre. Although still quite tricky, this was clearly the way to go. Once the two ropes were fixed, we abseiled back down to the tents – two blots of colour in a monochrome world blurred by drifting layers of cloud. As I followed Victor back along the knife-edge there was a sudden apocalyptic roar. 'What the hell is that?' Heads swivelled, trying to see what had caused the thunder that now filled the hanging valley. Then we saw the cloud, white on white, surging down from the ice tower, billowing higher and higher as it blasted across the cwm we had crossed that morning, then raced up the far wall on to the buttress we had negotiated the previous afternoon, where it finally dissipated in a distant shower of pulverized ice.

Victor pulled a long face. I said nothing, embarrassed that I had allowed us to spend so long beneath the tower just a few hours earlier. Once the dust settled, the tower looked no different – just the same old loose tooth, stuck on the side of the mountain. I wondered how many years it would take before it had rotted completely away? How many more avalanches sweeping across the cwm. We would have to move very fast on the way down.

The avalanche reinforced the conservatives' misgivings and back at the tents there was more talk of nooses. Bonington remarked that we really were out on a limb if anything should happen. I thought about his record of bold, necky climbs and asked about the Ogre – the mountain in Pakistan where Doug Scott in 1977 broke both his legs on the summit tower, 23,000 feet above sea level, just before a storm broke over the Karakoram. 'He had basically to get himself down,' replied the wily old survivor. 'I think if he hadn't been able to crawl on his knees, he would still be up there.'

He glossed over the vital part he, Mo Anthoine and Clive Rowland had played in helping Scott down, but the gist of his blunt assessment was correct – on that very steep, complex terrain the three men could probably never have manhandled Scott down through the storm. Sitting on our remote perch, isolated above a maze of unstable icefalls, I contemplated our own position. We were out on a limb and the weather was quite unsettled, but I still felt that we were in control. Despite almost daily snowfall, there had been no serious full-blown storm since we had arrived in May. Provided that the night temperature dropped to freezing, our summit climb should be perfectly safe and the descent, although long and difficult, was not going to be as hard as the Ogre. True, we had virtually no food and were now on half rations, but we had enough gas to melt snow for three or four days, should there be any crisis.

Far from feeling nervous, I was actually rather relishing our extraordinary isolation. Towards evening the clouds cleared slightly and warm sunshine percolated through the tent fabric. The two tents were pitched nose to nose. Framed in the adjoining doorways, I could see Sustad, long hair hanging over his face as he bent over, smoothing out a foil sweet-wrapper, then curling it into a miniature pipe, pouring in carefully the last, dusty, dessicated wisps of Golden Virginia. The man's a nicotine junky, I thought, then accepted eagerly as he passed the sordid contraption through the door and let me draw on the hot acrid smoke. Renshaw had a puff, then continued spreading our two rationed biscuits with a little cheese. The main meal was a meagre portion of soup and noodles, but I felt no real hunger, knowing that in a couple of days we would be back at Base Camp and very soon after that on the road back to Delhi.

It was Friday evening – midday in England – and I wondered what Rosie and Ollie were doing. Bonington had sent out a message with Graham Little, asking Wendy to phone everyone's wives and let them know that we were all fine and about to come home. We had now been gone for over six weeks and, although I was longing to get home, I was glad that we had made this final effort to climb one more peak, excited by the prospect of the next day's dash to the summit.

The background hum of Victor's chatter was interrupted by Bonington making an announcement. 'I've decided that I'm not going to come with you guys to the summit. You'll be much faster without me.' We remonstrated with varying sincerity, and he insisted, 'No. I'd much rather spend the day resting here. You're going so well as a team and I'll be really pleased if you make it to the top.' It was a generous gesture, particularly as he promised to eat none of the few remaining scraps of food, so as to leave something for us when we returned. In the meantime, he would have to endure a long, lonely day, with nothing to eat, nothing to read and nowhere to go, when he would much rather be heading down to the valley.

We discussed the rope situation. We would have to take both of them with us, dismantling the elaborate safety chain that kept us and the tents firmly on our eyrie. We would leave Bonington tethered by a long sling to the piton anchor and he would just have to hope that we returned safely from the summit.

I was grateful and relieved. Sustad and Renshaw had been very positive all along and even Victor now seemed quite fired up. Our summit day would be fast and efficient, with no nagging doubts to interrupt the flow. And it would be fun. On that happy note I snuggled deep into my sleeping bag to catch an hour or two of precious sleep. At one o'clock Bonington woke us with talk of cloud, but on closer inspection it seemed that it was thin and shifting, with more and more stars piercing the veil every minute. The snow outside felt crisp and there was a definite touch of frost in the air. The climb was on.

At 3.30 a.m. we were ready to leave. Victor waited to free the end of the rope, while Renshaw, Sustad and I set off, clipped into the safety line as we clambered stiffly along the knife-edge, isolating random details of rock and ice in the individual beams of our headtorches. Above us, cutting a black shape into the starry sky, Panch Chuli V waited silent and impassive.

Chapter Eight

'THIS IS JUST delighted – pure pleasure.' The curiously precise, articulated Seattle tones rang a clear note on the cold air, as an outstretched ice pick hooked a granite nubbin half smothered in crystalline white powder. Sustad was in climbing heaven.

We were now four ropelengths above the col and the magic alchemy of light was transforming the landscape. Apart from a few dark bands of cloud nosing round the back of distant peaks, the sky was clear. A friendly, promising cerulean blue. With the first peach glow on the peak opposite called Telkot. Marble textures on its gleaming snow flutes. Flamboyant, florid scrolls of its summit cornice. A warmth on the russet pinnacles where a ridge dropped in an elegant curve, to the narrow V of our col. The V framed by the dark shadows on our western side of the mountain. In the base of the V, the little dome suddenly illuminated on its crazy perch, yellow against the brilliant snow to the east.

We had collapsed the red tent in case of strong winds. The yellow one was weighted in place by our spare equipment – stoves, sleeping bags and so on – and by the elder statesman. After our departure he had dozed for an hour or so. Then pulled himself half out of his sleeping bag to greet the sunshine. There was a murmur of contented, purposeful voices above and he soon made out the four figures strung out on the shady side of the pillar. He felt a pang of regret for what he was missing. They were going well and would almost certainly make it to the summit. After all, when he was their age he was climbing Brammah, Changabang, the Ogre . . . carrying loads through the rockband on Everest. . . . He would have run up this peak. But, now, did he really have to prove anything? He had done well on Panch Two and the expedition had been an unqualified success. He had even beaten Victor at chess. And he had enjoyed that bridge session with Graham; he would have to do more of that in Greenland next year. No – there was actually no need to regret anything. Better just to enjoy a well-deserved rest day and be ready to help the others when they got back from the summit.

Two hundred metres above the tent, Renshaw was now following Sustad's hard pitch. Then it was my turn to grapple with the initial rock overhang, heaving over on to tilted slabs smeared with slicks of ice. Safe on a top rope, I hurried up the pitch, hooking confidently with the steel tips of my ice axes, revelling in the concentrated steepness and technicality of it.

We continued up the flank of the pillar, zigzagging to pick the easiest line through a maze of ribs and gullies, trying to fix in our minds the sequence of features we would have to abseil on the way back. After eight rope lengths I followed last up an awkward little chimney and climbed out on to the top of the pillar, to see Sustad ahead pointing his axe up at the foresummit. It seemed close and the ridge leading up to it looked like easy step-kicking snow. The cocky Lutheran shouted gleefully, 'Just walking from here.'

Some walk! We should have learned our lesson from Rajrambha, as we were soon back to the same scrappy crust over brittle ice. And the cornices here looked huge – far too frightening for bungee jumping. Conscious that I had been a passenger all the way up the pillar, I offered to take a turn in the lead and moved to the front of our two connected ropes to start a long weary crabcrawl, stopping every thirty metres or so to drive a titanium screw into the ice and clip in the ropes. Connected by these links to the mountain, the four of us moved slowly, sideways up the ridge.

Hours drifted by as the afternoon cloud proliferated, multilayered, reducing our glittering fantasy world to grey

opacity. My tongue was dry and my feet craved relief from the relentless clawing at toughened glass. Yet there was a kind of grim satisfaction – even pleasure – in pushing relentlessly forward, determined to maintain momentum. I looked back down at the heroic, black-and-white tableau of three figures linked by an arced thread, edging along a huge sloping roof. Behind, and now below them, the summit of Telkot was drowning in a froth of cloud. On the right the roof sloped away from beneath their feet, steepening as it dropped into the invisible cloud-filled cwm. On the left, just above them, it was cantilevered out into space, its cornices hanging, fragile, over another immense void.

The roof was actually tilted no steeper than about 35 degrees. With amenable snow it really would have been a walk. But in these conditions, where you knew that you could never self-arrest if you slipped, we just had to take it slowly and methodically, roped to the mountain. There came a point where I had placed all the ice screws and had to wait for the others – who removed them as they passed – to catch up and hand them all over for the next section. Victor was closest on the rope. As he reached my stance he warned, 'It's getting late. We'll have to turn back soon or we're going to end up benighted.'

'Yes, I suppose so, I'll try and press on faster.' As soon as the last man, Sustad, had arrived and handed over the screws, I continued. The slope was now curving up towards the foresummit and the crabcrawl metamorphosed into a straight cat's clawing up a tree trunk. The face steepened and I headed left towards a hollow, tempted to stop and rest. But no, I insisted, you mustn't be weak. Keep going. Keep up that momentum. Two ice screws left – one to protect this next section and then you'll be on the foresummit and can belay there.

The ice bulged out in a glassy boss. I kicked with rock-blunted steel crampon tips and longed for razor-sharp subtlety. Calf muscles screamed for relief and my arms ached. Foot by foot, forcing myself to concentrate, I hammered up the wall, trying to ignore the lengthening gap between me and the last ice screw. Then at last it was all over as I pulled out on to the broad dome of the foresummit and sat down gratefully to bring up the others.

Sitting with feet braced, facing down the mountain as I pulled in the rope, I kept twisting my head round, craning for a glimpse of the ridge ahead. Suddenly the clouds drifted apart and there it was – the final corniced crest to the main summit. So tantalizingly close. We had to make that final effort and get there.

'Look, there it is. I really don't think it'll take long now.'

'It's already two o'clock.' Victor was sceptical. 'Remember that every hour we go on is another hour added to the descent. As it is, we only have five or six hours' daylight left.'

Renshaw came to my rescue, recalling our summit day nine years earlier on Kishtwar-Shivling. 'It was very similar to this, wasn't it? I don't think we reached the top before four. The same conditions.'

'Worse, I seem to remember. It was a complete white-out. And we had to do all those scary diagonal abseils through the spindrift.' I thought back to that desperate fight with numbing cold – the malevolent hiss of spindrift, pouring in waves down the face, the grim concentration, the desperate groping through the blurred twilight, suspended over an invisible void . . . It had been horrible, but sometimes you have to struggle a little. As far as I could see, this afternoon cloud on Panch Chuli V was not life-threatening and Sustad also agreed that, having made such an effort to get this far, we should, despite the long delays on the ice ridge, complete the last bit to the summit.

Victor insisted on one proviso: 'Whatever happens, we turn back at three o'clock.' Spurred on by that ultimatum, Sustad seized the initiative and strode off down into the gap between the foresummit and main summit. I was now last on the rope, watching the others ahead, then following the pull on the rope as they were briefly obscured by swirling cloud. The rope was moving with brisk fluency and as I started to climb out of the dip I was thrilled to find soft snow underfoot instead of brittle ice. There was a brief hiatus as Sustad nicked his way carefully up one bare patch, then he was moving smoothly again, heading up a broad slope and I realized that he was actually on the final rise. It had been hard to judge scale from the foresummit but for once a summit ridge had proved shorter than expected.

I pulled back the cuff of my left mitten and glanced anxiously at my watch. Five minutes to three. But he was almost there. He stopped just back from the brink of a final jutting cornice. Moments later I saw three figures huddled together and knew that we had made it. At five minutes past three I walked out on to the summit and Sustad, the most understated and reserved of Americans, so far forgot himself as to shake hands on it.

I thought back again to that similar afternoon on Kishtwar-Shivling. There the summit had been the culmination of a long campaign, planned for months. Panch Chuli V was different – a surprise opportunity, seized serendipitously as an expedition afterthought – but there was the same foggy bathos, standing on a featureless, colourless lump of snow, lost in the clouds without a view, and wondering whether it actually had any value. Of course I knew deep down that it *did* have a value – even if that would only be experienced later. I also knew that escaping to enjoy that retrospective glow of fulfilment was going to be hard; just as we had done on that stormy evening nine years earlier, I steeled myself for a fight.

I was allowed two minutes at the most on the summit before Victor sent me hurrying back across the narrow strand to the foresummit. We reached it at four o'clock and stopped briefly to share some of our single litre of juice and two chocolate bars – the first food and drink we had had for over twelve hours. Blood sugar was low but adrenaline began to take over as we set off on the first of many abseils. As he started over the edge, Victor reminded us that it would soon be dark and that an open bivouac would be extremely unpleasant. Sustad looked phlegmatic. 'I think we're just going to have to keep going – even if it takes all night. Okay, it'll be cold and unpleasant, but we've all done this kind of thing before.'

Excellent fighting talk! Timed perfectly to coincide with the first swirling snowflakes, as the wind rose and the storm closed in. Somewhere over towards Nanda Devi thunder rumbled and soon the air on Panch Chuli was starting to buzz. One half of me was nervous – terrified of a repeat of the Rajrambha lightning strikes – the other half was strangely calm, accepting that there was absolute nothing we could do other than concentrating on the job in hand.

'The job' was tedious and painstaking. Most of the time having four people was a great strength but abseiling – when only one person can go down the ropes at a time – was frustratingly slow. Nevertheless, we persevered, even on the nearly flat ground, playing it methodically safe in the swirling whiteness rather than risk all moving together at the same time. We left behind ice screws for anchors until they had nearly run out, then we chopped bollards from the tough ice, taking turns to hack with blunted adzes, watching each other, checking and rechecking each time the first person set off down, making sure that the sling securing the doubled rope really was sitting firmly behind its bollard.

Ropelength by ropelength we reversed the icy crabcrawl,

listening fearfully to the thunder, hoping that the gap between flash and rumble would not narrow. At the end of the crabcrawl there was a short snowy section where we could traverse more quickly by the last glimmer of twilight. Then, beside a large rock near the top of the pillar, we stopped to pull headtorches from our rucksacks.

Peering into the limelight of my torch beam I scrutinized a crack in the rock, poking with a piton to find the precise slot where it could be hammered firmly to the hilt. This business of placing anchors was a fearful responsibility, and we always backed up the single anchor with alternatives, linking them loosely to the ropes, just in case the main anchor should fail. But on a long complicated descent, with all those icefalls still to descend the next day, we needed to conserve gear so, once the first three people had abseiled safely, the last man would remove the back-ups.

The hardest job was going first, particularly on easy-angled sections where the rope gathered in frozen tangles on the ground, rather than hanging amenably straight. It was weird, groping down through the darkness, tugging wearily on the ropes, swivelling one's torchbeam to seek out half-remembered landmarks, then, as the ends of the ropes drew near, searching urgently for somewhere to make the next anchor. For those who followed it was easier, but once we were all down there was nearly always a crisis pulling the ropes through. Almost invariably one of them would catch. Renshaw, the master disentangler, would hold out the two implacable ropes, playing them like the lines on a kite, then pulling with raw force on the lower one, exhorting the rest of us to add our weight. Sometimes there was a glorious moment when the snag succumbed to force and the ropes eased smoothly down again. But usually we just bounced ineffectually and someone would have to volunteer to climb back up in the dark and free whatever kink had jammed solid behind a malevolent rock. The volunteer at least had the benefit of some hard exertion to keep alight a flicker of warmth deep in the core of his body, sustaining him for the ensuing wait, as we took turns again to descend the next fifty metres. So, hour by hour, as Midsummer's Eve drew to a stormy close and merged imperceptibly with the darkness of Sunday, 21 June, we persevered with our laboured, crepuscular crawl down the mountain.

After watching the four figures climb the steep pitch on the pillar, Bonington shuffled back into the tent, grabbed a pan, then leaned out of the door to scoop up some sugary snow. He set the pan on the hanging stove then ferreted amongst a jumble of food bags and rucksack lids and all his pockets until he found the cigarette lighter and lit the stove. Half an hour later, after refilling the pan with snow a few times, he had enough boiling water for a brew. Feeling adventurous, he picked up a sachet of Chocolate & Peppermint powder.

Strange tastes that chap Sustad has, he thought. Still, I suppose he was only trying to give us variety. He eyed up the half-finished packet of oatcakes. Would they really notice? Couldn't he just take a couple? No, that wouldn't be fair – they're going to need every scrap available when they get back. He'd better go easy on the drinks too – make the most of this strange brew.

Later he dozed for a while, daydreaming about home – the comfortable, familiar routine of it all. The smell of fresh coffee in the morning. The cosy warmth of the Aga. The dog anticipating that run up High Pike. Precious evenings at home with Wendy. The comforting, familiar trust and easy conversation over a bottle of wine, free from the constant pressure to entertain, remember names, listen interestedly to some stranger's tedious tale of climbing Helvellyn. In two weeks' time they would be leaving for France on the canoeing holiday Wendy had planned – a glorious drift down lazy rivers, with no load-carrying and no heel-snapping ambitious young climbers.

He had to give it to them, though – they were incredibly determined. And they had bonded into a very strong team. Rather like Everest in 1982 with Dick and Pete and Joe – the same tight-knit intensity. Perhaps it had been silly to try and tag on – unrealistic to expect to fit into such a finely-tuned equilibrium. A team develops its own arcane ritual and language, which can be hard to share. But Victor was so welcoming. And Sustad.

Renshaw a bit cooler perhaps, but he's so shy you're never sure exactly what he's thinking. Venables less predictable. Those sudden explosions were a bit disconcerting and sometimes his singleminded drive was a bit worrying. I just wonder if he has pushed them too far?

At midday he looked out of the tent again, but the others had now disappeared beyond the top of the pillar. In fact they ought to be at the summit by now and starting back down. He registered the usual afternoon build-up of cloud but was not unduly concerned, inured now to climbing through indifferent weather. The afternoon passed quickly enough, contracting in the daydreams of a master at the Himalayan art of killing time. Only later, as the thunder started to reverberate through the hills of Kumaun did he begin to worry a little. The brittle patter of snow crystals on the nylon flysheet also gnawed at his nerves. At dusk, when he expected the climbers back, he stared up at the pillar, searching for movement, listening for voices. But there was nothing.

Darkness intensified his anxiety. Each flash of lightning was a stab of fear. His nylon shelter on the knife-edge suddenly felt desperately lonely. He allowed himself the solace of a weak, sugarless, milkless cup of tea, still hoping that the others would be coming back to consume the remaining rations. Then he looked out again into the black night to see if there were any lights up on the pillar.

Midnight and still no sign of them. He stared forlornly at the single nylon sling tethering him to the mountain. Alone and without ropes it would be a desperate descent. He thought back two days – no, three days now – to the tortuous sequence through the icefalls. Those huge, half-concealed crevasses. The crumbling snow bridges, weakening every day as the Monsoon's damp warmth grew closer. That horrible bit under the giant icicles. And what about Victor's waterfall pitch at the bottom of the gully? Maybe he would be able to avoid it by Venables's route. But then there would still be the lower icefall. And then the long, long stumble down the lower glacier and all those bushy ablation valleys.

He wouldn't get down to Base Camp before Monday, by which time Harish would be gone. So it would be another exhausting slog back to Munsiary before he could get to a telephone. Nevertheless, he was confident that he *would*, somehow, get down alive. It was the next bit that filled him with

dread. Tears welled up in a bitter rehearsal of a horribly familiar routine. It was nearly always right at the end, like this. Ian Clough on Annapurna. Mick Burke on the summit of Everest . . . that terrible radio call from Martin confirming the worst . . . the awful business of getting a message out to Beth, then struggling to say something for Chris Ralling's television cameras. Then Everest again – Joe and Pete in 1982 . . . promising Wendy he would never go back to Everest. But the worst of all was Nick Estcourt's death in the avalanche on the 1978 K2 expedition. He and Wendy had even shared a house with Nick and Carolyn. Nick had been his most loyal friend and for a while after the K2 disaster he had lost any desire to return to the Himalaya. And, as always, Wendy had been the one coping at home, fielding the telegrams and phone calls, soaking up all the pain and grief and aching loss.

With four of them it would be almost unbearable. How on earth was he going to face all the wives in turn? The only one he knew at all well was Dick's Jan in Cardiff. She had already experienced it by proxy when Dick came back early from Everest in 1982 and was at home when Joe and Pete vanished. In fact it was Dick who had to go up to Derbyshire and tell Joe's Maria the news. At least they hadn't had children. But Dick had a son. And . . . yes, a daughter as well. And what about Victor? Two sons. Wife – Maggie. The last time he saw them was when they stayed the night before Andy's memorial service. What about Sustad's wife Rose. Did they have a child? Yes, a little girl. And Stephen . . . that little house in Bath . . . there was a baby boy . . . and his wife was called Rosie. She came to Badger Hill that time . . . laughing in the garden with Wendy while we had our serious BMC meeting in the kitchen.

Lightning flashed again, but this time a more distant flicker towards the plains, hardly discernible through the tent fabric. Desperate to escape his gloomy forebodings, Bonington thought through the possible scenarios – an avalanche, a broken cornice, a simple slip . . . but surely not all four of them could have gone together? Surely there would be at least one or two survivors? Perhaps they had just been terribly delayed? Or had stopped to bivouac?

After hours of alternate hope and despair, at about one o'clock in the morning he suddenly heard a sound that might be voices. He rushed to pull his torso into the tent doorway and stared eagerly up at the black pillar. Silence. Perhaps it had just been the wind. His eyes swept the darkness above and then at last he saw a pinprick of torchlight puncturing the blackness near the top of the pillar. The torch moved a fraction. Then another light appeared, moving slowly, jerkily, from above to join the first light. Then, through the fading noise of the wind he heard it again and this time knew that it really was the wonderful sound of human voices.

He concentrated intently and was thrilled to realize that he could hear four people. Renshaw's voice was the lowest, slightly gruff, hesitant. Sustad was perceptibly American, even at this distance. Venables and Victor were virtually indistinguishable on the telephone and it was the same on a dark mountain, but they were definitely both there. It was impossible to decipher actual words but he could tell from the timbre of the voices that there had been no disaster. They were safely on their way home.

A few hundred metres above Chris we were still fighting the ropes. Heading diagonally down a vertical obstacle course of projecting rocks and ensnaring lumps of crusted snow, we were growing weary of freeing jammed frozen hawsers. Yet, apart from the odd grumble, tempers were restrained. During the long, long waits at the anchors, shuddering from the deep, bone-numbing cold, I comforted myself by thinking how efficiently we were coping. Having put ourselves in this situation, we were using our combined experience of at least seventy years in the high mountains to extricate ourselves safely. Everyone had taken his turn at the tough job of going down first. Each of us had climbed up at least once to free a jammed rope. At the change-overs we had a smooth routine to make everything both as fast and safe as possible. Victor had done a fantastic job of remembering the complex terrain from our ascent nearly 24 hours earlier. I felt proud to be part of this team – happy to be returning from a magnificent summit with some of the finest climbers in the world.

Comfort also came from the anticipation of warmth. And liquid. I could now see Bonington's torch light and knew that we would soon be down there, in the tents. As far as I could tell, we only had about two hundred metres to go – four or five abseils. The next was an awkward sideways job, horizontally over a sharp rib of snow, then diagonally down a steep gully. I was following last at this stage and when my turn came it felt uncanny, traversing horizontally in the darkness, completely isolated from the others until I had thrashed my way over the rib and started to descend more conventionally, with the life-supporting ropes cutting deep into the rib above.

When it was time to pull them through, they stuck. I volunteered reluctantly to sort out the trouble and Sustad handed me a camming Jumar to assist my climb back up the single rope. Fear and exhaustion vied for attention as I flailed back up near vertical powder, trying not to put too much weight on the rope. The others were safeguarding me with some slack from below but I had no idea what was holding the rope above and did not relish the thought of suddenly catapulting backwards.

I suppose it was the stuff of every climber's fear – this surreal night on a bare mountain. Retrieving an uncertainly jammed rope, in pitch darkness, ought to have induced sheer terror, but the best I could manage was a fatalistic nervousness. Again, it was just a case of doing what had to be done and noting, in a pleased sort of way, that one was coping. After climbing about twenty metres I found the kinked end of the frozen rope wedged in a narrow slot between two rocks. I freed it and re-set the abseil so that the same thing would not happen again. Ten minutes later I was back down at the anchor and this time the ropes came down like a textbook demonstration.

The warm glow from my exertions quickly faded. Our clothes were slightly damp from the afternoon storm and, even with down jackets on, we were all shivering. I suppose we could have survived a bivouac, but it would have been a hideously prolonged torture, so our decision to keep descending through the night seemed the right one. We had all suffered appalling bivouacs in the past. In 1974, climbing far too slowly up the famous Frendo Spur on the Aiguille de Midi, darkness had caught me on a tiny sloping ledge at the start of the final rock buttress, the hardest section of the climb. Nearly twenty years later, I could still remember the shivering huddle under a nylon sack, like a glorified dustsheet, perched on a granite knobble, trying to cook a meal on a stove balanced between us. I could even recall the smell of the dehydrated scrambled egg and cheese.

It had been too disgusting to eat, so we had chucked it down the precipice. Even worse than that had been Christmas night in 1976, drowning in spindrift halfway up the Supercouloir on Mont Blanc du Tacul, shivering, dehydrated and fighting a losing battle with the spindrift that eventually pushed me off my ledge, to dangle in my sleeping bag on the end of the rope. And then of course there was the bivouac on Everest, without even a comforting sleeping bag . . .

No – unplanned bivouacs were almost invariably unpleasant. Better to keep moving. In any case, we had to get down as soon as possible, knowing that it was now Sunday and we were due back in Base Camp that very day.

That long descent still to come – all the way down through those icefalls – was going to be such hard work. At best, we would probably only reach our first campsite on the lower glacier. Still, that would get us back to Base Camp on Monday morning. Harish would have gone, but he had promised to leave some food. Then there would be the forest. I wondered how they had got on, cutting a trail straight down the Pyunshani river to the junction with the Balati. Somewhere down there we had spotted a bridge on the way up five weeks ago.

Five weeks! Nearly seven weeks since we left England. And soon we would be back. How wonderful to end with this brilliant climax, extracting every ounce of potential right up to the last day of the expedition. What a contrast to my doubts and misgivings when we set out. How satisfying to return with this sense of fulfilment intensifying the pleasure of homecoming and the prospect of long summer days stretching ahead in domestic contentment. I wondered whether Rosie was pregnant. Tried to picture her at this very moment – perhaps just going to bed, perhaps out with friends, or sitting out in the garden with a bottle of wine, on the shortest night of the year, the air heavy with the scent of roses and honeysuckle.

The image was vague and generalized. Strange how hard it is to remember faces after such a short absence. I tried to visualize Ollie, asleep in his cot . . . or perhaps awake, demanding a bottle. He was now one year old. He would have changed. I grasped for nuances of expression but only retrieved a hazy approximation of his confident, boisterous smile.

The damp cold crept closer round my shoulders and down my back, settling in the clammy runnel of my spine. Knees sagged, yearning for horizontal relief. Parched throat imagined the sweet warmth of the first drink back at the tent. My mind kept fast-forwarding in anticipation. It was like the beginning of final exams – thinking ahead to the last sentence of the last hand-cramping essay, and imagining the moment of glorious, cathartic release. I stared longingly at the torch glow in the notch below, then turned round to the right, staring out over the cwm and down the valley towards the Goriganga and the far hillside. Lightning still flickered in the far distance, now a harmless and rather beautiful *borealis himalayensis*, but the clouds had lifted a little to reveal the lights of Munsiary, forty miles away. I wondered whether some insomniac villager was looking up at our trespassers' lights, high on the Pandava's sacred hearth, and wondering what on earth we were doing there.

How could they begin to guess at Sustad's joyful delight on this very piece of mountain yesterday morning? He was now on his way back down that steepest section of the climb, hanging directly over the big icefield that dropped to the cwm. Renshaw must have fixed the next anchor back at that same place, just beneath the steep bulge that had started the pitch. Remembering my pleasure at following the pitch, and the increasingly tough journey that had occupied us for so many hours since then, I turned to Victor and mumbled stiffly through frozen lips, 'I'm glad that we made the effort . . . that we actually climbed the mountain.'

'We're not down yet.' The brusque reprimand silenced me. Soon afterwards Victor disappeared down the ropes and then it was my turn to follow.

Chapter Nine

AT THREE-THIRTY on Sunday morning it was still dark. There was a faint red glow in the fireplace where the biggest log had survived the drizzle earlier in the night. A wisp of smoke still rose into the damp air. There was a gentle snoring from the large tent where Revatram and the other Kumaunis were sleeping. In one of the smaller domes Harish Kapadia woke briefly from a dream and registered that soon it would be dawn. Still, no need to get up for a while.

Before drifting back to sleep he thought back with satisfaction over the previous day and the vision of new panoramas at the Bainti Col. He had always wondered what lay over in that next valley. What a lovely way to end the expedition with Muslim and Monesh. And Khubram and Prakash joining them for the climb. And those two summits standing sentinel either side of the col – Panchali Chuli and Draupadi, shared wife of the Pandavas. Thank goodness they had started down by noon, when the weather closed in. It had been a long, wet, slithery slog back to Base Camp, followed by a stormy night.

Still no signs of the Britishers, but he had expected them to be late. What a pity that they hadn't been happy just to join the Bombay team on gentle summits. Presumably they had tried one of the main peaks. They must have been well on their way down before yesterday's storm. With any luck they would arrive today or tomorrow. There was a little rice and dal left. And a few potatoes. Enough food to get them down to Madkot. And the Harsinhs would look after them.

He shuddered in sudden recollection of yesterday's spilt pan.

A gush of water hissing on the fire. Harsinh Senior's sparkling eyes suddenly shadowed as he looked up towards the Pandavas' hearths and muttered something about bad omens. Superstition or an astute warning? Harish pushed back the dark thought and focused instead on the Alfonso mangoes which Geeta would by now have sent up from Bombay to Munsiary; then he drifted happily back to sleep.

Two-and-a-half thousand metres higher, Bonington was wide awake on his perch. Both stoves were purring inside the tent, their pans full of melting snow. The summit team had been gone for twenty-four hours and would be utterly parched. It was now at least two hours since he had first heard their voices. Soon it would be light: already there was a faint glimmer over Nepal although it was still pitch-black on Panch Chuli V. Yet again he looked across to the pillar to check their progress.

A single point of light was moving slowly down the blackness. Suddenly the light accelerated, falling in a great arc, faster and faster in huge leaping bounds. Then he heard the thud of flesh and bone flung against the mountain. And a harder, metallic clang of steel striking rock, as a trail of shooting stars fell into the abyss.

It was the noise that shocked me most. That terrible, strident, metallic din drowning out the distant moan that seemed to come from somewhere deep inside my lungs. That and the sheer force of the violent battering, as I was hurled backwards, sideways, upside down, sliding then swooping, somersaulting, flung this way and that, to bounce yet again with another crash of exploding light and sound.

Only once before had I experienced this passive acquiescence in the face of such gigantic, pulverizing force. Then I had been seven, up a wet tree in bare feet, ignorantly mistaking an overhead power line for a low-voltage telephone wire and shaking it for amusement. With intense concentration I can still recall every detail. The thick feel of braided grey steel in my hand. The satisfying ripple along the shaken cable. A gleeful shout down to my friend on the ground, suddenly cut short as my whole world was reduced to a multicoloured kaleidoscopic pattern of dizzy, pulsating, concentric circles. The same pulsation rang deafeningly in my ears, reverberating with the ringing force of an apocalyptic gong. There was a hot metallic smell of burning and my whole body was subjected to relentless pressure that seemed to go on, and on, and on, pounding wave after wave of malevolent energy through my entire being as I was hammered on the anvil of hell.

When I woke up I was lying on the wet grass beneath the tree. Gravity had saved my life. On Panch Chuli gravity was killing me, but there was the same sensation of watching from outside, as my body was subjected to some huge, previously unimaginable, malicious force. What was different this time was the adult knowledge that I was dying – first the resentful 'why me?' realization that the abseil peg had come out; then the more resigned, faintly regretful, acceptance that this was it – this was the big moment.

My life did not flash past me. At least there was no coherent narrative. However, during those few seconds outside time and space there was some vague collage of recognizable images. I wish that I could reconstruct them clearly, but I can only recall the memory of them happening. I think that there were images of people – friends, family, Rosie and Ollie . . . perhaps places and events as well – but all confused in a random, surreal jumble. Closer to the conscious tangible surface, everything was dominated by the crescendo of violence and my amazement that the body could continue to survive such colossal forces. Surely this crescendo must be building to a climax? Surely it must all end? Surely we must soon reach that final extinguishing *sforzando*?

Victor, Sustad and Renshaw were busy organizing the next abseil when they heard the rushing clatter in the darkness above. They were all clipped into the anchor Renshaw had placed when he had reached the bottom of the big steep pitch half an hour earlier. Perched as best they could on the sloping ledge, they were standing abreast, facing out over the valley, with the invisible cwm three or four hundred metres below. Sustad was on the right, closest to the line of the abseil. Closer in beneath the bulging rock wall was Victor. Further in on the left, Renshaw was wearily disentangling the frozen corkscrewed ends of the ropes, struggling to separate the two ropes and get the purple end (always 'pull purple') threaded through the loop on the anchor, ready to haul it through, yet again, for the next abseil, once Freddy was down. As usual the strands were horribly twisted and in the darkness the ends had got wrapped round one of his legs.

The thunder and lightning had long since faded, but the sudden rush of noise above felt like a jolt of electric current. Sustad shouted 'Avalanche!' and cowered close into the cliff. All three hunched fearfully into the corner as the rumble of falling debris grew louder. Facing now into the cliff, they glanced anxiously to their left, towards the fall line of the faint depression of the abseil route. There was a shower of sparks and then a terrible flash of realization as they saw a long dark shape flying past.

I never heard the final bang. The big moment was erased forever from my memory and in what seemed an instantaneous transition I awoke to dim grey light and a desolate silence. There was no joy at discovering that I was still alive, no cathartic rush of gratitude – just dull incomprehension. A feeling that this was all wrong. That I should be dead. And that in any case, if I were alive, where was I?

Slowly, wearily, my eyes registered the blurred shapes of cliffs, ridges and snowfields, just discernible in the murky light of a cloud-choked dawn. I reached down for my glasses, bent but miraculously unbroken, hanging from the elastic round my neck. The movement activated a dull ache in back and shoulders and as I pushed the wire frame on to my face I felt the slipperiness of blood on my nose.

With focused vision I could make more sense of my surroundings. I was the right way up and I was face down on steep half-frozen snow. The angle was about fifty degrees and as I turned my head to the left I could see across the slope towards a distant valley. I tried tilting my head down and realized that I could see the snowy bowl of the cwm far below me. I was lying – no, hanging – on the big icefield, the one immediately beneath the pillar. For some reason I was near the top of the icefield, not at the bottom.

There was sharp burning pain in my groin, where my harness was digging in under tension. The ropes were tangled round my body. Above me they stretched in a tight line towards dark rocks. I tried craning my neck to look up but could distinguish no human shapes – just a slender thread attached miraculously to something on the mountain. There was still no sound – just a bleak, grey emptiness. I seemed to be suspended in some gloomy limbo, alone and deserted. I wondered whether the others had been pulled off – whether they were all dead, or unconscious from terrible injuries, powerless to rescue me from this overwhelming sense of abandonment.

'The anchor's gone! Grab the ropes! Quick!' Victor's reaction was immediate and instinctive. With Sustad he grabbed at the ropes that were now whipping out after the falling body. If they could hold on to the ends they might just stop it cartwheeling all the way down the huge icefield below.

Iced perlon shot through Sustad's clenched mittens which dissipated some of the force. Braced next in line, Victor felt the lines burning into his overtrousers as they sliced across his thigh. Renshaw still had some python coils wrapped round his legs and the friction took some of the strain as he managed at last to get an end threaded through the anchor loop. As the few metres of slack were whipped tight and all three men were wrenched forward by the full force of the falling body, they clung with their hands in one final, courageous, melodramatic, B-movie gesture. To their amazement the whole system tightened to a standstill and Renshaw was left with the full deadweight of the body straining on his fists, clenched tight against the anchor.

The whole nightmare lasted a matter of seconds. Once it was over there was total silence. No one moved. No one said anything. But as the first glimmer of dawn illuminated their faces they stared at each other, and in each shattered grey face they could see the same look of horror. A long time seemed to pass before anyone dared to move. Then, slowly and fearfully, they began to reinforce the anchor and make themselves secure, escaping the torture of the ropes and transferring the strain on to the anchor. Then they shouted down. There was no reply from the deadweight on the ends of the ropes.

We never established how long it took me to wake up. I certainly never heard the others' shouts. Hence my terrified sense of abandonment. And puzzlement. Why wasn't I lying crumpled in the bottom of the cwm? And in any case, why hadn't the fall down the rocks killed me?

For the first time a wave of pure distilled fear poured over me. I didn't want to find out anything more – didn't want to discover the terrible paralysing damage. There must be some horrific head injury, or a broken spine – something about to snap. The whole of my torso felt brutally pulverized. At the very least there must be broken ribs. I just didn't want to know.

But eventually I forced myself to get a grip and be brave. It was time for a complete checking of parts. I felt up to my head and found the helmet cracked but still intact. I was conscious and my vision seemed fine, so perhaps my skull really was undamaged. Arms and hands seemed to be working. Ribs painful, perhaps broken, but if there were a spinal injury I would surely know about it by now. What about the legs? Always useful for getting off mountains.

I tried to move my right leg. Hot pain seared through the knee. I tried to bend it, but again it was racked by agonized spasms and it was obviously locked solid. I pulled off a sodden mitten and prodded gently, sensing the rasp of torn tissue inside the joint. Then I found the gash on the inside of the knee, where three layers of clothing were ripped open, allowing fingertips to explore a warm, sticky hole underneath. I thought I could feel bone. I could definitely feel blood running through my fingers. Another wave of terror washed over me with visions of compound fractures and severed arteries.

'Is anyone there?' I shouted weakly. There was no reply. I tried again. Still no reply. Then a third time. This time there was an answer. They were still there! They were alive! I craned my neck to stare up, but it was still too dark to see the faces above me. But I could make out the dark shapes of the cliff – could register that I had fallen over eighty metres, starting far above the others and finishing down here, forty-five metres below them, saved miraculously from a further 300-metre plunge.

Victor shouted down to ask if I was all right. 'I've broken my leg. I can't move it.' Unheard by me, Renshaw noted darkly, 'Can't move his leg ... he's probably broken his back.' But Victor put on his best bedside manner and shouted encouragingly, 'Don't worry, we'll get down to you very soon.'

'I'll try and get my weight off the ropes. Give you some slack.' My voice was weak and breathy, vocal cords tensed by fear and shock. But I had somehow to rise to the occasion and conquer squeamishness. I thought they needed some slack to attach an abseiling device to the rope. In any case I was desperate to relieve the burning pain in my groin where my harness was digging in. I managed to unwrap part of the rope tangle from my shoulders, then reached down for my ice axe, still lodged securely in its holster with no hint of the sparks it had struck during the fall. I thrust the shaft into the snowface, then used it to steady myself as I tried to stand up on my undamaged left leg.

The experiment failed. There was a sharp ache and a slight grating sensation in my left ankle. That explained the crampon ripped from the boot, hanging from its safety leash, with one forged steel spike bent through 90 degrees. The foot did not seem to be connected to the leg in the usual efficient manner. So I actually had two broken legs. This really was serious. I was going to have to tackle the problem another way: without a leg to stand on, it was now all down to my arms. Biceps and pectorals have never been my strong point and at this particular moment, battered and bruised from the pounding on the rocks, my whole upper body was even weaker than usual. But I had to try.

First I hacked at the slope above to scrape out a ledge level with my chest. Next, twisting painfully, I managed to pull the other ice axe out of its holster. Then reached high to plunge both axe shafts into the snow above the ledge and pull as hard as I could. My arms were too weak so I bent my left leg and tried kicking in the heel for some extra push. There was the same grating sensation as in the right knee, but the pain in the left ankle was bearable, so I carried on pushing and managed to flop up into a half-sitting position on the ledge.

It wasn't good enough. The ropes were still stretched tight on the harness. So, after a panting rest, I repeated the laborious process all over again, forcing myself not to think about what might be happening inside the ankle. Gasping with the effort, wrenching every sinew in my body, I heaved frantically towards the second ledge, fighting back waves of dizzy nausea, forcing myself not to give up until I could flop, utterly drained, into the shallow snow scoop.

This time it worked. At last I could sit in comparative comfort and wait for the others to take over. Blood seeped into the snow. Dizzy nausea washed over me again. Still thinking ignorantly that an artery might be severed, I whimpered at the thought of bleeding to death. I wallowed in a morass of self-pitying guilt. This was the end of climbing – the end of all those self-deluding dreams. This was the unthinkable disaster which should never have happened. This was the vindication for all the critics who talk of moral responsibility and the sacredness of life.

Almost from the first moment of coming round I had been thinking about Rosie and Ollie, realizing painfully that, but for some miraculous trick of fate that had spared my spine and skull, a baby boy would have just lost his father. I pictured the parting vignette of the two faces watching bravely from the doorway. Tears pricked my eyes and when Victor arrived at my side I pleaded, 'If I don't get out of this alive, will you say "sorry" to Rosie for me?'

'Don't talk nonsense. Of course we're going to get you out of here.' Whether or not he believed it, it did the trick and from that moment I was convinced that somehow we were going to escape. I vowed never to say anything rude about Victor again, as he cared for me with just the right balance of professional efficiency and tender sympathy. He assured me that the bleeding, however spectacular it might seem, was nothing like the geyser effect of a severed artery. From his rucksack he pulled out a first aid kit I had never realized he was carrying and found a sterile dressing. He bandaged it in place and secured the whole arrangement with a rather elegant elasticated sleeve of what looked like fishnet stocking. Then for good measure he wrapped a spare sock round the whole lot to soak up the excess blood.

A rolled foam sleeping mat, secured tightly with nylon slings, made a serviceable splint. He asked tenderly, 'How does that feel? Okay?'

'Yes – well done. Although – aargh – ouououw – it's fucking painful if I move it.'

'I know. Let's try sticking the whole thing in this rucksack. Then when we lower you we can tie the rucksack to the rope . . . try to keep it held up off the slope.'

Already the leg had metamorphosed into a foreign body, a completely separate encumbrance which had somehow to be dealt with. Moving this encumbrance sideways across the slope to the camp on the col would be virtually impossible, so the plan was to lower it all the way down the icefield to the base of the cwm. Sustad had now joined us and was about to set off unroped for the col to tell Bonington what had happened. The two of them would dismantle the camp and carry everything down to the cwm, while Victor and Renshaw lowered me, ropelength by ropelength, down the long slope.

Before he left, Sustad swapped my mittens for his, which seemed marginally drier. Seeing my violent shivering, he also removed his thick down jacket and helped Victor put it on over the top of mine. Then Victor said, 'Let's sort out these ropes.'

What had been the top end of the ropes was now the bottom. The joining knot was jammed up hard against the abseiling brake on my harness, obscured in a tight clump of frozen kinks. I had descended five or ten metres from the knot when the anchor failed. At the end of the fall the ropes had begun to come tight at the same moment that I hit a final glancing blow against the top of the snow-covered icefield. Then I had slid a few metres further

the remaining slack was wrenched through the abseiling brake,
nally jamming tight on the knot and bringing me to a halt.

'Ah, here we are!' exclaimed Victor, holding up a three-inch
ngth of forged chrome molybdenum. The peg was still attached
the ropes by its red nylon sling. 'I still can't work out why it
ame out. But I think there may have been a bit of a sideways pull
n it.' Ever curious, he was already theorizing. 'And I can't think
hy you're still alive. You should have seen the sparks – like a
atherine wheel going past. We all thought we were going to find
stiff on the end of the rope.' By now he had fixed up an in-
ependent anchor just above us on the iceface and unclipped me
om the ropes, leaving Renshaw free to abseil down and join us.

The companion who had shared so many climbs in the past
oked profoundly shocked. Watching it all happen seemed to
ave affected him more deeply than the other two. Perhaps, also,
ne strain of being anchor man – the one who had so
ourageously stopped my fall – had induced a kind of post-
raumatic shock. He was subdued but, like Victor, worked
nrough the shock to get everything ready for the long lower to
ne cwm.

I was fearful of the journey ahead. Terrified of the pain.
nxious about what would happen during the following days
nce we reached the cwm. I succumbed to another wave of
izziness, then forced myself to swim clear, remembering all the
ther people who had had to cope with these situations – Doug
n the Ogre; Lindsay Griffin braving unspeakable pain from
vorse injuries than mine; Joe Simpson crawling out of the depths
f despair in the Andes; soldiers at war, who have to cope with
ar worse injuries under heavy bombardment. If they could do it,
could too. Still, some kind of pain relief would help. I asked
victor what he had.

'I'm afraid we don't have anything very strong. The morphine
vent back to Munsiary with the main medical kit, but you can
ave some paracetamol tablets. Here – have this sweet to help
hem down.' I crunched the sweet between my teeth, alleviating
he gagging bitterness of the pills, then scooped a handful of
now into my mouth, using the resultant trickle of liquid to force

it all down my parched throat, hoping that somewhere along the neural chain there would be some perceptible numbing of nerves.

'Okay, let's get going. I can use this left foot a bit to help; just, please, try to make it smooth – no jerks.' And so we started, Victor descending the fifty-degree slope beside me, clipped into the same rope paid out from above by Renshaw. I sat facing outwards, using my left heel for stability, ignoring the dull ache of the broken ankle, which was tightly braced in the plastic boot. The right leg – the encumbrance – hung down in front of me, sliding smoothly until it jarred on any slight protuberance, sending splinters of pain shooting up my thigh.

After fifty metres we stopped while Renshaw dealt with the knot joining the two ropes. 'Don't want to do a Simpson,' remarked Victor, referring to the Andean incident when Joe Simpson's partner was unable to get the knot past his friction brake. Dragged inexorably towards the abyss by the helpless weight of his injured friend, he was forced in the end to cut the rope and send Simpson plummeting into a giant crevasse. Here, by securing the lower rope with a prussik loop, Renshaw was able to take the weight off the knot, while he unclipped from the friction brake and re-attached the second rope. Then we continued down the next fifty metres.

As we neared the end of the first one-hundred-metre lower, Bonington and Sustad appeared above us to the left. Each was moving very carefully down the steep slope, laden with a bulging rucksack. Victor cut me a ledge and I wedged myself on sideways, glad of the rest. Bonington arrived, full of cheerful sympathy. For the first time the strained muscles of my face relaxed into a smile. Then Sustad joined us, took off his rucksack and pulled out a full litre of tea. He unscrewed the lid and handed me the bottle. Hot, milky and saturated with sugar, it was true Indian chai and it was the most delicious thing I had ever tasted.

We had now been on the move for nearly thirty hours and during that time we had each had just a quarter litre of juice. We still had a long, hard day ahead of us and that sudden coursing of blood sugar through the veins made all the difference. 'See you,' shouted Bonington, as he carried on down, swaying slightly

under his top-heavy load. 'We're going to try and set up a safe camp somewhere in the cwm.'

Lowering the encumbrance was back-breaking work for the chief lowerer, so Victor and Renshaw took turns as winch man. It was also exhausting for me, bracing myself constantly to try and keep my bad leg clear of the slope. Every fifteen metres or so I begged for a rest and slumped on to a hastily-cut ledge. Then, reluctantly, I would agree to continue, sliding off the ledge and waiting for the rope to pay out again. Climbing rope is quite elastic and by the time we had nearly one hundred metres paid out there was a lot of stretch in the system. I would sit immobile while my minder shouted up impatiently, 'Slack! Slack! Pay it out! Come on! What are you doing?'

'What the hell do you think I'm doing?'

'Well pay out more then.'

'All right; all right.'

Then there would be an explosion of angry expletives as we shot off down the slope, my bad leg bouncing and juddering in front of me, each excruciating jolt producing another hysterical outburst.

Meanwhile Bonington followed the Lutheran down into the cwm, braced under the weight of his top-heavy load. He was still about 150 metres above the bergschrund – the typical big crevasse at the bottom of the iceface – when a footstep collapsed. 'Instinctively I grabbed my ice tools which were planted in the snow, but they pulled straight out. Then I got hold of my ice axe in both hands to use it as a brake, but the pick just cut straight through the snow. I was gathering speed, my crampons must have caught in the snow, and I flipped over. Suddenly I was cartwheeling down the slope, all orientation gone, just aware of a mad, bouncing rush.

'I was vaguely conscious of being in mid-air. I had shot the bergschrund, and was bouncing and rolling once again. I tried to adopt a foetal position, hugging my arms and drawing up my legs, to avoid damaging my limbs. The motion became slower. And then I was still. Winded, frightened, pinned down by my heavy rucksack, which was still on my back.'

He had tumbled about 500 feet. Sustad was just above him, and saw it all: 'It was the most horrible thing I've ever watched. I just thought "He's had it." Even if he did survive, how the hell would we cope with two injured people?'

Renshaw saw the figure far below pick itself slowly up, then sit motionless for half an hour, head in hands. But eventually Bonington picked up his rucksack and continued across the basin to join Sustad and pitch one of the tents as far as possible from the threat of avalanche. Then the two of them came back across the basin to meet us at the foot of the face.

Foot by weary foot, we slid our way down the slope. It was tempting in gloomier moments to think 'interminable slope' but the bergschrund did slowly creep closer. As we veered slightly to the left into a conveniently smooth, varnished ice runnel, I noticed red dabs on the surface. 'Oh, no, the bleeding must be really bad.' I could feel it gathering soggily in my right boot but, on rational reflection, I couldn't see how it was seeping *ahead* of me in isolated blobs. It was only when I was finally lowered across the bergschrund, manoeuvred with infinite care like some fragile treasure into the waiting outstretched arms, that I noticed the cuts on Bonington's face and he announced proudly, 'No – that wasn't your blood; it was mine.'

That brief flourish was his only mention of a terrifying fall, from which, thank God, he had escaped with nothing worse than cuts and bruises. Already he had put it behind him and was intent on getting me to safety. Now that we were down off the ice face it only remained, for today, to get me across to the waiting tents, about two hundred metres away in the middle of the cwm. At my suggestion they fetched one of the tents to use as a hammock-cum-stretcher. With one person at each corner, they could just about half-carry, half-drag me towards the campsite.

I thought back nostalgically to the gentle smoothness of the ice slopes, with its merely occasional stabs of pain. Here the ground was undulating and strewn with half-frozen chunks of avalanche debris. The stretcher bearers stumbled and swayed. Every lurch shot a spasm of pain through the shattered tissue of my knee. I screamed and cursed. Then cried with tears of pain and laughter as we collapsed in a drunken sprawl. Then Bonington would try to hold my leg steady as Renshaw took command for yet another forward lurch: 'One, two, three – Heave!' And so it went on, lurch by lurch. Yet again, I shouted in pain. Then groaned, 'Sorry . . . I'm sorry I'm being so pathetic.'

'You're not being pathetic,' reassured the elder statesman, 'you're being incredibly brave.'

Bless him, I thought. What a diplomat! Why had I been such a self-centred bastard on the way up? Why are these people being so kind and patient? Between the therapeutic screams I just had to concentrate stoically on the job, knowing like the others that eventually it – or at least this phase of it – would be over. All the while I was periodically craning my head backwards, peering through the gyrating viewfinder of a handheld, ground-level camera, in my surreal, low-budget, upside-down movie of the cwm. In the far corner of the frame the pale yellow blob of the waiting tent grew mercifully closer.

The tent was the promised land. Once we were there nothing would matter any more. We would escape at last from this weary treadmill. We would drink and drink and drink. And sink into

warm blissful sleep. Guilt, fear, gratitude, regret, homesickness –
all those abstracts were subsumed in the simple animal craving
for rest.

On the final stretch I resisted the urge to look round. Only at
the last moment did I steal one last upside-down glance and see
the tent fill almost the whole frame of my vision. The others
stood up yet again from their hunched respite, lifted their
shoulders and with three more heaves deposited me on the
flattened snow beside the tent door. It was exactly thirty-six
hours since we had started our climb to the summit.

Chapter Ten

'MY GOD – IT'S as big as your head.' Victor was bent over my right leg examining the puffed balloon that had been my knee. 'Wonderful, isn't it, how the body protects itself? All that swelling is to stop the broken bits inside from moving around – the leg's own internal splint.'

'Yes, Victor – another of Mother Nature's little miracles.' I was still slightly resentful at the gleeful way he had chopped off the end of a brand new pair of fleece salopettes to get at the mess inside. Propped up on a pile of sleeping bags, I stared at the two medical exhibits stretched out in front of me, pasty yellow in the tent's filtered light. The left ankle, released now from its plastic boot, was also ballooning spectacularly. The foot ended prematurely with calloused stumps in place of the toes I had lost on Everest. Poor body. I must try to look after it more carefully.

'I'm going to take your *right* sock off now. Tell me if it hurts.' With infinite patience Victor eased off the soggy sponge that had been soaking up fluid all day. 'Pffuhh . . . yuk . . . it smells like an abattoir in here.' Now that he mentioned it, I noticed the sickly stench for the first time. So it was true. Blood really *does* smell.

With help from Sustad, he cleaned up the knee and prepared a clean dressing. Before they applied it, I allowed curiosity to overcome squeamishness and leaned forward to peer nervously at the gash on the side of the knee. It looked like the Sunday joint and I wondered what bacteria were congregating on the raw meat, so close to the bone. If only we had the antibiotics. I was worried, but only in a mild, unurgent sort of way, not registering the full extent of the risk. For the time being it was just so blissful

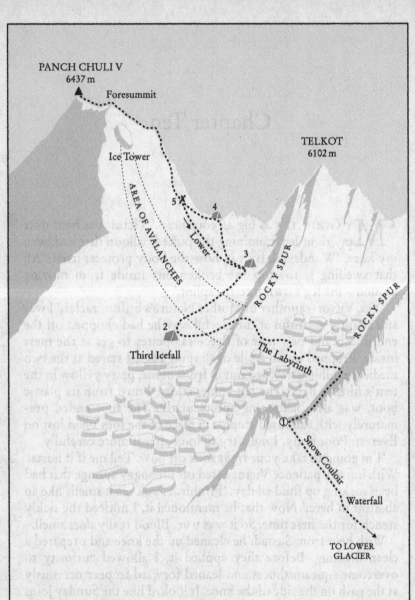

PANCH CHULI V
6437 m
Foresummit

TELKOT
6102 m

Ice Tower

AREA OF
AVALANCHES

5

4

Lower

3

ROCKY SPUR

ROCKY SPUR

2

Third Icefall

The Labyrinth

1

Snow Couloir

Waterfall

TO LOWER
GLACIER

1 Lunch stop on approach. Later site of food dump.
2 Camp in the cwm on the way up.
3 Camp where Renshaw, Saunders and Venables waited.
4 Top camp on the col, where Bonington waited.
5 Scene of the accident.

to be resting in the tent, feeling the warmth flow back into my body, savouring the exquisite sensation of food and drink.

Once the dressing was complete, Victor and Sustad cushioned the giant knee with socks, then splinted both my legs together, wrapping them securely in a foam sleeping mat. The tent was pitched deliberately at a tilt, with my feet high and the blood draining back towards my heart.

Sustad patiently re-arranged rucksacks and spare clothing to prop up my head in the dip, then made me another mug of hot tea. Yet again I marvelled at the robust compassion of these wonderful people who were saving my life. Beyond my uptilted legs, in the other tent, I could hear the infinitely sweet music of human voices exploring all the possibilities of escape. Even Bonington's voice sounded musical, rising above the others with a new authority. For the first time he seemed to have adopted the role of 'Leader'; having been drawn rather reluctantly into this trap he was going to take charge of our escape.

'I think two of us ought to go down,' he suggested. 'And I think it's best if I'm the one who goes all the way down to Munsiary to tell Harish and help put pressure on the authorities. Perhaps Sustad should come with me.'

'Yes, fine,' agreed the amenable American, 'but it's probably best if I stop at Base Camp. In fact I'll probably have to come back up with some food.'

'Yes, of course. We don't know how long Victor and Dick are going to have to wait up here.' We had been on half rations for some time and now were down to the last few scraps of food. Victor suggested a halfway dump: 'You know the place where we stopped for lunch – at the top of the couloir. If you could leave something there – say within the next three days – we could go down and pick it up. We'll just have to leave Freddy on his own for a while.'

I relished my new passive role. I was a contented child, secure in the care of kindly adults. I subsided into beatific slumber as Sustad tucked me up in bed, giving me his sleeping bag – the only one with a full-length zip – and telling me to call him if I needed anything. Only later in the night was my sleep troubled by a nagging dream about a forest. Fine, strong indigenous trees threatened by a foreign intruder. Diseased timber that had to be cut out. Dead wood. Thwarted attempts to hack it down, but it only loomed larger and more tiresome ... finally dragging me into a confused consciousness with its insistent pain. I woke Sustad with a plea for painkillers and he noticed quickly that I was shivering. 'Here, we need to warm you up. You're probably still in shock. I'll get the stove going.'

What a brilliant nurse! He let the flame roar uncovered for twenty minutes, warming the tent to a cosy fug, then put on a pan of ice chunks to make some hot tea. In the other tent they were still talking. Bonington's mind was racing, ideas spilling aloud through the tent walls. 'Maybe we can get the army to help ... teams of stretcher bearers taking turns. But would they have the experience? We'd have to guide them through the icefalls. No, we must get a helicopter. I'm sure Harish will fix it. But does he have that much clout with the military? Actually ... no ... yes, I know – yes, that's it: I should get through to *The Times* in London – I mean, it's a great story – and get them to pile on the pressure. Just imagine! If the public knows that Stephen's stranded on a remote glacier ... critically injured ... '

The man's energy was astounding. As I dozed, semi-conscious, his voice continued to reverberate through the darkness as he prepared for the long, dangerous descent to the Pyunshani Base Camp. Just before dawn he set off with Sustad, taking one of the two climbing ropes. There were goodbye shouts, a ringing rattle of ironmongery, the receding crunch of footsteps in the snow and then they were gone.

I woke later to yellow filtered sunlight and the sound of Victor and Renshaw tramping around in the snow outside. The pain in the bad leg had receded to a dull ache and I looked forward eagerly to the first day of my new life. There was plenty to keep us busy and the time passed quite quickly. The first job was to repitch my tent with a less extreme slope. While I made encouraging noises, the other two shovelled snow, packing it under the groundsheet to level the base. Then we had some breakfast, eking out a couple of biscuits with a hot drink. Later that morning Victor was summoned by a shout: 'I need to have a crap. Sorry.'

He appeared in my tent with a spare saucepan. Greater love hath no man than that he give up his own billy can ... the receptacle was adequate but, with my inability to squat, we had to arrange some kind of seat. A sturdy climbing boot wedged either side of the pan did the trick, then Victor and Renshaw manoeuvred me into position before retiring discreetly outside.

Victor emptied the bedpan uncomplainingly in a crevasse, cleaning it thoroughly with snow; nevertheless it was reassuring to have a second, unpolluted, pan for lunch – a simple snack of soup and a couple of biscuits. After lunch I dozed for an hour or two, exhausted by all the morning's activity, but eventually I was woken by backache. 'Victor ... Dick ... can you help roll me over, please? Yes – grab the legs. Aarghhh! Fucking hell! Not so hard ... that's better. Good. Right just hold it there ... No! Careful – '

'You're very brave, you know, but you do make a terrible fuss about the little things.'

'Sorry, Victor. I just had to get off my back. The whole of my torso feels as though it's been run over by a lorry. Sore bum as well.' It was only the first day after the accident and already I was proving a lousy patient. Propped up on my side, facing left into the tent wall, with the bad leg balanced on top of the better one, I retreated into the ritual of camera-cleaning, eking out each little mindless activity, from polishing the lens mount to working a tight-furled point of tissue into every corner of the camera body. It appeared to be quite unharmed by the huge tumble on my back, but the spare telephoto lens was now in two irreconcilable pieces – a token sacrifice to the forces of gravity.

Details like the destroyed lens jerked me back to the horrible events of the previous day, reminding me that I was actually stuck high on a remote mountain, seriously injured, with no certainty of rescue – or at least no certainty of a successful rescue. Somewhere along the line there was going to be struggle, danger, fear and acute pain, which might all end in disaster. But there was no benefit in thinking about those things, so I buried myself in trivia, dusting, polishing and air-blowing the camera to showroom perfection before returning it finally to its case. Just as I was wondering what activity to choose next, Renshaw asked, 'Do you fancy a brew?'

'Yes, what a wonderful idea!' Every little treat had to be relished and the hiss of snow in the pan had all the sensual promise of drawing a moist-squeaking cork to release the rich, dark, multi-layered secrets of some ancient claret. Victor tempted me with a dazzling array of choices. 'Would you like tea, Freddy, or one of these other things? Orange and cinnamon ... Colombian coffee with vanilla ... Chocolate and peppermint ... Where does he find these things? Do you think this is what they drink in Seattle? How about hot chocolate with a hint of strawberries? Or Blue Mountain coffee with *Schwarzwaldertörte* –'

'Ah – *Schwarzwaldertörte*. One of our Swiss friends taught my mother to make it. Huge quantities of hazelnuts and whipped cream and grated dark chocolate – completely different from that caterers' muck they call "Black Forest Gateau" –'

'I seem to remember you talking about puddings years ago,' interrupted Renshaw, 'something you had in France – '

'Oh, you mean the log Béatrice made. Now, let's get it right. The centre was ginger biscuits soaked in brandy; then round that there was a layer made from chestnut purée and chocolate; then a thick layer of whipped cream with grated chocolate sprinkled over the top. And that was *after* the fondue!' I groaned with olfactory yearning, longing for wine-cooked Gruyère to wash away the pervading smell of old caked suncream, stale farts and blood.

On the second day the food ran out. For Victor it was almost a relief to finish the dried potato powder. 'God I hate this stuff. No matter what you do to it, it always tastes like sawdust. Or wallpaper paste.'

'Yes, ghastly,' I sympathized. 'I remember we had some on the way down from Everest. When we were dawdling at Camp Two, trying to find the energy to get on with the descent. We hadn't really eaten for two days and it was all we had left. I knew we desperately needed the calories but I only managed a couple of spoonfuls. I don't think Ed or Robert touched it.'

I could still recall the foul metallic taste of ketones in my mouth as my body had begun to consume its own reserves of muscle. What had started as such a determined, organized climb had degenerated into a pathetic retreat. After the gruelling ordeal of our open bivouacs near the summit, Robert Anderson, Ed Webster and I had waited a whole day when we returned to our tents on the South Col, desperate to lie down, having only slept a total of about ten hours in the previous five days. By the time we had eventually set off back down our route on the East Face, we had become perilously weak. We had lost another whole day, dawdling in our sleeping bags at Camp Two, wallowing in the enervating heat which is the Himalaya's most potent weapon. When we did finally force ourselves to leave the next morning it took me nearly an hour to stand up. I knew that no one in the world could come and rescue me and that if I failed to stand up I would die. The choice was entirely up to me.

I had made the choice to live and, during the next seventeen hours of downward struggle without food or water, had found myself dredging up a new, previously unimaginable level of reserves. Four years later, shortly before leaving for Panch Chuli, I was asked to take part in one of those television studio discussions which assembles selected members of the public for a themed free-for-all. The topic that day was 'Survival'. The outdoor adventuring fraternity was well represented and included a good sprinkling of *mutilés de montagne*, some of whom performed with predictable self-importance. All fine entertainment, no doubt, but what made it all rather embarrassing was the way our experiences were linked to those of other contributors who had experienced the deepest horrors of human oppression. Amongst the latter were survivors of Auschwitz. Attempts to equate our self-inflicted little dramas with their unspeakable suffering seemed obscene. At best all one could say is that, having experienced, very briefly and artificially, a measure of physical hardship outside the normal luxuries of modern life, we might have some very vague inkling of the kind of physical privations faced by those who have suffered political and ideological oppression. But we cannot begin to imagine the despair and horror and sense of abandonment in the face of human evil, for landscape is not evil, however much we try to anthropomorphize mountains. A mountain is just a dangerous piece of geology on which we tread at our own peril.

On Everest a combination of circumstances, largely of my own making, pushed me quite close to death. Getting myself out of that position was some kind of vindication of personal drive, but what really sustained me, once I had made the decision to stand up and move on the final day, was catching up with Ed and Robert and drawing strength from their own determination. During the four years that had passed since that extraordinary day when we returned to life, I had often wondered whether I would have made it on my own. Or whether, with no one to share the ordeal, I would have exhausted my mental resources. Here, on Panch Chuli, I was utterly dependent on my companions. And what was so remarkable was their lack of complaint. Victor and Renshaw had the hungriest, most boring job of all – waiting, stranded for God knows how many days, now without food, in a precarious campsite high above a dangerous maze of collapsing icefalls. The two tents were at the upper, enclosed end of the cwm, almost encircled by snow-laden slopes. Small avalanches were slithering towards us all the time. None reached the tents, but a big storm could change everything.

That afternoon we finished the last of Sustad's exotic drink sachets. After a last supper of soup and one biscuit, we had a final cup of tea, adding the last granules of sugar. Halfway through melting the snow the stove fizzled out and Renshaw screwed on the last gas cylinder. Once that ran out it would virtually be impossible to produce water.

At dusk the other two retired to the red tent, leaving me to lie on my back and wait for sleep. I had now perfected a technique of rolling my hips to swing the splinted legs over on their side, with only a brief tweak of pain in the mangled knee. Over and over again I swapped from my side to my back, trying to trick the bruised muscles out of their nagging ache. Trying to ignore the other empty ache in my stomach. Dreaming of home – of being in the garden with Rosie . . . of crawling round the house chasing Ollie as we had done on the last morning, when he shrieked with delight. I wanted to hear his flamboyant laugh. Wanted to see that giggling, trusting shine in his dark eyes as he gazed out from behind his cot bars at bedtime. Just wanted this waiting to be over.

I had no doubt that it *would* be over at some stage – that I would be mended and crawling with ease, safely home again. When or how that was going to happen was not a question I bothered to address: I just knew that Victor and Renshaw, and Harish and Bonington, and everyone else would make sure that somehow it did happen.

On the third day the hunger gnawed deeper. Victor took a photo of Renshaw and me hunched in the end of the tent with glum empty faces. Whilst we tended to retreat inside ourselves, he tried to tease conversation out of us. I was the least forthcoming and sulked wearily while Victor forced Renshaw to disclose the technical minutiae of the abseil building work which supplemented his earnings from sculpture. That led them on to a mutual friend called Cho and a complicated story involving a church spire in Shropshire.

Every two or three hours we would have a drink, melting some snow and re-squeezing the last two tea bags in the tepid water, examining it earnestly for a change of colour. Victor peered up with one of his inquisitorial looks. 'You two got quite hungry on Kunyang Kish didn't you?'

'No, that was the first expedition, when Dick didn't come,' I corrected him, recalling the 1980 attempt on the giant mountain in Pakistan. 'It was just Bartlett, Wilkinson and me – waiting in the snowcave at 7,000 metres. The storm lasted five days and we waited a sixth day to give the snow a chance to settle. Each morning Wilkinson would hand us a cup of thin gruel, with a few oatflakes floating around – '

'Wilkinson – ah, yes I can just imagine it,' shrieked a delighted Victor.

'Yes – staring at you with those big owl eyes – telling you to eat it up because it was good for you. Then we would have an interminable wait for lunch. Counting the hours until we could each have one biscuit with a thin slice of cheese. You know – the processed stuff in the blue tins you get in Islamabad. We used to savour every crumb. It tasted like Stilton … Roquefort … Gorgonzola – '

'Do you know my favourite Italian recipe book,' interrupted Victor. 'I had it somewhere at Ferntower Road. What was the man's name. Giuseppe Someone? Or was it Giorgio? I don't think it's in print anymore, but it had wonderful recipes. Particularly good on quick snacks. He had a brilliant recipe for a quick instant pizza, using ciabatta for a base. And beautifully written – you know – witty, discursive, poetic …' He continued to taunt us for a while then turned to the man who lived in Cardiff. 'What about you, Dick. Do you know any good Welsh recipes?' After a long pause Renshaw came up with a valiant description of laver bread, but Celtic seaweed was no match for the riches of the Mediterranean.

Silence descended again on our confinement cell as we each wrestled with our nagging hunger. I longed to escape the foetid yellow prison, yearned painfully for comfort and normality, clinging to the belief that somehow they would get me out. Then doubts crept in again and I remembered the moments of dark fear, all those years earlier on Kunyang Kish, when I had worried about being marooned for ever, cut off by storms and avalanche, sealed in a frozen catacomb.

Memories of the cave revived the conversation which I managed at last to steer away from food. 'At least in the snowcave we had something to read. Wilky brought a copy of *The Magic Mountain* from Birmingham Central Library. We had to break it into three parts to share it out, so you didn't necessarily read it in the right order. Still I'm not sure that that makes much difference with Thomas Mann. Some of the pages had to be used as bog paper once everyone had read them, but Wilky took most of the book back to the library after the expedition. I think he was a bit offended when they asked him to pay a fine.'

'What was that D. H. Lawrence we had on the second

Kunyang Kish trip when I came?' asked Renshaw. 'Carlos was quite puzzled by it.'

'Carlos who?' queried Victor.

'Buhler,' I explained. 'Nice American man who was on the first ascent of the Kangshung Face.' A couple of years before his triumph on Everest he had joined our 1981 expedition in Pakistan. He had found the Lawrence – I think it was *The Rainbow* – a bit perplexing and on one occasion had asked, 'What's this word "fecund" the guy keeps using?' Renshaw had replied in his most deadpan Yorkshire voice, 'he wanted to write "fuck" but he wasn't allowed to in those days, so he decided the closest he could get was "fecund".'

For hours these strange, random drifts of memory sustained us in our grey limbo, cut off from the rest of the world by the clouds that hung over the mountains of Kumaun. The occasional sibilance of a wet snow slide, or the lazy thud of a stone falling to the glacier, would remind us where we were. At eleven o'clock that morning we heard a louder roar from further down the valley and wondered if it was a big avalanche on Panch Chuli II. But the noise persisted, fluctuating unnaturally, daring Renshaw to suggest tentatively, 'Is that a helicopter?'

'I think you may be right.' Victor stared intently into our eyes. 'But I can't hear it any more now ... it seems to have stopped.' The noise had died completely and we wondered whether we had been fooling ourselves. 'No, I think it *was* a helicopter,' insisted Victor. 'Perhaps they're landing a rescue team on the lower glacier. With this cloud they wouldn't be able to fly up here.'

If Victor was right this was the first thrilling hint that someone was trying to get to us. It was also confirmation that Sustad and Chris had descended safely. But nothing was certain and, even if we *had* heard a helicopter, we had no idea how soon it – or a stretcher team – might get to us. In the meantime we were quietly starving and hoping that Sustad had succeeded in making the promised food cache beside the second icefall. Victor and Renshaw discussed going down to look, but were worried about the soft, melting snow, so they decided to wait for colder conditions at night.

As dusk settled over the cwm, they prepared to leave. Both felt weak and apprehensive. Before leaving Victor said, 'I hope we'll be back by dawn, but if there's no food cache I don't think we're going to have the strength to climb back up here, so we'll probably have to carry on down to Base Camp to find out what's happened. We're also nearly out of gas here, so you'd be better off on your own if we can't get more. Those two bottles are full of water and I've left a full pan of snow where you can reach it – here. And more snow in this bag. Here's the cigarette lighter. The gas cylinder's about half full, so you could probably eke it out for three or four days if you had to. And look – here are the last two distalgesics in case the pain gets bad.'

He zipped shut the flysheet door and with a shouted goodbye the two of them disappeared into the darkening night. Alone now, bound in my foam rubber chrysalis, I knew that if things did not work out I could remain lying here until I died. I was strangely unafraid of that possibility. The fall through the darkness, four days earlier, had shown me that the actual moment of dying – or at least of believing that this was the instant of death – was not as frightening as one would imagine. Now that I had in fact survived the fall, of course I wanted to stay alive – I longed desperately to return to earth – but it was reassuring to know that if that were not possible, death itself was not frightening; it was not such a big deal after all. I lay on my back, staring at the fading colour of the dome above my face, concentrating on its blank nothingness, emptying thought and emotion from my mind and trying to ignore the cramped pain of my back and the duller ache of hunger.

Sleep came quickly and my dreams were reassuringly mundane until they were shattered by the harsh roar of pulverized masonry and wet cement falling out of the sky. Electric shocks pricked my scalp and fingertips as the blood was sent racing in a shudder of pure terror. I stared helplessly into the impenetrable blackness, braced for annihilation as the avalanche filled the whole cwm with its implacable thunder. I had no idea where it was coming from and at first the noise seemed to be immediately above me. Only when it began to die away did my heart slow down. It was the ice tower shedding a few thousand tons more of its rotten superstructure. I knew from five days earlier that it would be sweeping the cwm well below the tent.

Safe and secure again, I drifted back to sleep, only to be woken an hour later by the same roar of destruction. This time I knew immediately that I was safe and hardly bothered to emerge from the complacency of slumber, returning quickly to a deep sleep, only to be woken yet again – this time by voices. 'Victor! Dick! So the cache was there. You made it! What was it like?' Victor said nothing. Renshaw unzipped the flysheet and shone his headbeam into the tent. 'It was very, very frightening. Did you hear the avalanches?'

'Yes – it was a relief they were not too –'

'They completely wiped out our tracks –'

'You mean . . .' How stupid! How insensitive and complacent! Wrapped up in my solipsistic cocoon, it had never occurred to me that the other two might have been in the danger area. The first avalanche had swept the cwm as they arrived at its lower lip on the way back from the cache, just in time to see their tracks from the previous evening being obliterated. Once the dust had settled they had had no choice but to fight their way up through all the debris scattered over the basin. They had only just cleared the disaster zone when the second avalanche crashed down behind them, wiping out their tracks for the second time that night.

'The whole mountain is falling to pieces.' Victor's voice was edged with a weary hatred. He just wanted to get away from this horrible place. 'Nothing was frozen properly and the labyrinth had changed completely. And the Venus Flytrap –'

'The what?'

'You know – the overhang with the giant icicles – '

'Oh Victor, you're such a poet.'

'Shut up. Anyway, we've got the food. We're just going to have a bit of sleep, then we'll cook a meal. Thank God Sustad made it.'

When Sustad and Bonington left the cwm in the early hours of Monday morning, they knew that everything depended on their safe descent to Base Camp. Sustad drove himself forward on adrenaline, ignoring the hunger and exhaustion of the 36-hour journey to the summit and back. Bonington was oblivious of the cuts and bruises sustained in the previous day's plummet down the icefield. Fear metamorphosed into a positive determination to climb carefully, every sense focused on the dangers ahead.

In the labyrinth they managed to find a detour round the long jump. Traversing beneath Victor's Venus Flytrap, they hurried urgently, tending the rope with a new alertness. At the bottom of the big snow couloir four days' melting had enlarged the waterfall gap. Sustad stopped to set up an abseil. 'We'll have to leave the rope fixed in place for when I come back with the food.' As he began to hammer in a peg, Bonington asked, 'How come you've got that sling already tied to the peg?'

'Ah, that's *the* peg – the one that came out. At least we get to re-use it.'

'Yes, well make sure you hammer it in nice and firm.'

The peg held and they both abseiled quickly through the waterfall. Then they headed across the top rim of the lower icefall, Sustad leading with tense alertness now that they had left the rope behind, every sense tuned to the risk of concealed crevasses. As the slope broke away into the valley they were confronted by a changed landscape. Snow bridges had rotted away. The ice had wrenched open new crevasses. Grit-blackened towers had crashed down leaving fresh, raw, turquoise stumps. The whole of the lower icefall was falling to pieces, and the old route up its edge no longer existed. Sustad improvised a new line through the shattered chaos, forced to work right out into the middle of the icefall, before he could find a way through to the flat calm of the lower glacier. There the strain eased, but they still had a long way to go, forcing their aching legs down the interminable ice highway, then up on to the moraine and into the ablation valley. They were thrilled by the sweet green novelty of grass and flowers, and the running streams, but this final stretch felt infinitely longer than it had on the way up. Whole new sections seemed to have been inserted provocatively into the landscape, forcing them to walk on and on and on.

It was late afternoon when they crossed the last stream, slipping on wet boulders and stumbling out of the gully to see a thread of smoke rising from the camp amongst the trees. Harsinh Senior's kind smile soon turned to alarm as they pointed up to Panch Chuli V, gesticulating and miming the events of the last two days. Dhansinh and Harsinh Junior built up the fire and filled the large kettle. After several mugs of tea they then cooked a huge pan of rice and dal for the two exhausted sahibs who could barely stay awake to finish their meal.

Bonington left at dawn the next day, striding down the Pyunshani valley with Harsinh Senior. Sustad longed for a rest day, but after a meagre breakfast he began to pack up virtually all the remaining food at Base Camp. There was not a great deal of it but, rummaging through his personal belongings, he found a tin of smoked mussels – a treat from his wife Rose which he had been saving. After a moment's salivating indecision, he added it to the bag of provisions for the others.

It was now Tuesday and Victor and Renshaw were hoping to pick up the cache the next day. He would have to start immediately. The previous evening, struggling with sign language and wishing that he spoke Hindi, he had asked Harsinh Junior to accompany him. Travelling unroped through the icefall once was risky enough, and he didn't want to do it again. He would use the spare rope left at the first glacier camp a week earlier, and tie Harsinh on to that. Now, as Harsinh tried to pad out a pair of spare climbing boots three sizes too big, Sustad wondered if there was any point. He would just have to see how far Harsinh could get.

Early the next morning, groping back up through the icefall after camping on the lower glacier, his doubts changed to anger – anger that this shepherd with no technical climbing experience should be dragged into such danger. Why should his life be risked to help frivolous foreigners out of a trap of their own making? Seven years earlier Harsinh had overcome his fear to traverse granite cliffs – the only way out from the Terong valley. But this wasn't just about overcoming fear – it was dangerous.

Only two days had passed since he had come down this way

with Bonington, but already the icefall had changed again. At one point Sustad reached a dead end and had to shout to Harsinh to reverse back across a teetering blade of ice. He untied to scout an alternative route, eventually found an escape and returned to tie Harsinh back on the rope. Above the icefall the snow lay like sticky clay on the long traverse to the base of the couloir. The waterfall was now an even bigger torrent and fear twisted the edges of Harsinh's nervous smile. Sustad wondered about teaching him to climb the rope with a Jumar, then thought better of it.

'Okay – give me the load.' Sustad pointed at Harsinh's rucksack and took out the supplies to add to his own rucksack. He pointed to a protected hollow, making a downward motion with his palms, instructing Harsinh to wait there. Then gulping with the icy wet shock of it he pushed up into the waterfall, bracing cramponed feet wide on sloping rocks encrusted with half-frozen mush, fighting the dragging weight of his rucksack, relieved that he had had the foresight to leave a rope fixed.

He hauled himself patiently to the top of the icefall, stopped to get his breath back and wring out sodden mittens, then continued up the familiar treadmill of the couloir to the old lunch stop. Before making the food safe from choughs and ravens under a pile of stones, he wrote a note to leave with the food:

> Sorry for the low volume of food. It's all we had at Base Camp and it's also all I could carry on my own. Should have fresh supplies in 2 days at base and so it will be 4 days from now till next delivery. Bottom icefall is now very dangerous. At 2/3 on way down turn sharp right at flattish area into centre of icefield and then down. Be careful. Heli could come any time. Sorry no books. I am just too weak to carry much more. Hope all is well. You're in my thoughts. Stephen.

Descending with Harsinh was even more worrying than the journey up and it was only late that night that the two men returned exhausted to Base Camp.

'Wake up Freddy. It's breakfast time.' It was light and Victor had the stove going. 'How about potatoes – *real* potatoes, with onions.' He made a sort of stew, with a soup packet for stock, and it tasted utterly delicious. Calories coursed through the collective metabolism, soothing our hunger and filling us with warmth and hope. We still had to ration ourselves carefully, but my minders agreed to a couple of biscuits for pudding. And unused tea bags to flavour our hot water! Even a spoonful of sugar! The future was bearable again and I felt that I could wait here for several days longer. The lump of meat lying in front of me was now causing little pain and although Victor had detected the beginnings of infection when he inspected the wound the previous afternoon, I hoped blithely that it would take a while to spread.

I seemed to have forgotten about the contemporary from Cambridge who lost his leg on the Petit Dru, above Chamonix. It was in the early seventies and he was attempting the soaring granite precipice of the famous Bonatti Pillar – in those days an extremely ambitious route for young students to tackle. A single rock, falling from hundreds of feet above, landed on his leg, smashing through bones and ligaments, leaving him in agony and unable to move. He waited for several days, perched on a ledge while his companion, Mick Geddes, tried desperately to signal to the cable-car station at Les Grands Montets. By the time a helicopter came to winch him off the pillar, gangrene had rotted his leg to the core and it had to be amputated above the knee. A year later he made the first one-legged ascent of Joe Brown's legendary Welsh rock climb in the Llanberis Pass that goes by the cheerful name Cenotaph Corner.

I had no desire to become a one-legged climber. In fact I seemed blissfully unaware of the risk of losing my leg, and now that the awful yearnings of the stomach were assuaged, I felt confident in holding out longer if necessary.

We were just finishing our tea, enjoying our new calm repleteness, chatting contentedly, when Renshaw interrupted Victor. 'Shh – what's that.' It was coming from somewhere down towards the main glacier. That roaring noise again. Except this time it was coming closer and it was definitely not an avalanche.

Chapter Eleven

SALT SWEAT MINGLED with the rain pouring down his forehead and stung his eyes. His knees ached with the strain of the relentless, lurching adjustments as feet slithered on mud, skidded over the dark slime of dead tree trunks, tripped on rogue bamboos. His ribs heaved with the strain of hard panting. But he must keep going – must stick to that wiry, lithe figure in front. Without Harsinh Senior he would have lost the temporary trail of slashed branches and churned mud, switching from bank to bank of the Pyunshani – would never have found that scary tree trunk over the main river to rejoin the Balati trail.

Filthy weather. Must be snowing up at the high camp. Avalanche risk increasing every day. Must try and get a helicopter up there by tomorrow morning. It's already Tuesday afternoon now. Don't know how long they can hold out.

Bonington forced himself on down the valley, pleased to notice that they were bypassing the climb to Ringo village and heading straight down the river to Madkot. But even this route had its irregularities. Bending forward, panting hard, he ran up yet another torturing rise on the trail, hardly stopping to rest at the top before plunging down after Harsinh. Not bad for a fifty-eight-year-old, he thought. In a strange way he was enjoying himself, revelling in the urgency, the surge of adrenaline, the intensity of purpose, the determination to make sure that everyone came down alive.

At three o'clock in the afternoon, having covered thirty miles through the forest, a third of that distance along a new, roughly improvised trail, he arrived at Madkot. With Harsinh's help he managed to find a telephone but the line was continually cut off and no one at either end spoke English. For two hours he struggled to make himself understood, desperate to get things moving.

Harish, Monesh and Muslim had reached the hill-station early that morning. After a shower and a huge late lunch, they were now relaxing on the verandah outside the Dak Bungalow. Cloud hung thickly over the Panch Chuli range across the valley, but here it was dry and they were all enjoying the novelty of freshly laundered clothes, as they sorted through a sheaf of papers, finalizing the expedition accounts. Suddenly a boy came running up from the village. Perhaps he was bringing that paan they had ordered – the first delicious, spicy, betel digestif for six weeks. But no, he was running far too fast for that. And there was a gleam of excitement in his eyes. The boy staggered on to the verandah and between gulping breaths told Sri Kapadia to hurry to the post office to take an urgent phone call.

'Harish . . . Harish . . . is that you? Ah, thank goodness. Chris here. I'm in Madkot. There's been an accident. Stephen – Stephen Venables – has broken both his legs.' Harish's face darkened and the joyful, celebratory sparkle went out of his eyes, but he asked calmly, 'Where is he?'

'Stuck up on the glacier – right up under Panch Five, with Victor and Dick. They're above some desperate icefalls – very difficult terrain. We have to try and get a helicopter in there.'

'*Achha.*' Harish remained imperturbable. 'Okay, Chris, I will alert authorities immediately. Once that is done I shall come down to you with a vehicle.'

Muslim and Monesh had now joined Harish under the whirring fan in the hot little office. Within seconds of putting down the phone the three of them were setting the rescue in motion. First they summoned our liaison officer, Wing-Commander Anil Srivastava, who had escorted Vijay out from the Balati two weeks earlier. Harish explained the bare facts of this new accident and asked him to get a message immediately to the nearest air base, two hundred miles away at Bareilly, down in the plains. He had no idea whether a helicopter could ever get in, with the cloud cover increasing every day. It might take several days, and in the meantime he had to prepare for a possible land rescue. Monesh took Revatram on a frantic shopping spree, buying up supplies for a ground party to restock Base Camp. In just an hour the party was ready to drive down to Madkot.

Bonington looked ghastly. His face was hollow, grey and muddy, with dried blood still caking the gash on his cheek. Choking with emotion, his voice rasping from the strain of the last three days, he told the whole story. Harish got out the Air Force map to pinpoint the exact location of the tents and get the co-ordinates for Anil to report to Bareilly. 'They're in a *desperate* position,' Bonington stressed. 'The tents are pitched on a slope in an avalanche-prone basin, with steep walls all round. But they must try and get in there because if we have to send up stretchers, through the icefalls . . .' He faltered, terrified at the thought of a huge unwieldy team lurching through that tottering chaos.

'Don't worry.' Harish put a solicitous hand on his shoulder. He had always admired Bonington from a distance and, ever since meeting him in Delhi in 1983, he had been trying to lure him on a joint expedition. He was moved to see his hero so vulnerable to emotion.

Before dark Muslim started back up the Balati valley with a party of seven carrying supplies for Base Camp, resigned to postponing his return to Sabina and the baby in Bombay. Harish and Monesh took Bonington up the long dusty hairpins to Munsiary for a richly-deserved shower, meal and sleep. On Wednesday, 24 June, he rose early as usual. Harish was already up, cross-legged on the verandah, meditating. His closed eyes faced east, across the Goriganga to the Pandavas' hearths. Bonington's narrowed eyes, still puffy from sunburn, exhaustion and bruising, scanned the diffuse horizon, glimpsing only ephemeral wisps of mountain behind a shifting miasma of cloud. Even at dawn there was a heavy dampness in the air.

Throughout the day Harish played the imperturbable foil to Bonington's anxiety. Communication with the outside world was fitful. The telephone lines were down in Munsiary and messages had to be relayed through the radio of the local chief of the India Tibet Border Police. Information was scant and no one mentioned that already that day, less than twenty-four hours after the alert, a helicopter was doing a recce up the Pyunshani valley. Only later did Harish get the news that the thick cloud had stopped the pilots from locating the tents.

Meanwhile the two men made contingency plans. If after three days a helicopter had not managed to get through, the India Tibet Border Police would provide twenty men to assist with a ground rescue. It would only be a last resort, for Bonington had made it quite clear how difficult it would be for a large party, including comparatively inexperienced climbers, to manhandle a stretcher out of the trap on Panch Chuli V. It would put many people in danger and would be excruciatingly painful for the victim – if he were still alive by the time they arrived.

As we listened to the helicopter climb closer, Victor and Renshaw rushed to get me ready, packing a rucksack with a few essentials and strapping a climbing harness around my waist so that I could be clipped to the winch. They were just about to drag me out of the tent when the sound began to recede. We paused, listening nervously, hoping for that glorious sound of an internal combustion engine to roar closer again. But it dwindled to a distant hum then vanished. Renshaw stuck his head out of the tent to see thick banks of cloud piled over the icefalls below us. Higher layers wreathed the summits above. Trying to be stoical, trying to ignore the bitter disappointment, we reverted our collective mindset to the patient, hopeful game of waiting.

I told myself that it had all been too good to be true. I shouldn't have hoped to get out so soon. After all we had only just begun our fourth day of waiting and I was very lucky that a helicopter had got anywhere near us. Perhaps our first supposition was correct and they were landing a ground party below the icefalls. Or perhaps they *were* going to do an air rescue, plucking me painlessly to instant safety. Perhaps plucking all of us, if the helicopter was big enough.

Fortified by our generous breakfast, we chatted with new energy and optimism. Hopeful that the helicopter might return in the next day or two, Victor and Renshaw discussed how to prepare me when the time came. In their dreams the helicopter arrived complete with paramedic winchman, who would land beside the tent and strap me into the comforting embrace of a stretcher before clipping my vulnerable body to the wire. I suggested that we retain my makeshift splint, but Victor insisted, 'No, the winchman will sort you out with his own stuff.'

'Of course you've been through all this, haven't you, Victor?' chipped in Renshaw. Victor retreated behind his sunglasses, still embarrassed by a winter rescue, many years earlier, from the infamous 'Spider' four thousand feet up the North Face of the Eiger. In fact he had been plucked involuntarily from the wall, forced to accept defeat when his companions succumbed to the bitter cold which had already snapped the brittle tips of several essential ice tools. 'It must have been infuriating to have to stop, but quite fun riding on the chopper,' I coaxed.

'Terrifying,' replied a re-enthused Victor, 'It's an extraordinary situation. One minute you're minding your own business, perched securely on this fifty-degree icefield, tied to an ice screw. Then the winchman clips you into the wire and unclips you from the mountain. He actually gave me a shove –' his voice rose in outrage, 'just pushed me off. Suddenly you're hanging in the air four thousand feet above the ground – well actually you're looking about *eight* thousand feet straight down to Grindelwald. And they don't winch you up at first: they just fly out horizontally dangling you on the end of the wire.'

Victor returned later that year to make a complete winter ascent of the Eiger North Face with his friend Stevie Haston. 'It was Renshaw's winter ascent with Tasker that made me want to do it. You've done it in summer, haven't you Freddy?'

'Yes – well September. It was perfect – plastered with snow and ice and well frozen. We hardly heard a single stone fall. I did it with Luke – you know, just before I came to live at Fernytowers and joined his workshop. It must have been almost the best climb I've ever done. We enjoyed it so much we sang *Figaro* most of the way up. I think we were both in love with Susanna. Do you know that bit in the last act? The sexiest music ever written.'

I rambled on. Later Victor returned to the subject of rope

access work, quizzing Renshaw, who reminisced fondly about a job with a climber called Tut Braithwaite, who had been quite a hero when he came to lecture to me and other callow youths in Oxford. Twenty years on, Renshaw, whose achievements had also inspired me, talked about mellow summer evenings after work, feeling strong and fit, romping up climbs with Tut, attuned serenely to the form and texture of the rock which glowed steadily redder as the sun dropped in the sky.

Talk of climbing – of its most treasured memories – made me equivocal. Four days earlier, in the immediate dark awakening from the accident, I had assumed that that was it. Final. The end of climbing. The irrevocable decision to pack it all in. But now, already, I was realizing that it might not be so easy to abandon something which had provided such intensity of experience. Already I was less certain about the immorality of unnecessary risk. Perhaps, it was justifiable after all: perhaps the dangers of mountaineering were only an extension, to a higher level, of the risks everyone face from the moment of birth. Perhaps there was even some benefit to gain from confronting one's own mortality so brazenly, choosing not to make survival to a secure, prosperous, comfortable old age an all-consuming priority. Then I remembered Ollie, the baby who had so nearly lost his father, and I longed contritely for the helicopter to come back and take me home.

Bonington paced urgently down the muddy street that linked the Dak Bungalow to the police office. Harish struggled to keep up, urging breathlessly, 'We just have to wait patiently. It is in the hands of the authorities – and God.'

'But what's happening? Why has the helicopter gone all the way back down to the plains. It's Thursday now. Stephen's been up there with a serious injury for four days. The wound must be infected by now – that's if he's still alive. Maybe they've been wiped out by an avalanche and there was actually nothing for the helicopter to find.'

'I think there is probably a problem with the cloud,' reassured Harish. 'Maybe they'll try again in the afternoon.'

They had now reached the office. The chief of the border police offered them chairs and ordered the inevitable cup of tea. Bonington bridled at the inscrutable charmingness of his hosts. 'Harish, can't we get a message to London? I think I should speak to the Prime Minister – John Major – get him to put on some pressure.'

The police officer smiled politely. Harish laughed. 'Chris – it would make no difference at all. This is India! Now drink your tea and have some of these biscuits.'

At Dharchula, in the Kaliganga valley fifty miles south of Panch Chuli, Squadron Leader P. Jaiswal was eating an early lunch in the officers' mess. He looked out through the window to the clipped lawn, the white posts, the neat bungalows with their red corrugated iron roofs and the tarmac landing pad where khaki-clad figures were busy checking and re-fuelling the helicopter, its dark green panelling blending with the forested wall of the valley immediately behind it.

He hardly spoke to his companion, Flight-Lieutenant P. K. Sharma, who was scooping dal hungrily with a folded corner of steaming fresh chapatti. They seemed to have spent most of the last two days in the air. Yesterday, they had flown all the way to that glacier – or as close as they could get before impenetrable cloud had turned them back. They had flown here to refuel, and then continued all the way to Bareilly.

Then today they had been up at dawn to run through pre-flight checks before setting off again at 5.20. All the way up to those Panch Chuli mountains, with just a map reference to go on. At least this time they reckoned they had located the correct branch of the glacier, but the terrain had looked horrible – peaks hemming in the valley all around; steep walls doing unpredictable things to the air currents; cloud moving fast at different levels; glimpses of complicated upper branches of the glacier, with huge icefalls.

Neither of them had liked it and although they thought they could now tell roughly where the casualty was, they hadn't dared get any further into the cloud and had been forced to fly back here to refuel. At least on the Siachen Glacier, up in Ladakh, the terrain was more open; and they normally only flew in good conditions. And the pilots there were supplying their own troops, not risking their necks for a British climber.

'Shall we eat the smoked mussels?' Victor opened the tin to add rich flavour to our otherwise rather bland mid-morning lunch. 'Do you realize these were a special present to the Lutheran from Rose?'

'I wonder if I would have done the same. I think I might have been tempted to eat them myself.' Yet again I was struck by Sustad's thoughtful generosity. He shunned publicity, never writing or lecturing about his climbs, which was probably just as well because he usually only had the vaguest idea where he had actually been. He tended to leave the promoting and planning and organizing to other people, presenting a shambolic persona to the world; but you knew that if there were a crisis you could not wish for a better companion.

'Mmmm, that was excellent.' Victor licked his engrimed fingers. 'Just a shame about the smell. I'm really looking forward to being somewhere that doesn't smell of blood. I don't think I'm ever going to be able to walk past a butcher's shop without thinking of this tent.'

'Ah yes – the associations of smell. Like going back to your old school.'

'Proust was always going on about it wasn't he? Each little tiny smell sending him off on some interminable, tedious reminiscence. Have you read Proust, Dick?'

'What – oh Proust.' Dick emerged wearily from his private musing. 'Yes, we had volume one when we went to Kishtwar. I rather enjoyed it.'

'I liked the bit about the hawthorn blossom,' I interjected. 'Pages and pages of it. Rosie liked it too. In fact we used to joke that we would call our first child Hawthorn. I suppose it would have been rather an imposition. Still, better than Lupin – '

'Lupin?'

'You know – Lupin Pooter. Now there's a funny – '

'Shhh! What's that?' We froze, silent.

'Yes – they're coming back. Quick, we must get you ready.' As the engine's promising roar grew closer, we rushed through our preparations. Once again, Victor and Renshaw worked the climbing harness round my waist, buckled it up and attached a long sling with a karabiner. I removed my normal spectacles and put on sunglasses for the snow outside. Then, still coping patiently with my cries and groans, the others untied my splint and fed my legs into a sleeping bag to keep me warm while I waited outside. Then they helped me get my aching torso into Sustad's red duvet jacket for extra protection.

'Come on, it's time to get you out.' They dragged me out of the tent and for the first time in four days I blinked at the unaccustomed brightness of high altitude sunlight reflecting on the snow. As they dragged me across the slope I thrilled to the air and light and end-of-term excitement. I was going home!

Sitting in my sleeping bag I looked round at my now unfamiliar surroundings. Behind me on the left, new avalanche runnels scoured the face of Telkot. I turned right, to the crescent silhouette of the col where Bonington had waited in his tent. The summit of Panch Chuli V was engulfed in cloud but I could see the dark rocks on the flank of the pillar. I stared up at the scene of the accident, gauging metres against the impassive mountainside, looking for the last time at the long icefield where Victor and Renshaw had lowered me stoically, hour after hour, and registered the long slick runnel where Bonington had tumbled down the face. Then I stared hard, peering down the cwm towards the valley, scrutinizing the diffuse snow and cloud for some visible sign of the growing noise.

At last I saw it. A tiny object. A miraculous insect emerging from the shifting clouds into sunlight, gleaming metallic as it zigzagged backwards and forwards above the icefall, growing steadily larger as it came towards us.

Chapter Twelve

THE BALL BOUNCED with a puff of dust and tore out a makeshift willow stump. The boys shrieked with delight and one of them rushed up to take a turn with the bat. A few yards away the man from Bombay shouted in Hindi, urging them on with tales of miraculous sixes, double centuries, astronomical batting averages, legendary catches and all the myth and glory of India's adopted national game.

The other man – the Englishman – smiled distractedly. He was dressed incongruously in bulky, bright-coloured mountaineering gear and he carried a rucksack full of food and equipment. He kept staring out over the rough turf of the sports ground to the green immensity of the distant gorge and he was the first to hear the sound of the helicopter coming up the valley. The children abandoned their cricket and screwed up their eyes, trying to detect the tiny distant object.

'There it is.' Bonington had already spotted it. 'They're going straight into the Pyunshani valley. Why can't they stop here first?' Since the unsuccessful early morning flight he had been trying to get a message to the pilots to take him up with them. At least then he could show them the exact position of the tents and drop some supplies if the helicopter was unable to pick up the casualty. 'Harish – if they don't succeed this time we've got to get them to come back here and pick me up. I've got to get up there!'

'Achha – we will try.' Harish was also getting increasingly worried. The pilots were obviously having problems and he was now pushing for a land party to go in. The constant problems with radio and telephone communications had made it very hard to know what exactly was happening. And his resolve had been shaken momentarily by critical mutterings from some of the locals: if the famous, experienced one with the grey beard had had the sense not to continue to the summit, why had the other four gone on recklessly? Look what had happened! They had obviously been taking stupid risks. Why should other people now be put in danger to rescue this irresponsible Englishman?

Harish had deflected the criticisms with joshing banter, and spared Bonington a translation, relaying instead the more helpful comments. He had tried to put through the request for Bonington to accompany the pilots and hoped that next time they would land in Munsiary and whisk him off to the high cwm, assuming that they had room on board.

For the third time Squadron Leader Jaiswal headed for the dirty rubble snout of the Panch Chuli Glacier. It was 11.20 a.m. Beside him the co-pilot kept switching his gaze from the map on his knees to the real version outside the perspex bubble. This time the detail was clearer and they continued beyond the last scattered trees, up the grey highway of the glacier, heading straight for the wall of the Panch Chulis until they could swing right towards the most distant upper corner of the glacier.

The helicopter was a Lama – a hybrid of the Alouette II and Alouette III. In India, where it is made under licence, it is called a Cheetah. As it climbed up the narrowing defile it was getting close to its official service ceiling of 6,300 metres – the level at which the climb rate is reduced to less than 100 feet per minute. The rules can of course be stretched. In 1972 an extremely bold French pilot called Jean Boulet removed everything he could – including most of the instruments, the batteries and the starter motor – from a Lama, and, with no one else aboard, coaxed it to 12,442 metres above sea level – 40,820 feet! However, the lack of a starter motor proved embarrassing when, shortly after beginning the descent, the engine stalled, forcing Boulet to complete a record autorotative descent – a sort of airborne free-wheeling – all the way back to earth.

No one had repeated that particular stunt and Jaiswal knew

that he would be stretched just to operate at the official ceiling, with the fuel tank still over half full, two pilots on board and, he hoped, a third, rescued, passenger weighing about seventy kilos. As long as a helicopter is moving forward, its momentum compensates partially for the thinness of the air at high altitude. But the critical point is its hover ceiling. All sorts of factors come into play, but the recommended hover limit for a Lama is 5,600 metres – the exact height of the spot on the map which Sharma and Jaiswal were now trying to locate.

Sharma held up a gloved hand to wipe condensation from the bubble as they climbed into colder air. He peered out left at the pleated snow curtain hanging so horribly close, where his colleague had flown as near as he dared to the wall of Panch Chuli IV to squeeze through a gap in the clouds veiling the icefalls. Now, as they climbed through the gap, the tortuous, fractured ice rose with them, horribly close beneath their fragile transparent shell. Flying straight from Bareilly, at only 150 metres above sea level, Sharma and Jaiswal had no acclimatization and as they approached 5,000 metres, they made a point of taking turns to breathe deeply on an emergency oxygen mask. They both knew that if they crashed up here, even if they survived, they would soon weaken from hypoxia and would be very unlikely to get out alive.

As they crested the icefall and for the first time saw the elusive cwm, Sharma suddenly spotted a tiny red blob at the head of the basin. Staring into the cauldron, both men flinched. The snow floor was riven by dark slots. Between the crevasses avalanche debris littered the surface. The basin seemed to rise steadily, with no discernible level area and it was horribly narrow, enclosed on three sides by menacing walls. Anxious not to stick his head irrevocably in the noose, Jaiswal took the helicopter on a long rightward tack, heading away from the cwm to gain more height and get a better feel for the air currents before committing himself to the final approach.

Incredulous despair engulfed me as the helicopter disappeared, apparently heading back towards the Goriganga, or perhaps searching one of the other branches of the glacier. We had no idea how well – if at all – the pilots had been briefed and I began to resign myself to another long aching night on the mountain. But then the noise returned again and suddenly there it was! Nosing back round from behind the retaining wall of the cwm, zigzagging purposefully towards us again. Now I could begin to

make out clearly the profile of the thing – the improbable transparency of the front bubble, the solid engine housing in the middle and the fretwork sketch of a tail, fragile as a child's Meccano construction. But the solid, pulsating throb of its engine filled me with confidence and, as the noise grew to fill the basin, I felt tears of relief and gratitude prick my eyes.

The noise grew louder and louder. The friendliness metamorphosed into menace, recalling the Conradian horror of Vietnam soundtracks. Mesmerized, I photographed the giant insect's single, bulging, transparent eye as it pressed aggressively close, hanging just a few feet in front of us, its wings scything the air with unimaginable power. The pulsating noise thudded in our ears and snow was whipped in our faces. Victor and Dick clung to me and stared anxiously at the hovering beast. They searched for some sign of a winch and held up the karabiner on my waist sling, waving it hopefully.

From behind the bulging eye we could see two brown faces and as they edged deafeningly closer we could see the whites of their eyes – the anxious glances up and down, left and right, as the man in the starboard seat kept wiping the fogged perspex. As the co-pilot put the oxygen mask to his face, Victor gesticulated down the valley, pointing towards an area that seemed slightly flatter. But the difference was only marginal and there was no escaping the fact that everything was tilted at about thirty degrees. The bulging eye backed off a little and the tail swung round into profile again as the insect hovered tentatively backwards and forwards, testing the air and searching the snow surface just a few feet below the two steel skids.

Our blithe assumptions about a simple winching operation had been hopelessly naïve. This was not Chamonix or Grindelwald and, although these were highly experienced pilots,

they were not mountain rescue experts. They were also flying dangerously close to their craft's altitude limit.

The eye came closer again, this time staring at us from just a few metres away. Victor and Renshaw stared back, once again waving the karabiner forlornly, for want of anything better to do. The pilots looked even more worried. Then the co-pilot gesticulated with rapid sideways crossing of his hands and a down-pushing motion. That's it, I thought, they can't do it. They're just saying, sorry mate, there's nothing we can do. You're on your own. The gesture became more emphatic, almost hysterical, but the helicopter showed no sign of moving away. Then we noticed the starboard man pointing to the red tent. 'Ah – of course. He wants us to take down the tent,' Victor shouted at Dick through the din. 'I think he wants to land on the tent ledge.'

They had already dismantled the yellow tent and secured all loose objects. Now, shouting 'Don't slide away, Freddy,' they dashed back to the red tent. From my sloping perch I watched over my shoulder as they collapsed the poles frantically and bundled them up with the baggy fabric. The co-pilot pointed away from the tent ledge and again made the hand-crossing-palms-down motion, emphasizing that nothing must get sucked into the rotor blades. Then he pointed at me and back to the tent ledge.

While Renshaw held down the baggage, Victor stumbled backwards across the snow, dragging me in my sleeping bag back to the ledge were I had spent the last four days. Gasping from the effort he looked up at the helicopter for approval and the hands behind the perspex pointed towards the back of the ledge, urging Victor to pull me into the far corner. There we huddled as the helicopter edged closer.

At this point I suddenly decided that I didn't want to be rescued any more. Just leave me here, please. Don't worry, we'll find some other way of getting out. Just go away and don't turn us all into mincemeat. Hunched in terror, I glanced up to see the whites of the pilots' eyes, staring with intense concentration as they nudged the perspex bubble closer and closer and swung the tail round until it was parallel with the slope. Victor and I huddled like paralysed rabbits as the blades scythed right over our heads, compressing the air in pulsating thuds. Slowly the green steel bar of the starboard skid pressed on to the outside edge of the snow ledge and rested there.

Squadron Leader Jaiswal focused with desperate intensity on the altitude indicator. His hands on the joystick were attuned to every nuance, feeling nervously for any sudden air current that might send them all spinning to oblivion. Landing like this – holding the craft stationary and then taking off again – used every ounce of power available at this altitude. Even on flat ground it would be risky, but here, with just one skid resting on that snow ledge and the tips of the rotor blades slicing less than a metre from the slope, it was going to take all his years of training to avoid calamity. Anxious about the sudden imbalance of an extra seventy-kilo loading, he decided to back off and try again before committing himself to the actual rescue.

I exhaled with relief as the the predatory insect backed away. But a minute later it crept closer. Once again the blades sliced within inches of the slope and Victor hugged me close to the ledge, tensed for instant annihilation. For thirty seconds – perhaps a minute – the beast hung there, seeming to paw at the mountain, testing nervously, unsure whether or not to commit itself. Then again it backed off. This time it came in facing the other way. Again it backed off.

Four or five times the pilot tested his ability to hold the helicopter stable in the thin air, all the while remembering to keep his brain clear with regular gulps of oxygen. Cowering a few feet away, battered by the deafening noise of the engine, we watched anxiously for a sign, acutely aware of the pilots' own fear. Then at last the flimsy side door was flung open and the co-pilot pulled down his intercom mouthpiece to shout at me to get in. We waited hopefully for him to come and help us, but quickly realized that he was fully occupied on board the helicopter. We were going to have to do this on our own.

Passive compliance was no longer enough. For the first time

since the immediate aftermath of the accident, over four days earlier, I was going to have to be brave. I was going to have to subject myself to intense pain.

The co-pilot was shouting at me to get in quickly. Victor helped as best he could, dragging me over to the metal skid. Hard steel pressed into the wasted flesh around my pelvis. A blast of exhaust fumes filled my nostrils. The demonic thud of the rotor blades brought back the Vietnam images. Victor's eyes had the desperate pitying stare of the GI buddy powerless to help. 'Get in!' he screamed, pushing on the less badly broken leg, now unzipped from the sleeping bag. I reached behind me and pulled at the vibrating metalwork, wincing with the pain of stretched muscles, heaving my weight on to the upper framework from which the skid was suspended. Exhausted by the pain and exertion I then slumped back to rest.

'Get in! Get in!' Victor and the co-pilot were both shouting. I twisted my head round into the cockpit, still impossibly far

op left: Sustad leads the way into the labyrinth during the tortuous approach to Panch *huli V.*

op right: Two hours later he looks back to see Bonington, Renshaw and Saunders (circled) *arting* across. The food dump was later left at the pointed rocks below and to the right of *ae* tiny figures.

fter a twelve hour day the team finally reaches the elusive cwm and pitches tents for the *ght.* Tracks can be seen coming in from the left and further down in the labyrinth, behind *ae* yellow tent.

Top: At daybreak Renshaw takes first lead into the cwm, crossing debris from the ice skyscraper and heading for the saddle on the centre skyline.

Left and above: It proves to be a precarious campsite, requiring serious construction work before the team can relax in the tents and let Sustad make afternoon tea on the hanging stove.

Right: Telkot glows at sunrise the next day. Bonington waits at the tent, just visible in the notch bottom left, while the other four climbers head for the summit of Panch Chuli V.

Above: It is some time after sunrise and the tiny figures photographed by Bonington are still only halfway up the rock pillar. It was from just above this point that Venables fell nearly 20 hours later.

Midday cloud boils up over Telkot as the team claws its way slowly over brittle ice slopes (above) and it is already 3.30 p.m. when Venables leads the way back across from the main summit to the foresummit (left).

Driving snow, icing up Sustad's glasses (below), turns the long descent into a hard struggle (right) that continues through the night.

Above: Venables forces a smile at the start of the long lower. Blood stains the snow at the foot of the rocks he tumbled down.

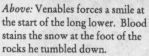

Right: A grim dawn as Saunders administers first aid to Venables.

The lower down the ice slope takes several hours, but the hardest part is dragging Venables across the glacier to the distant waiting tent.

Top: The camp where the three climbers waited four days. The accident happened on the skyline cliffs immediately above the tents, while the threatening ice tower is high on the far left.

Inset, top left: Saunders photographs Renshaw and Venables starting to get very hungry.

Above: Meanwhile Sustad re-uses the fateful piton during his descent with Bonington.

Above left: Venables and Saunders are just visible cowering on the tent ledge, as the helicopter makes its terrifying single skid landing.

Left: Moments after being lifted from the cwm, Venables stares down into the giddy depths of the icefalls.

A joyful return to Munsiary. The pilots, Sharma and Jaiswal, look on proudly wh Bonington, still bruised from his own fal is overcome by emotion. Within minute the whole population of Munsiary gather to watch while Bonington and Kapadia catch up on four days news.

above me, where the co-pilot looked more frightened than ever. No, I thought, I can't do it. I'll just stay here and let them take off with me draped over the skid – limp prey dangling from the eagle's talons as it soars out over the mountains.

'Get in!' Victor prodded, forcing me to rise to the occasion. Again I reached up into the cockpit, this time grabbing the steel frame of the canvas passenger seat above my head and dragging my bottom on to the actual sill of the doorway. Pure, distilled pain poured through the right leg now hanging unsupported in front of me. I cried out with self-pity as the co-pilot shouted from behind, insisting that I had to get right inside the cockpit, which was easier said than done, because the tiny space behind the pilots' seats was filled by the canvas contraption two feet above the floor. Somehow I had to get myself one level higher.

I shouted at Victor, pointing urgently at my left boot and at the skid superstructure, making lifting motions. He twigged – bright boy – and lifted the left boot high on to the metal strut. With that knee bent I now had some leverage to push myself upwards and backwards. But it was going to hurt. For a moment I shrank from the task – reverted to helpless eagle fodder, whimpered, failed the test. But no, come on, you have to do it. This is the only chance you're going to get. The others have all done their bit – tried their utmost, put their lives on the line. You mustn't let them down.

One. Two. Three. Push! Every wrenched sinew cried out in revolt, as I heaved myself up, catching my harness on the corner of the canvas seat, fighting to get free and pull further back into the cab. The right leg – the encumbrance – flapped in the air like a dead branch. Splintered bone grated deep in the swollen pulp of the knee. As I screamed triumphantly, Victor reached up and gave me a push and at last I slid back into the hot fug of the cockpit, emitting a final shriek as the door slammed shut against the mangled leg.

There was no time for Victor to hand in my rucksack. Without waiting a second the machine had backed off from the ledge and I was looking out through scratched perspex at two waving figures, receding in a world that was already completely separate. Heaving with sobs of relief, laughing, crying, and panting to get my breath back, I slumped back across the canvas seat, my back resting against the door on the other side of the helicopter. The co-pilot turned round and shouted, 'Please no – be careful', checking the catch on the flimsy panel. I had almost fallen back out of the other side of the helicopter!

My heart thudded as I pressed my nose to the window to stare down at the dizzy, plunging nightmare of the icefalls immediately beneath us. Determined to record the full horror of what I had been spared, I twisted round to point my camera down at the shattered chaos below and tried to imagine the enormity of descending that battlefield in a stretcher. Then, as Sharma turned round to hand me my ear-protectors I shouted, 'Thank you very much. You are very brave.' He smiled and Jaiswal also turned round momentarily. His face was relaxed for the first time and he insisted gallantly, 'It is *you* who was brave. And it is God we must thank.'

The two men turned their attention to the panel of black-and-white dials in front of them. I sat back to enjoy the hot smell of aviation fuel and the throbbing vibration which had filled me with such terror two minutes earlier. Outside our perspex pleasure bubble the glacier was now disappearing. I looked down at the area of Base Camp and tried to find the tents where Sustad and the Harsinhs would be staring up, but the land was racing past too quickly. In seconds we had left the grey world behind and our bubble was wrapped around in vibrant, beautiful, life-affirming green. It was the greenest green I had ever experienced. It felt as though I had been gone not for a week but for years. I was the Ancient Mariner escaping from the deadly clutch of the ice, but instead of bringing a tale of lingering horror, I rode on a surge of grateful joy.

I wanted to be down there in the forest, instead of skimming past, wanted to smell the earth and feel the smoothness of the bamboo. I even felt a pang of regret for the slithery path down the Pyunshani that I would never see. Already now we were flitting over the confluence with the Balati. Straight ahead, past the pilots' helmets, the soft cushioned forest canopy began to break up into yellow fields dotted with ochre and whitewash walls. Then we shot over the bare shoulder of a great ridge and the land suddenly plummeted beneath us, far down into the wrinkled glitter of the Goriganga. The river passed beneath us and another great wall of land raced towards us, this time lined with the steps of endless terraces. The wall lay back on to a broad shelf crowded with houses and the roar of the engine began to moderate as we skimmed over their roofs, slowing, veering left, circling, then descending towards a circular expanse of dusty grass. The playing field was almost empty but on the left-hand side there were two figures – one upright, slightly stout, alert, with dark skin; the other paler, taller and bearded, dressed in mountaineering gear. I stared out through the scratched perspex. They stared back at the two khaki figures in the helicopter. Then they saw the bright red duvet jacket at the back of the cockpit and their faces broke into huge smiles of relief.

Chapter Thirteen

OUTSTRETCHED ARMS LIFTED me tenderly from the silent helicopter and laid me down on the warm flat earth. Revatram the cook was there. And Pasang, Monesh and Muslim. They all looked so clean and scrubbed. Harish was beaming, his eyes bright with emotion. He knelt down beside me with Bonington, whose face still looked battered from the fall. 'Oh, I'm so glad you're down. I'm so relieved.' His voice cracked tearfully and I was touched again by the man's emotional vulnerability. And again I regretted my impulsive outburst on the way to the col in that distant time six days ago. Now was the great cathartic moment of redemption and I wished that I had the eloquence to do it justice. We needed poetry. We needed Shakespeare. We needed the final chords of *Figaro* soaring above the squalid reality of a bloody leg lying in the dirt.

The chorus gathered for the final tableau – a huge crowd engulfing the helicopter as the entire population of Munsiary turned up for the most exciting event they had witnessed in years. Jaiswal and Sharma stood modestly beside the Cheetah, helmets under their arms, smiling proudly. Someone brought a tray and laid it beside me on the ground. Harish poured tea and pushed a plate of food towards me. I nibbled a couple of nuts, then toyed with a slice of mango. 'Come on, Mr Venables, you must eat. You are looking very thin.'

'Yes, Harish, but I can only manage a little.'

'It is very rude to refuse our Indian hospitality. Come on – eat!'

I tried another biscuit but I was too excited to swallow much and my stomach was still shrunken, despite the meal in the tent that morning.

That morning! I was still dazed by the miraculous speed of it all. Ten minutes earlier I had been lying in the snow on Panch Chuli V at 5,600 metres. Now I was safe in the village at 1,500 metres. Safe with friends. Free to carry on where we had left off and enjoy the gentle journey back to Delhi and Bombay, once the rest of the team had returned safely to Munsiary. Like Ed Webster, who deluded himself after Everest that he would stick to his planned romantic holiday on Hawaii, despite gangrenous, frostbitten fingers, I imagined fondly that the others would accommodate my mangled leg on the long road and train journey back south, allowing me to share all the celebratory feasting. So I was rather put out when Bonington handed me a bag of clean clothes and told me that I was leaving immediately for the military hospital in Bareilly. 'You can't possibly travel on the roads! It's two days to Delhi from here, assuming there are no landslides. You need to be in a hospital.'

'But what –'

'Don't worry,' Harish interrupted, 'Muslim will be coming by road to join you in Bareilly tomorrow. Then he will get you back to Delhi. He'll bring your passport and air ticket and arrange to get you home.'

So this was it! After all that tense, patient waiting on the glacier, my expedition was to end instantly, with no gentle unwinding from mountain to plains. I complied reluctantly as they slid me back into the Cheetah. The huge crowd backed away to the field's perimeter, the engine roared to life and we rose into the air, speeding back over the great gorge of the Goriganga. As we turned south I glanced out to the left, but the Pandavas' hearths were lost behind rolling banks of clouds and there was no sign of the high cwm where I had so recently left Victor and Renshaw.

They hardly said a word once the helicopter had left them alone in the silent basin. There was a tacit understanding that they would not wait for morning, but would leave immediately, that very afternoon, and escape this horrible place before the mountain disintegrated completely. They quickly packed up the tents, stuffed sleeping bags into rucksacks, folded up the stove. 'What about this?' Renshaw held up the crampon with the brutally bent steel spike.

'Better take it. He might want it for a souvenir. But I think we can leave the sleeping bag.' Victor wrinkled his nose at the blood-soaked mess and threw it into the pile of rejected gear. What they could not carry was all dumped down a deep crevasse. The rest went on their backs and within half an hour of the helicopter leaving they too were on their way down, resigned to a long exhausting journey.

They hurried through the previous night's avalanche debris, glancing fearfully up at the ice tower. They waded through thigh-deep slush to get back over the buttress and down into the labyrinth, which had already changed since the night. The couloir below the cache was a weary test of their ability to concentrate after two days with virtually no sleep. Then they found Sustad's rope down the icy waterfall and continued on to the final icefall. They tried to follow Sustad's instructions, but the shattered landscape had changed yet again, and by the time they finally emerged from the glacier on to the soft earth of the ablation valley, night had fallen. They carried on down regardless, stumbling in the dark through an eternity of scrubby bushes and ankle-tripping boulders, finally reaching Base Camp late that night. Two days later everyone was reunited in Munsiary.

As the helicopter flew south I opened the overnight bag and took out a polythene bag full of letters. Every single one of the expedition mail runs to Munsiary had coincided with a public holiday, so all our incoming letters had been piling up at the post office, unread. There were four from Rosie which I saved for last. The others were of no consequence, apart from one letter from a climbing acquaintance replying to some suggestions for a possible future expedition. Reading his thoughts on a huge unclimbed face in the Karakoram, I wondered whether I would ever set foot on a big Himalayan climb again. It now seemed so irrelevant and futile.

I arranged Rosie's airmails in order, slit open the edges and began to read a catalogue of disasters. There were the usual cash flow problems at the bank. The holiday in Kenya had been quite successful, but the hideous package flight home – complete with statutory five-hour delay at Athens airport – had been a ghastly trial with an eleven-month-old baby. Ollie had got ill immediately afterwards, had been in excruciating pain for two weeks and had been diagnosed with salmonella poisoning. The only light relief in that letter was the news that Rosie was pregnant, just as we had hoped. But in the next letter, as Ollie began to recover and regain weight, Rosie announced that she had had a miscarriage. So there would be no baby brother or sister that winter.

I could not have been away at a worse time, yet I still failed to register at this stage that my homecoming was going to be difficult – that my little drama on Panch Chuli, even with its brilliant rescue, might be viewed not as a glorious escape but as a bloody nuisance – the final insulting inconvenience that was going to wreck what was left of the summer. Instead of contemplating that reality, I floated in a green, solipsistic blur, enthralled by the beautiful miracle of my magic carpet ride over the Himalayan forest.

After flying for twenty minutes we slowed and descended to Dharchula, alighting on the tarmac to refuel. Sharma asked if I would like some food. Now I felt ready to eat, and moments later an orderly handed up a thali – the classic compartmentalized tray with different vegetables, dals, rice, yoghurt and chutneys. The air was languid. Huge broad-leaved trees rose above the airfield perimeter. Tropical birds called from the forest. The orderly returned to offer me a second cup of tea and again I was touched by the impeccable politeness of the Indian armed forces who had gone out of their way to help a foreigner in trouble. This was not the Alps. They were not part of a professional mountain rescue service, trained specifically to help climbers stupid, or unlucky enough to get hurt. Yet these people had spent two days of expensive flying time, risking their lives to get me out.

Once the fuel tanks were full we continued south for another hour and a half, steadily losing height in our journey over the immensity of the Himalaya. The hills beneath us were luminous with banana palms, purple convolvulus, gleaming stands of maize, vibrant orange and yellow gourd flowers. Then suddenly the last hill ran down abruptly to the edge of the great northern plain and our shadow sped across flat ploughed fields, still waiting, dusty brown, for the Monsoon. Children stared up at the throbbing machine, ox carts lumbered under the spring harvest, bicycles wavered along the rutted edges of irrigation ditches and cattle egrets flew just beneath us, brilliant white against the dusty earth.

A military ambulance was waiting at Bareilly. I said a final good-bye and thank you to Jaiswal and Sharma and was then driven to the hospital and left in a dark waiting room. Even with ceiling fans, the air down here, almost at sea level, was oppressively hot and I felt a little overdressed in my layers of fleece and Sustad's down jacket. I waited patiently while doctors clerked me twice then sent me through to the X-ray department to join the queue next to a young jawan (an army private) holding up a bloody bandaged finger.

There was another delay, then I was wheeled over to the X-ray machine. A chitty was handed to the radiologist who glanced perfunctorily at the strangely-dressed foreigner, examined the chitty and said, 'Please show me your index finger.'

'He's the one with the finger! Look – it's my *legs* that need X-raying.'

'*Achha.*' The radiologist gave the orderly a withering look, asked for the correct chitty, then had a more thorough look at my body. He manoeuvred me on to the X-ray bench and photographed legs and torso. Later, in the ward, a doctor came to tell me that my chest seemed fine, with no broken ribs. However, I had a fracture of the medial maleolus on my left leg. He held up the X-ray and pointed out the hairline crack through the inner knobble of the left ankle. Then he showed me the right knee. As always with X-rays, I found it hard to equate the tiny irregularities in the photograph with the devastation they were supposed to represent. The knee was apparently in quite a mess. The patella, first cracked nineteen years earlier in the Avon Gorge, was now shattered into about thirty pieces. No wonder it had grated so disconcertingly when I moved it. The gash on the inside of the leg *had* started to turn septic and would need watching very carefully because the infection was spreading into a fracture of the tibial plateau. For the time being they would immobilize the leg with a temporary plaster and start me on a course of antibiotics.

The plasterers were two cheerful Tamil youths from southern India whose dark faces flashed white-toothed smiles as they chatted and joked over their work, treating me with the same kindness that seemed to run right through the hospital. Back in my bed I pleaded for hot water, desperate to wash off ten days' accumulated grime and change into my precious clean clothes. As I began to peel the foetid climbing gear from my pale withered body the nurses withdrew hastily behind curtains and someone explained that in India this kind of job is left to male menials. A skinny youth in a loin cloth came over to help me and soon I was tucked up in bed, floating in a glorious haze of well-being, savouring the delicious luxury of being clean, moderately comfortable and safe.

The morning ward round was led by a female major in uniform, who explained apologetically, 'I'm afraid that our hospitals are not up to the standard of yours in Britain, but we will try to do our best for you.' She then apologized for making me sleep in a communal ward and had me transferred to a private room before I could explain that this kind of thing was unheard of in the NHS. In lonely splendour I whiled away the next few hours, occasionally remembering Renshaw's story about the time he was alone in a Delhi hospital, receiving treatment for his Dunagiri frostbite injuries. They had nursed him with punctilious care until one afternoon, when someone accidentally plugged an intravenous drip into muscle, instead of a vein. Dick had watched with increasing alarm as the fluid seeped into his arm, inflating it into a huge balloon, while he shouted desperately for someone to come and remove the needle.

I was just starting to feel rather lonely in my private room when Muslim arrived from Munsiary, bearing gifts. By way of an anaesthetic-cum-sedative, Bonington had sent down his Jilly Cooper blockbuster. The only problem was that my glasses were in the rucksack Victor had not managed to get on to the helicopter. So, too shortsighted to read unaided, I had to use my prescription sunglasses, peering dimly at the small print held two inches from my face, while presenting to the startled nurses at the foot of my bed the jauntily explicit cover photo of a lascivious hand stroking a tightly-jodphured buttock. Invisible behind my glacier sunglasses, I steamed incredulously over the incessant, rampant couplings of Jilly Cooper's county heroes until I drifted into an exhausted sleep.

Rosie was with friends at the Royal Crescent that night, sharing a generous allocation of free tickets to an open air recital by José Carreras. She returned late, her head still buzzing with Verdi and Puccini, to find a message that Wendy had phoned. A few days earlier, on the first occasion Wendy had phoned, Rosie had frozen in terror, knowing what an unscheduled call from Wendy Bonington usually meant. She had only stopped trembling several minutes after the end of the harmless message that everyone was fine and would be coming home soon. So this time she was unfazed by the call and expected nothing sinister. Wendy was disconcertingly vague, saying that Stephen had 'hurt his leg'. Then Muslim phoned from India with equal vagueness. Anxious not to alarm Rosie, he said that I was being looked after in hospital and would be coming home in a day or two. 'I think that perhaps you should try to get some crutches,' he added hesitantly.

'So do you mean he can't walk?'

'Well, not very well.' Five thousand miles away the diplomatic brow furrowed. 'I think you might need to get a commode also.' Rosie tried to work out how I could walk on crutches and need a commode. For someone who had just 'hurt his leg' her husband seemed to be strangely incapacitated. On the assumption that Muslim had underplayed my problems, she decided wisely to play safe and hire a wheelchair.

On Saturday, one week after our summit day on Panch Chuli V, Muslim sprang me from Bareilly hospital. Revatram was waiting ouside with the 'ambulance' – a minivan with just enough room to fit me in longways in a half-sitting position, facing backwards as we careered and swerved our way west down the Great Indian

Trunk Road. Proud of his sudden elevation to paramedic status, the van driver rarely took his hand off the hooter, forcing his way self-importantly through the dense afternoon traffic. Frantic to secure the spring harvest before the Monsoon broke, trucks lumbered under bulging loads of grain three times their height, competing for space with overloaded buses, bullock carts, bicycles, rickshaws, handcarts, scooters and kamikaze pedestrians. A yellowish pall of dust and diesel fumes hung over the road and the noise was incessant. Beside me in the back of the van, Muslim smiled encouragingly. Revatram dispensed cigarettes to give our lungs an alternative to the clogging fumes. I don't know how many cigarettes we smoked on the seven-hour journey, but they helped pass the time and induce a certain fatalistic acceptance. There was just no point in worrying. Even if we did pass the mangled remains of an upturned bus or truck every few miles, we had to remind ourselves that they were hugely outnumbered by the *unmangled* vehicles completing their journeys safely. And, as our own manic 'ambulance' driver hooted his way through yet another diminishing gap between hurtling lorries, I kept telling myself that he probably wanted to stay alive too.

At dusk we reached the confused sprawl of Delhi. With many stops for directions, Muslim navigated patiently to the house of Romesh Battacharjee. I had heard much about this Catholic who works for the Indian customs service – a sort of roaming VAT man, who specializes in out of the way places, such as the far north-eastern marches of Arunachal Pradesh, and who nearly always travels by motorbike, pushing it where no bike has gone before. He had already booked me into a private clinic nearby and showed us the way.

The following day Romesh came back with Muslim and entertained me with tales of the impenetrable jungly mountains of the North-East Frontier. He brought fresh food and asked what else I would like.

'Any chance of some beer?'

'My God – alcohol in a hospital!' exclaimed a scandalized Muslim, but they smuggled it in nonetheless. Other visitors dropped in: Sudhir Sahi who had hosted my lecture in Delhi two years earlier, and Captain Motwan Kohli, a well-known mountaineer and former director of Air India, who promised to use his muscle to get me on the next day's flight to London.

The doctor continued my course of antibiotics and gave me a new, sturdier plaster for the journey home. An FRCS who had trained in London, he explained that the infection would have to stop before anyone could do much with the knee. The fracture, he said, was a serious one requiring major surgery and would probably need a bone graft and steel plate where the tibial plateau was chipped.

At dawn on Monday, I said goodbye to Muslim and was wheeled through the airport departure gate. On the aeroplane the cabin staff were wonderful, putting me in the front row with room for my leg to stretch out. They kept up a steady supply of gin-and-tonics, politely ignoring the growing collection of full pee bottles under the discreet blanket covering my lap. At Heathrow the airport officials took one look at my leg in the doorway and started muttering disdainfully about 'emergency exits ... well, what do you expect with an Indian airline!' Welcome home to Little England. Another, less petty, official produced a wheelchair and took me through to the arrivals lounge, but although we had arrived, Rosie had not. The man left me parked in a corner and went in search of a tannoy operator. Then I saw her, twenty yards away, looking at me across the crowded hall. Instead of a welcoming smile she just gave me a look of anxious, nervous shock.

It was only much later that she explained: 'After Everest I had always thought that you were indestructible – after surviving that night near the summit. When you went to Kusum Kanguru, it never occurred to me that you might not come back. And it was the same when you went to Panch Chuli. Then I arrived at the airport and saw you sitting in the wheelchair, like a little old man – this pathetic withered husk.'

'Well, I didn't feel like a husk!'

'You looked terrible! And then we had all that ghastly business of trying to get you into the car – with the wheelchair man – and we could only just fit you in ... and I thought why on earth couldn't you have got an ambulance.'

'But I thought that you would want to see me.'

We were driving past Reading when she eventually asked, 'Well – what happened?'

'The abseil peg came out. I fell about three hundred feet.'

'What!' The car swerved towards the hard edge and Rosie went very pale. I begged her to concentrate on her driving and tried to change the subject, but her news was not much better.

Coming home was proving to be harder than I had expected, but there was a nice interlude after we left the motorway and got lost trying to take a shortcut, ending up unexpectedly in the quintessential chocolate-box village of Castle Combe. We stopped in the ridiculously pretty street, outside a rose-festooned pub, and Rosie took pity on me, asking, 'Would you like a drink?' She came back with a pint of bitter and we completed the last part of the journey in a mellower frame of mind.

But the angst kept resurfacing. Friends helped carry me into the house, but I was insufferably impatient, frustrated at not being able to move, not go upstairs, not even make a telephone call without Rosie having to drag me across the room. I wanted to know why she hadn't got a lavish welcome-home dinner prepared and only understood reluctantly that she had been rushed off her feet as it was, organizing a wheelchair, driving to the airport, finding a babysitter for Ollie . . .

I slightly dreaded seeing him. How would he react? Would he scream and hide as he had done when I returned from Kusum Kanguru – an unwelcome stranger? Would I recognize *him*? Would he be the same person?

I was sitting at the far end of the room when Rosie led him in from the garden. At first he *did* look different – bigger and sturdier, but also more beautiful. He had made an amazing recovery from the salmonella and was positively glowing – golden from long days in the sun. He eyed me tentatively, curiously . . . stared intently, thinking carefully about the haggard man in the corner, looked back briefly to Rosie for reassurance, then smiled – not a nervous smile, but a wide, open, happy glow of recognition.

Chapter Fourteen

'THERE WAS NOTHING in the marriage vows about emptying commodes.' Rosie was getting increasingly disenchanted with the Florence Nightingale role, forced on her when I had insisted on being allowed just one night at home, determined to cling to this brief domestic interlude before being banished to institutional exile. I had promised the doctors who clerked me in at Bath's Royal United Hospital that I would come back in the morning.

So, with some relief, Rosie installed me in the Trauma ward to await my first operation. The hospital PR man arranged for a photograph and the gaunt wounded hero duly appeared in the local paper that afternoon, smiling optimistically from the hospital bed which would be his home for the next five weeks. 'No wonder he looks so happy,' commented our elderly next-door neighbour, 'he's got the prettiest nurse on the ward holding his hand.'

They were all extraordinarily long-suffering for I was a difficult patient: in fact I was horribly *impatient*, no longer content with the passive role that had sustained me in the tent on Panch Chuli V. Despite my incredible good fortune at surviving the fall, despite the miracle of escaping from the remote glacier 5,000 miles away and reaching my hospital bed in just nine days from the morning of the accident, I was irritable and frustrated. I cursed the surgeons for delaying the first operation, leaving me to take my place in the queue behind the incessant road accident emergencies. Then I fretted whilst waiting for the second operation, unconvinced by the explanation that every trace of infection had to have vanished before the surgeons could risk working on the bone.

When the main operation was finally completed I lurched back to consciousness in a filthy mood, indignant at the throbbing pain in my mauled leg and furious with a doctor who had applied the plaster too tightly. By coincidence Charles Stewart, the curate from Bath Abbey whom we knew well, had dropped in to see me. He smiled tolerantly, whilst Rosie winced with embarrassment at the semi-conscious torrent of foul language pouring from the bed.

Other friends came to visit. All of them brought food to supplement the unappetizing, calorie-challenged starvation rations which hospital nutritionists seem to think are conducive to recovery. One evening a vinophilic climbing friend came over on his motorbike and appeared in the ward in full leathers. Creaking his way over to my bed, he pulled out a corkscrew and a bottle of sumptuous claret. The duty nurse provided a pair of tooth mugs and told us to be discreet.

Rosie brought Ollie to see me and she brought a huge vase, overflowing with roses, irises and mallows from the garden. My parents brought strawberries from their garden. Geoffrey Grimmett, the man who had witnessed Paul Beney's sudden violent death all those years ago in Chamonix, when the abseil sling broke, brought books, including a copy of Oliver Sacks's apposite *A Leg to Stand On*. I had been spared Sacks's baffling neurological symptoms, where his leg seemed to become totally separate from his body – at one point he was convinced that the nurses had taken it away – but there was a similar sense of an alien object – of the unfamiliar encumbrance that I had been dragging around ever since I awoke from the accident. Whilst the broken ankle on the left leg healed quickly once it had been screwed together, the right knee had seized up totally. The smaller fragments of patella had been removed and the larger remaining pieces cobbled back together with wire, while the tibial plateau now sported a piece of my hip bone held in place with a metal plate and eight screws. The unwieldy limb was stuck periodically on a flexing machine designed to help ease movement back into the knee, but the leg remained obstinately rigid.

In the meantime I had work to do. Our sponsors at *Photo Plus* brought in a computer for me to write the promised article and helped me sort through two thousand slides. I also had two after-dinner talks booked, for British Gas and Henley Management College. Summer is usually a lean spell for freelance lecturers and I couldn't really afford to lose the fees, so I listened politely to the surgeons' urgent advice not to risk infection, ignored it equally politely, and got Rosie to drive me eighty miles to each venue, wheeling me on to address the perplexed managers before returning me in the early hours to my hospital bed.

After about three weeks I felt ready for further outings, so one night we procured a wheelchair for Rosie to take me off to the pub. The NHS did not run to sporty self-drive models, so I was dependent on Rosie's pushing. She in turn had to put up with my impatiently shouted instructions as we tilted dangerously on Bath's steep cambers. It was wonderful to escape the claustro-phobia of the ward, but patients had to take turns with the one available wheelchair. The following night a young road accident victim emulated my initiative, but returned very late and very noisy, with twelve pints of lager inside him. Pub visits were banned after that.

My first physiotherapist was a fierce woman impatient with my wimpishness. The first time I tried to hold my legs vertically I almost fainted. The idea was to stand on my left leg, supported in its weight-bearing plaster, and with the help of crutches do a short round of the ward, dangling the right leg. From the knee down it burned with a terrible throb and I despaired of ever walking again. This horrible, withered, scaly object, with the great eighteen-inch stapled incision running up over the bulbous dome of the knee, seemed quite unrelated to the leg it had once been – the leg that had pushed and flexed and kicked and balanced up the world's highest mountains, which twenty years earlier had leaped down the sides of Scottish glens with such speed that my brother mistook my distant, bounding form for a deer.

In the heat of crisis immediately after the accident, I had

managed to be brave. Now, as summer approached autumn, and the future lay in my own hands, I found it much harder; but I *had* to start forcing the leg back to life. Gradually I overcame squeamish distaste and began to feel a hint of response from long-redundant muscles. One afternoon, enjoying a day out at my parents' house, sitting in the garden, I suddenly shouted for joy as my heel rose an inch from the lawn in my first successful straight leg raise.

With that barrier broken, confidence returned, although Ollie did learn to walk before me, taking his first unaided steps in the Trauma ward, entertaining the nurses with his proud laughter and occasional crashes to the ground. He made fast progress, but I was still wheelchair-bound when Rosie arrived one day with a huge bundle of papers from the VAT people. I had written to warn them that the trifling amount of tax I owed would be late and that they should not pester my wife while I was stuck in hospital.

'What do you mean by doing this? It's the last straw! The neighbours were watching!'

'Watching what?'

'The bailiffs! They came round last night threatening –'

'The bastards! How dare they!' I cursed petty officialdom, transferring the blame where it belonged, but Rosie was unimpressed. She heaped the papers on to my lap, suggesting 'You had better sort it out,' and wheeled me out into the middle of the hospital lawn, then walked off in peals of laughter, leaving me to sift through reams of gobbledygook, stranded under a blazing sun until a nurse eventually came to rescue me.

While ranting at the callous intransigence of the Customs & Excise office, I paused occasionally to number the blessings of the much maligned Welfare State it helps sustain. Despite the delays and frustrations and appalling food, it did seem miraculous that I could spend week after week being looked after by teams of experts, receiving hugely expensive treatment, consuming vast quantities of expensive medicines, dressings, plasters, braces, washing materials, and all the other paraphernalia of a modern hospital – all without paying a single penny on top of my taxes. In fact, the hospital seemed so keen to nurture my rehabilitation, long after I felt competent to leave, that towards the end I discharged myself for most of each day. Desperate for decent food, I stayed out for dinner most nights and on one occasion, returning after the midnight door-locking, had to be manhandled back through a window. After that it seemed simpler just to come back after breakfast, checking in briefly for the doctors' morning ward round, and spend the night at home, making up for lost time; the miscarriage had upset Rosie terribly, we were both keen that she should get pregnant again as soon as possible and we weren't going to let a couple of broken legs spoil our fun.

Seven weeks after the accident I was at last officially discharged from hospital and sent home to rebuild my life. A past master on the crutches, I could move much faster than most uncrippled people can walk; but I had to force myself to make the right leg work again on its own. A new physiotherapist took me on at Outpatients, shaking his head gloomily at the waxy lump that had once been a serviceable knee. 'To be quite frank,' said the candid Scotsman, 'I'd be very surprised if you get ninety degrees bend.'

'What?! Not even ninety degrees.'

'You've had a very bad injury. You had to wait over two weeks before it was operated on . . . you've had a bone graft and the patella's full of wire . . . the whole thing's just seized up. Anyway, as the surgeon said, at least you'll be able to sit at a desk and drive a car.'

'What!?' I exploded again. 'I'm not even forty and they're expecting me to spend the rest of my life as some kind of sedentary slob!'

'Well, you know what surgeons are like.' The physiotherapist gave me a sympathetic look. 'I'm sure we can do better than that. We'll try, anyway, but I think you're going to have to be a wee bit brutal with it.' With that, he took the joint in his hands and began pressing hard on the lumpy remains of the kneecap, showing me how to force it down, bullying it into a travesty of its former sliding motion, working it over the roughness of the joint. Then he put me on my back and told me to grab the foot, pulling the heel back towards my bottom as hard as I could. Each time I reached a wall that seemed totally solid, but with wilful concentration I could detect a faint weakness in the barrier.

Over the next few weeks I chiselled away at that weakness, gradually forcing contracted tendons to stretch, kneading mobility into the glutinous mess clogging the joint and slowly rebuilding the muscles either side. Soon I was able to discard the crutches and started visiting the local gym to use the weights machines, marvelling at the dedicated regulars. Some were merely narcissistic; others seemed to be nurturing some pathological lust for violence. One young man in particular, complete with Union Jacks on his special weight-grasping gloves, seemed to sublimate oceans of pent-up hatred as he strained against gigantic forces, every vein bulging red in his shaven head. It can't have been good for him.

Bicycling was a lot more fun. I also enjoyed carrying Ollie on my back up to the Iron Age remains of the fort on top of Solsbury Hill, just above our house. Whenever I needed encouragement I would telephone Lindsay Griffin, the man who had suggested my first Himalayan expedition all those years back, in 1977, and whose recovery from past accidents had inspired me to grit my teeth manfully on the Panch Chuli ice slope. By a strange irony, while I was being mended in Bath, he too had suffered another accident – this time in the outer marches of Mongolia. He had been walking down an apparently innocuous scree slope when an enormous boulder had rolled over, crushing his leg and leaving him pinned to the ground. The story of his rescue, organized by Julian Freeman-Attwood and my Everest companion Ed Webster, was as dramatic as my own and Lindsay had come dangerously close to losing his leg.

Now undergoing repair work at Gobowen, in Shropshire, Lindsay approached his own rehabilitation with his usual cheerful stoicism. Having been through this kind of thing several times before, he was an unwitting orthopaedic expert. He could talk bone grafts and traction and muscle flexion with the best of them and he listened patiently to my own progress reports, questioning me on every detail of my exercise routine and offering huge encouragement. Joe Simpson, who has built a legendary literary career out of spectacular accidents, was equally encouraging. However, I never dared follow his example of getting extremely drunk, dancing wildly and then falling over with a sudden, tissue-ripping wrench to the knee, gaining twenty degrees extra flexion in five seconds.

By March 1993 I was just touching ninety degrees, and was feeling quite proud. Then Harish came over from Bombay and scolded me for my lack of progress. 'Ever since I broke my hip in the Nanda Devi Sanctuary, I have done yoga *every day* and I have no trouble. But you are *very* stiff – I had expected you to be better by now. Now, look – I'll show you the five basic exercises.' He proceeded to give a display of wondrous suppleness, completely unhindered by his prodigious paunch. I dutifully tried the exercises and although I never achieved anything like his flexibility – nor his regular discipline – the knee did subsequently bend well beyond the magic figure of ninety degrees.

Harish was in England to give a talk at the biennial British Mountaineering Conference in Buxton. Chris Bonington and I were also doing a talk, to mark the fortieth anniversary of Everest's first ascent, and the day after the conference we drove over to the gnarled gritstone outcrop of The Roaches, in Staffordshire. Bonington led someone up a climb. Then I asked him to send down a rope for me. It was a foul, blustery day, with rain streaming down the cold rock, and I had on big bendy walking boots, but I still managed, thrilled to be climbing again for the first time, a little nervous but moving competently nonetheless. It was 21 March, exactly nine months after the day of the accident. The gestation was over.

A fortnight later I spent a day with friends on the Tremadoc cliffs in North Wales. This time the sun was shining. Rooks and jackdaws were noisily busy with their nests. The first emerald foliage was just unfurling. The pale lichen-patterned rock glowed warmly and the old familiar outlines of the Rhinog mountains, rising beyond the Portmadoc Estuary, seemed lovelier than ever. I stuck cautiously to easy climbs but after following one route, I insisted on leading the next, glad to be back on the sharp end of the rope, taking control.

My first tentative steps back on to the rock coincided with the birth of our second son, Edmond. With a two-year-old and a baby now to look after, further climbing trips were limited to the occasional evening in the Wye Valley, usually finishing in the dark with a mad dash back to the pub at Tintern Abbey. Beyond that, as yet, I had no definite plans to return to the big mountains. I wasn't even sure that I wanted to. For the moment life at home seemed much more important and in any case it seemed imperative that I stay alive, at least for the time being.

The accident on Panch Chuli had affected all of us to varying degrees. Victor was now immersed in completing his training as a mountain guide, committing himself to a life of easier, less extreme climbs and ski tours, where the client's enjoyment had to take precedence over his own aspirations. Sustad soon returned to the Himalaya, but this time as a twosome with the most talented of all our contemporaries, Mick Fowler, to climb an awesome tower which I had admired hopefully from Kishtwar-Shivling back in 1983. Between expeditions and guiding commercial treks, he was busy at his workshop in Oswestry.

Harish was justly proud of the rescue, which was a tribute to his negotiating power and his co-leader's international prestige. The next time they organized a joint expedition, Indian and British climbers went together to the summit, which was something we failed to achieve on our more disjointed Panch Chuli venture. However, for Harish summits became less and less important as he poured ever more of his formidable energy into long journeys over unknown passes, continuing to fill in the myriad details of his personal map of the Himalaya, devoting increasing time to expeditions, while delegating more of the cloth business in Bombay. Monesh, Bhupesh and Vijay continued their expeditioning but soon after the Panch Chuli trip Muslim, alarmed by growing Hindu fundamentalism, which seemed to be destroying a long tradition of ecumenical tolerance and threatening his children's future in Bombay, decided to emigrate to Canada.

With Muslim's departure from India, Harish lost a loyal friend and sharer of so many Himalayan experiences. His Kumauni helpers remained faithful to the continuing odyssey, but Harsinh Junior was adamant that in future he wanted nothing to do with dangerous glaciers. The resupply mission with Sustad had forced him out of his depth and afterwards, when Victor and Bonington suggested flying him over to Britain for a mountain training course, he had just shrugged, 'what's the point. I don't want to climb. I'm a shepherd and I want to get back to my sheep.'

Bonington remained as generous as ever towards me, continuing to say nice things about my writing and lecturing, sometimes passing lucrative work my way; but he did not invite me on any more expeditions, sticking instead to less troublesome companions such as Graham Little, Victor and Jim Curran, his personal film-maker and biographer – 'Bonington's Yes Men', I called them. Although his own expeditioning continued to flourish with unabated success, he would still become very emotional talking about the accident, fighting back tears even after several years. He had come to terms with danger and death long before Panch Chuli, deciding resolutely that even the loss of friends would never deter him from his passion, but the accident still seemed to touch a deep resonance of loss and sadness that will always be there.

Although I never felt as able as, say, Victor to relax with Bonington, the expedition reinforced my admiration for what he has achieved during a mountaineering career now approaching fifty years. Very few British mountaineers before him managed to make a well-paid career out of their vocation. Even men like Edward Whymper, who made the first ascent of the Matterhorn, and Frank Smythe never achieved the same single-minded, sustained success, never shaped their own destiny so forcefully. But what was most impressive was his capacity for enjoying himself and his ability to drop out and say 'no' when he realized that he was no longer enjoying himself – and his ability to do so graciously, without rancour. As for the subsequent rescue, he showed all the strength and skill of men twenty years younger, and had the added advantage of being able to pull rank down in the valley.

After we returned to Britain, the Kusum Kanguru and Panch Chuli expeditions were nominated for a *Piolet d'Or* award in France, along with four or five other climbs of the previous twelve months deemed noteworthy of shortlisting for a dinky toy ice axe. We did not get the award, but I wrote an article for the sponsoring magazine, mentioning how lucky I had been, after nearly killing myself on Panch Chuli, to be with four of the world's best Himalayan climbers. The French editor could not conceive of British climbers being amongst the world's elite, so changed the text to 'Britain's best Himalayan climbers'. I tried to laugh off the Gallic chauvinism and just reminded myself that they really *were* amongst the world's best. And that that had been proved by the way they reacted to the accident, rising to the occasion with skill, compassion and humour.

Out of all the team, Dick Renshaw had done the most over the years to keep me alive in the mountains with his wary sense of survival. He also seemed the most affected by the accident. Although he had been a driving force on Panch Chuli V, participating with all his usual determination, I already had the sense in the early days of the expedition that this might be his Himalayan swansong. Despite Harish's humorous cajoling, he had seemed slightly disenchanted with expedition life and afterwards he admitted that all the travelling and hassle and watching and waiting had began to pall. 'I think I had had enough of all that sitting around and reading. There were other things in life that I wanted to get on with, like my sculpture. But I think what really clinched it was getting back to Bombay at the end of the trip. There was an old man – a beggar, I suppose – lying on the platform. And he was dead. Someone had covered his face with a newspaper and all the people were walking round him. It seemed so sad and pathetic. It made me think, "what's the point?" There we were, with our expedition, having gone to all that trouble and expense, just to put ourselves at risk, while this man was dying on a station platform.'

I wish that I could have been so unequivocal. It was not as if Renshaw's argument about futile waste was not reinforced. Soon after I came home from hospital I received a card from the famous French mountaineer, Pierre Béghin. We had never met, but I had always liked the sound of this hugely ambitious man and we had been corresponding for a couple of years. The fractured English of his letters had a poetic, joyful panache and I had been flattered when he suggested climbing together one day. He seemed to have sensed – and probably overestimated – an ambition in me that might complement his own drive. We had discussed various ideas but nothing had yet come of them. He said in his card that he was sorry to hear about my accident and was just leaving for Nepal with a single companion, Christophe Lafaille, to attempt a new route on the huge South Face of Annapurna. I wrote a quick note back, saying 'Good luck' and 'be careful on the abseils'.

A month later I had to write his obituary for *The Times*. Thwarted by bad weather, several thousand feet up the face,

Béghin and Lafaille decided to retreat. Pierre placed a camming device for the first abseil anchor. Lafaille suggested that a peg hammered home would be more secure, but Pierre insisted that they would need all the pegs lower down during the long perilous descent. Lafaille was unhappy and remained unclipped from the anchor while Pierre set off on the first abseil. He had only descended a few metres when the camming device ripped from the crack. Lafaille saw Pierre slip, try to catch hold of a rock, then gather speed as he disappeared from sight, plummeting over two thousand metres down the mountain.

I mourned the man I had never met, who now lay lost and buried in the avalanche debris beneath Annapurna. I mourned the great projects that we might perhaps have attempted, then wondered whether, actually, we *would* have attempted them – whether Panch Chuli had not changed all of that irrevocably. Reason told me that I should have made a simple decision to abandon the risks of high altitude mountaineering, and stick to home territory. But then I thought of Andy, dying not on a great Himalayan face but during a weekend on Lochnagar. Then the news came through that some of Britain's top mountaineers, four of them bound ironically for the South Face of Annapurna, had just been obliterated when their airliner crashed on the approach to Kathmandu, before they even set foot in the mountains.

It all seemed so random and haphazard. Andy had suffered fatal head injuries, but my skull had been spared. I had been incredibly lucky. And yet, it seemed extraordinary bad luck that the peg had come out in the first place, having just held three other people. Evaluating risk seemed such an inexact science and, short of staying home and never going anywhere, it seemed hard to avoid danger. Life seemed inherently precarious. The American climber, John Harlin, put it in perspective as we were chatting one serene autumn afternoon at the top of a cliff in New Hampshire. He had been nine when his father of the same name fell to his death during the first ascent of the Eiger Direct in 1965. Recalling his childhood in Europe, he said, 'We saw a lot of Chris and he said something like this to my father: "Doing one particular, difficult, dangerous climb is not going to kill you, but going repeatedly on difficult, dangerous climbs, you're likely to get caught out in the end." That's why I've tried to ration my own climbing, particularly on big glaciated mountains.'

The rationing approach seemed a bit of a compromise, but it made sense and fitted my own indecision. Incapable of the bold gesture, terrified of turning my back irrevocably on something that had been so central to my life, I just put expeditioning on hold, waiting to see how events would develop. In the meantime I continued to work on my leg and at least enjoy the tactile pleasures of pure rock-climbing when I got the chance. In the absence of grand Himalayan projects, in October 1994 I spent three weeks on a lecture tour of South Africa and Namibia. Thanks to the hard work of the organizers I was kept very busy, earned good money and between lectures did some fantastic rock climbs, including the great 400-metre-high sandstone wall of the Blouberg, the Blue Mountain in the far northern wilderness of the Transvaal. It was a marvellous working holiday, revelling in the light and colour and floral exuberance of the southern spring, tasting the prolific wines of the Cape, journeying into the desert of Namibia, enjoying the thrill of entertaining enthusiastic audiences and reviving friendships from my earlier visit in 1991 – but it was an indulgence only justified by bringing home a large cheque, for in the previous few months events at home had made any concerns about my injured leg and the future of my expeditioning seem irrelevant.

Ollie had been a golden picture of health when I returned, battered and shrivelled, from Panch Chuli. Ten months later, when he was just coming up to two, his self-confidence took a slight knock when Edmond was born. However he quickly adapted to having a younger brother and during that summer of 1993 he talked more and more, delighting himself and us with his ability to grasp new ideas, make connections, construct a picture of the world around him. He loved stories, adored naming pictures, was even beginning to recognize printed words. He was starting to experiment with sentences. He loved to try to play the piano, copying me. Now approaching forty, I began to understand what all the fuss was about. This was the real excitement of parenthood – as one's own brain cells were starting to die off by the million – witnessing the astonishing speed with which a young mind can learn and expand and grasp ideas.

Ollie's rapid recovery from salmonella while I was on Panch Chuli indicated a robust constitution. However, soon after I returned, despite his normal development, he became suddenly prone to viral infections. They started at fifteen months when he had his compulsory MMR vaccination against mumps, rubella and measles. Over the next year the bouts of flu-like illness increased, each time seeming to check momentarily his mental development. Nevertheless, he was otherwise normal and seemed bright for his age. Then, at Christmas 1993, he became particularly lethargic with a bad viral infection. He had always seemed acutely sensitive to the mood around him, and he picked up on the prevailing atmosphere of crisis. I had just returned on crutches from a second stint in hospital to have the metalwork removed from my legs. A dangerous post-operative infection had given me a high fever and Rosie enormous anxiety. The family car had finally died, to be towed ignominiously away. Then Rosie's mother had fallen down the stairs, breaking her hip and sinking into a physical and mental decline from which she was never to recover.

It was a grim Christmas. Ollie spent most of the time in bed and was indifferent to his presents. Ill and feverish, he talked little; in fact he almost seemed to have forgotten how to talk. After Christmas the illness passed, but he seemed a different child. His favourite toy, a duck, became 'dawk'. His pronunciation of other words changed. Then he just stopped saying the words at all, and at the same time seemed to find it hard to understand what we were saying. His whole hearing seemed radically altered, so that he became terrified of the vacuum cleaner and even fearful of the rustling of dead poplar leaves on the trees at the local playground. He became obsessed with switching lights on and off. His behaviour veered between manic hyperactivity and lethargic retreat. His play dwindled to a strange ritualistic lining up of toy cars, with his head on one side, staring intently at the geometric patterns, apparently oblivious of everyone around him.

By the spring of 1994 Ollie's burgeoning vocabulary had dwindled to fewer than ten mispronounced words. The world outside had become increasingly a place filled with incomprehensible terror and it was hard to take him anywhere. Having failed to convince the doctors that anything serious was wrong, at Easter we phoned a climbing friend and distinguished neurologist, Charlie Clarke, who used his clout to get us an appointment with our local community paediatrician the next day.

One or two friends had already mentioned tentatively a word about which I knew absolutely nothing – autism. After a brief examination the paediatrician came up with the same word, later producing an official diagnosis of 'pervasive developmental disorder on the autistic spectrum'. Dazed and shocked, we had suddenly to learn about a whole new, mysterious, baffling world called autism, then convert shock and despair into some kind of positive action. Virtually all the initiative came from Rosie as we embarked on a series of experiments with diet, vitamin supplements, psychotherapy and home education programmes. Edmond was farmed out increasingly to child-minders, so that a part of his life was lost forever to Rosie as she focused all her attention on Ollie, grieving for the child we had lost, whilst trying to start the long process of getting to love the new person he had become. At the same time, with the help of the home education programme we had to try to retrieve what was left in the scrambled wiring of his neural pathways and cling to the remnants of the old personality which still shone through the fog – the old Ollie, with his defiant sense of fun and adventure and his luminous smile.

Ollie's defiance and capacity for joy would continue to be an inspiration, even after 1996 when he almost died from leukaemia and started three long years' treatment with chemotherapy and radiotherapy, all endured without the controlling power of speech. His courage made a mockery of mountaineers' artificial, vicarious struggles in the mountains and at the moments when he was teetering on the edge of life I was forced inevitably to question the morality of self-imposed risk. But at the same time I still had to earn a living and as my income was generated solely from the world of mountains and expeditions, it seemed sensible to top up the reservoir of exploitable experience. I was also determined, despite my reservations about the morality of it all, to banish the demon of Panch Chuli, overcome my fear, and prove to myself that I could still climb a remote, glaciated mountain. Before leukaemia added another complication to Ollie's and our lives, it seemed justifiable to embark on a short expedition to an objective that posed no obvious, unreasonable dangers. The fact that someone else initiated the project somehow made it easier to take the step.

The invitation came out of the blue from Jim Wickwire, an attorney from Seattle who has managed to juggle professional career, family life and an ambitious mountaineering programme with extraordinary success. His greatest moment was in 1978 when he fulfilled his country's fifty-year quest and became, with Lou Reichardt, the first American to stand on top of K2, which at that time had only been climbed by two other parties. While Reichardt hurried down, Wickwire lingered to savour an almost mystical hour on the summit, then, like me on Everest, he was caught out by darkness and had to survive a solo bivouac near the summit. The following morning the second team of Rick Ridgeway and John Roskelley were pleasantly surprised to find him alive and making his way competently back to the top camp, urging them to continue themselves to the summit.

Roskelley and Wickwire remained good friends. Many years later, attempting the North Face of Everest, they met friends of mine, with whom I had climbed the East Face in 1988. Listening to stories about Paul's and Robert's stubborn English team mate, and about the fun and camaraderie of our East Face expedition, Wickwire decided that I might make a suitable companion for a future expedition. He had wanted for years to travel to the southern tip of South America and explore the mountains of Tierra del Fuego. And so he invited me to join him and Roskelley in the austral autumn of 1995, attempting a new route on the spectacular twin summits of Monte Sarmiento, a stunningly beautiful ice peak named after a Spanish adversary of Captain Drake, which stands sentinel over the Straits of Magellan, lashed by the almost incessant storms of the mis-named Pacific Ocean.

I too had long dreamed of visiting Tierra del Fuego's mysterious icy summits, rising from the maze of intricate waterways on Chile's convoluted coastline. I wanted to taste the bittersweet red berries of the 'Calafate' berberis that had once sustained the vitamin levels of the indigenous Indians, and I wanted to see for myself the Nothofagus species – the gnarled, lichen-dripping southern beeches which dominate some of the most beautiful and extensive temperate rainforest on earth.

I was also intrigued at the prospect of meeting Wickwire's old friend John Roskelley, who in the late seventies and early eighties had been one of the world's truly outstanding Himalayan climbers. Apart from his phenomenal climbing record, he had a reputation for abrasive, shooting-from-the-hip, straight talk and I wondered how this legendary redneck was going to take to the rather effete, semi-crippled Englishman joining the team. Awed but curious, I decided that I would go along and see what this Roskelley man was really like. To add a bit of new-mannish gentleness to the team I suggested that the fourth person should be the vegetarian Australian, Tim Macartney-Snape, whom I had recently got to know and whom the other two had met a decade earlier on Everest, when he had made the first Australian ascent, by a new route up the North Face, and without oxygen. In 1990 he had returned to the mountain, this time approaching on foot all the way from the Bay of Bengal – the first ever ascent of Everest from sea level.

It all added up to a good story – a diverse bunch of high altitude veterans heading for a beautiful, remote, mysterious mountain, all of 8,000 feet above sea level, in a region once famously called 'the uttermost ends of the earth'. The appeal was heightened by our approach to the mountain. Instead of nipping over the Straits of Magellan from Punta Arenas in a chartered fishing boat, we would sail the long scenic route from the south-east, making our way up the Beagle Channel in a fifty-foot yacht. And, to complete the veteran cast, the skipper was an eccentric American expatriate climber called Charlie Porter, whose name was a legend on the hallowed granite precipice of El Capitan in

Yosemite. In the early seventies, before taking to the sea, he had pioneered some of The Chieftain's most famous big wall routes, as well as creating spectacular new climbs on the giant arctic walls of Alaska and Baffin Island.

This was the team that would meet in Ushuaia, the most southerly port in the world, in April 1995. From January to March I was hectically busy, finally completing the illustrated history of modern Himalayan climbing which I had inherited from Andy Fanshawe, pleased to see that I was still capable of surviving on four hours' sleep a night. At the same time I was having to devote some time to helping Rosie set up Ollie's home education programme. With the house remortgaged, we now had a fund to employ helpers and people would be working with Ollie most of every day. In theory. But there were inevitable gaps and absences and there was still Edmond to look after, now nearly two. It would be very hard for Rosie but she did agree hesitantly that it would be good for me to get immersed briefly in a new adventure.

There was a last frantic flurry of activity between my study in Bath, the designers in Frome and Maggie Body, my editor in London. The last maps were sketched, captions corrected, and introduction written. The proofs arrived just in time for a final check and then it was time to leave. This time there were three people to say goodbye to. Because I had to leave very early on a Sunday morning they remained in bed and there were no faces smiling bravely from the doorway as I hauled my luggage up the path to the waiting taxi. It seemed better that way.

Chapter Fifteen

A HUNDRED MILES FROM Cape Horn, no sunlight touched the South Face of Monte Sarmiento and the snow wall fell from beneath us in billowing undulations of soft blue. Only far out beyond the mountain's shadow was there a whiter light, illuminating the crisscross pattern of crevasses and the jagged spine of the ridge where we had left our tent that morning, lashed firmly to the rock to withstand the next onslaught from the Pacific. The night had been stormy and just before daybreak the wind had risen to a new level of fury, hammering against the thin fabric, threatening to tear us from the mountain. But then, suddenly, it had died away to reveal a silent pastel dawn, with only a hint of peachy cloud wreathed benignly over distant peaks. After three weeks of almost continuously filthy weather, we were finally blessed, on this last day of the expedition, with total calm for our one and only try at the summit.

Roskelley was busy on the icewall above. Macartney-Snape – or Carpetsnake, as his Australian climbing friends call him – was standing beside me, tied into the same aluminium snowstake and alone with his own thoughts, staring down into the valley of the Lovisato river thousands of feet beneath us, where it emerged from a dammed lake at the snout of a great glacier. White icebergs, streaked black with rubble, floated incongruously in the middle of the forest. Below the lake the river meandered chalky green, like Chinese celadon, carving lazy curves through the trees, which made their own abstract patterns of dark evergreen and deciduous yellow and amber.

On the far side of the valley an old glacier was smeared thinly over the mountainside, receding to reveal the bare bones of smooth, scoured rock. Now, climbing higher, we began to see south and west beyond that ridge, tracing the line of our voyage, all the way up the intricate thread of the Beagle Channel, into the Bahia Desolada, which now looked benignly sunny, through the maze of little islands around the Brecknock Peninsula, almost out into the Pacific, where we had felt the surge of waves that came all the way from Australia, before heading back east, up the Cockburn Channel and into the dark fjord of the Seño Negro, right to the foot of the mountain where we now stood.

It had been a strange voyage. The unequivocal emptiness of western Tierra del Fuego, deserted totally since the native Indian tribes were wiped out in the last century, could be overwhelming and at times I found it almost unbearably melancholic. The persistent rain and squelching dampness of it all didn't help, but my subjective reaction to the landscape probably had more to do with a slight unease amongst the team. Our skipper, Charlie Porter, was unimpressed by his landlubber crew, apart from Macartney-Snape, whom he treated as the blue-eyed boy of the team. In fact Tim, for all his strength and competence, was quite subdued. He had recently been getting some bad press in Australia, where his idealistic outdoor courses for young people had come under attack. The attacks were misguided and malicious, but his livelihood depended on his public reputation, so he took them seriously. He looked tired and preoccupied – quite unlike the photos of the carefree young greyhound who had raced up Everest with such panache eleven years earlier.

John Roskelley, the redneck local hero of Spokane, was much mellower than the reputation that preceded him. But he seemed restless and it was obvious that his heart was no longer in expedition life. He loved to talk about his home, his wife and children, his voluntary work in the fire service and his planned new career in local politics. When he *did* reminisce about his famous Himalayan achievements the stories were self-deprecating, flippant, anti-heroic. He laughed about the time he set off bravely to solo the gigantic Great Tower of Trango and dropped the bag containing his entire rack of big wall climbing equipment into the Braldu river. Wickwire joined in when Roskelley told the story of K2 – returning exhausted from the summit to the top camp, only to have a gas stove blow up as he changed the cylinder, destroying a tent and leaving four men to share a tiny single tent and two sleeping bags at 26,000 feet.

That shared epic on K2, in 1978, had been Wickwire's defining moment of profound fulfilment, but it came in the middle of a five-year period when he seemed jinxed by disaster. Twice he saw friends fall to their deaths right in front of his eyes. On another occasion, attempting the remote Wickersham Wall of Denali, in Alaska, he had had to listen helplessly all night to the delirious ravings of his companion freezing to death forty feet beneath him, injured and jammed irretrievably inside a narrow crevasse. At home in Seattle he had had to pick up the pieces when a colleague and his family were murdered in their home on Christmas Eve. It seemed that, for all his professional success and the huge love and support of his wife Mary-Lou and five children, Jim had experienced his fair share of tragedy and the mountains did not necessarily bring solace. Several times he had tried to give up serious mountaineering. Once he had even taken the dramatic step of cancelling the dangerous-sports premium on his life insurance, only to re-instate it a few months later when he decided to return to Everest; but now, at fifty-six, his chances of reaching the top of the world were receding. In fact he had said that Sarmiento would probably be one of his last expeditions.

Perhaps we had all become too old and wise to abandon ourselves to the thrill of adventure? Or perhaps we were just trying too hard – clinging stubbornly to the withered remnants of glory? Roskelley's frequent allusions to the calm purposefulness of his home life certainly made me wonder what on earth we were doing down here, sailing past the dripping bogs and forests, whiling away the hours with books and idle chatter. I thought guiltily about Rosie, struggling to co-ordinate all the helpers working with Ollie in his special playroom, coping with endless meals, changing both boys' nappies on her own, trying to snatch moments with Edmond and find time to buy presents for his second birthday. It would have been easier if I had felt more committed to what I was doing, but on the rare occasions we glimpsed some malevolent glacier glowering down through a break in the clouds, I wasn't at all sure that I even *wanted* to climb anything. All I could feel was a kind of dull dread. I wondered whether Panch Chuli had poisoned everything, blighting for ever the magic of wild places.

Then, fitfully, the magic returned. I think it was almost through a conscious effort – a realization that I was actually incredibly lucky to be here and that, if I was going to desert my family for a month, I ought at least to have the decency to enjoy myself. I began to value again those 'moments' that didn't necessarily have any direct connection with the actual climbing process, such as rowing ashore at the enchanted anchorage of Caleta Olla, where we were startled by white-striped Fitzroy dolphins dashing exuberantly around the dinghy; or, a few days later, making our first reconnaissance beneath Monte Sarmiento itself, and hearing the whirring drone of the air parted by immense wings as condors sailed past, a few yards from where we sat. Down at Base Camp I even grew grudgingly fond of the insolent fox that pissed in our drinking water and stole the salami.

Our camp was a just a few yards up from the beach, hidden inside a fantasy forest that was Arthur Rackham, Tolkien and Grimm all rolled into one. The huge Nothofagus trees were encrusted with exquisite jade lichen and, where light penetrated the canopy, brilliant pink *Philesia buxifolia* – a sort of epiphytic fuschia – sprouted from the host trees. Above Base Camp, we toiled to build a bridge over the Lovisato river, hacked our way through the forest and trudged across bogs, carrying luggage up to the base of Sarmiento's west ridge. The therapy of hard physical work began to take effect. I was relieved to see that my knee was coping with the heavy loads, thrilled to experience again the primal physical satisfaction of moving through difficult country. It was also good to experience again the contented glow of tired warmth after a hard day, sitting round a fire with a huge meal and mugs of local red wine, watching orange sparks drift up towards the forest canopy and just occasionally, if we were lucky, glimpsing stars beyond. The wine also knocked off some of the rough edges. We began to laugh and talk more openly and I started to feel an increasing warmth for my companions. I was cheered by the discovery that expeditions could still be fun and remembered a comment Charlie Clarke had made the previous year. Amidst all the consultations and discussions about what might be happening in Ollie's mind, Charlie had said during one telephone conversation, 'whatever happens, you mustn't give up climbing.'

The clinching moment of rehabilitation came when we reached the glacier and for the first time in almost three years I strapped crampons to my boots, noting the shiny new section that had replaced the spike bent so brutally during my fall. Although I had been rock-climbing several times since the accident, ice tools seemed emblematic of a nastier, riskier world of big mountains. At first I moved tentatively up the glacier, not even attempting to keep up with the others, then the rhythm returned and I began to enjoy the reassuring crunch of steel on ice.

That day we reached the site for our second camp, excavating a platform from a snowdrift sheltered by rocky crags. Although the sun was shining for the first time on the expedition, the wind remained as histrionic as ever, coming at us from a cloudless sky in fitful, unpredictable blasts, with no protection once we started back down to Camp One. One of these blasts caught Wickwire off balance. He shot across the ice, crashing into a boulder and spraining his ankle. The next day exactly the same thing happened to Porter, except that he was less lucky and dislocated his shoulder.

It took several hours to rope him down to Camp One in what was beginning to look like a replay of the Panch Chuli disaster. In the shelter of the largest tent we tried to put back Porter's shoulder. Macartney-Snape had once had to reduce a dislocation in a remote bush hospital and was confident he could remember what to do. As a trained paramedic, Roskelley was also prepared to give it a try. While they stood over Porter, working the arm, Wickwire sat on his legs and I held down his head. In the absence of morphine, he chewed on a piece of beef jerky and dug his fingernails into Jim's calf muscle.

It was ghastly. Tim and John heaved repeatedly on the arm, lifting and twisting until they felt the ball and socket on the cusp of realignment. But each time they had to give up when they failed to make the final connection. Charlie was extraordinarily brave, subjecting himself time after time to the same violent torture. I thought it was like witnessing childbirth all over again, feeling wimpishly relieved that I was not the one having to face all the pain.

As the torture progressed the beef jerky in Charlie's mouth was reduced to pink pulp and Wickwire's leg was lacerated by the anguished fingernails. It was a bizarre scene. The low torchlight had the effect of garish footlights on some perverted sado-masochistic ritual, with five grown men locked in a contorted struggle, one of them periodically screaming in pain. Conscious of how odd we looked, Roskelley suddenly announced, 'I think I'll just shut that door.' Perhaps he was worried that the neighbours might start talking.

After about thirty attempts, Tim finally admitted defeat and we all agreed that Charlie would have to get professional help. Down at the anchorage the next afternoon we surveyed the shambolic ruins of our expedition. Our time was nearly up. Wickwire was unfit for climbing. Porter was in excruciating pain and needed urgently to reach the nearest hospital, a hundred miles away in Punta Arenas. As he discussed the arrangements to sail that night I realized selfishly how much I wanted to climb Sarmiento. After all my fears and doubts I now wanted to see this thing through. Even the thought of leaving the darkening southern autumn and returning home to emerald spring foliage, lengthening evenings, Rosie and Ollie, Edmond playing in the sandpit ... even the knowledge that there might be some unstable ice cliff or cornice up there, waiting to take all those things away from me – none of that altered the realization that I wanted to finish the job, to see the thing through. In the end any climb, no matter how extraordinary, or beautiful, or frightening, or dangerous, or absurd, is a project to complete and it doesn't always help to ponder its purpose too deeply. Like most of the jobs and hobbies and pastimes and holidays and other irrelevancies with which we pass our lives, it doesn't always bear up to scrutiny. Sometimes it's best to suspend disbelief, accept that 'this is what I have come to do' and immerse oneself completely in the doing.

The doing was now threatened. Porter was anxious to get to hospital as quickly as possible and really wanted a full crew. It was only after some persuasion from Macartney-Snape that he agreed generously to go with just Wickwire and the ship's cook, Minos, who would help him navigate our boat, *Gondwana*, across the Straits of Magellan. Wickwire, who had worked so hard to make the whole expedition possible, gave us all his support, encouraging Macartney-Snape, Roskelley and me to snatch this last chance at the summit and promising somehow to return and pick us up in five days' time when we would all be due to catch flights home. He never once hinted at his own disappointment.

With poignant irony the sky was completely clear that evening. For the first time we could see the mountain from sea level, its two peaks glowing violet. I felt sad to be parting, but also excited to be paddling ashore in the inflatable, with the silence broken only by the dip of our oars and the distant chug of *Gondwana* as her navigation lights headed north for the Straits of Magellan.

Roskelley was more practical. 'He wouldn't even let us take his outboard motor. You know, it sure as hell spooks me when I can't hear the sound of an internal combustion engine. I mean, we are *marooned* . . . If Wick doesn't manage to come and pick us up, we're just stuck on this peninsula with nowhere to go.' His lukewarm enthusiasm cooled further when normal stormy conditions returned in the morning, but Tim and I kept the heat on, cajoling him back up to Camp One, determined to have his company on the climb. Tramping through the drizzle, I talked for the first time about Ollie. I had long since realized that beneath the redneck caricature there was a highly intelligent, kind, generous Roskelley longing to get out. Hearing about the the baffling mysteries of autistic behaviour, he was predictably sensitive, touched by what our family was going through, sympathetic without resorting to sentimentality.

Camp One was swept by rain and the next day the weather was

no better, but we managed to talk Roskelley up to Camp Two, where we lashed the tent firmly to the rocks. The wind rose steadily through the night and just before dawn the tent nearly took off. Then suddenly it all died away and we realized that our gamble had paid off as we emerged to a miraculously clear morning. Once again, at the eleventh hour, on the last day of an expedition, I had a chance to snatch my summit.

It was all down to speed and efficiency and I felt glad to be with two such superlative climbers. They took turns at leading, moving with cautious stealth, reading the mountain's surface with fine-honed instinct, weaving a line from hummock to hummock, seeking out firm ice and avoiding the drifted powder in avalanche-prone hollows. Icicle-fringed crevasses and glinting towers broke the monotony and as we climbed higher the massed summits of the Darwin Range appeared gradually in the east, floating in a sea of harmless billowing cloud.

At the start of the climb there was a tacit assumption that Tim and John would share the leading. In fact, Roskelley seemed slightly surprised that he was not doing *all* the leading. This was the man who had forced through the route on the North-West Ridge of Nanda Devi; who had insisted on climbing every single pitch on the first ascent of Cholatse, in Nepal; who had sent back his companions on Makalu because they were moving too slowly, and had continued alone to the world's fifth highest summit. He did not suffer fools gladly and he liked to be in charge, but the apparent arrogance stemmed from a deep instinctive sense of survival. He had the air of a wild animal – wary, alert and attuned to every possible danger – and he did not want anyone else leading him into trouble.

I respected his skill, but I was also quite an experienced climber and, if only for the sake of my own self-esteem, I was determined to take a more positive role in this climb. Ever since my first regular roped climbs at eighteen I had always shared the lead – on one expedition, to the 8,000-metre peak Shishapangma, I had led virtually every pitch of the route – and that was the way I wanted to continue. It would have been all too easy to use Panch Chuli as a reason to opt out and defer to the others, but I wanted to prove to myself that I could still take charge. I didn't want to spend the rest of my life as a passenger.

So, soon after Roskelley led his steep icewall, I asked to take over. Tim suggested, 'why don't I do this next section of trail-breaking and you can take over when we get to the interesting bit.' For 'interesting' read steep; but, even though I couldn't match the Carpetsnake's long-legged stride, I insisted on doing my stint of deep-snow footslogging, before getting on to the steep ice, where the face reared up to about seventy-five degrees. The ice was in good condition, so the climbing was not particularly difficult; nevertheless it was wonderful, after three years' absence, to be balancing up on the steel tips of my crampons, with the rope dropping away beneath me.

I stopped to bring up the others and Tim led through, continuing up on to a sloping ramp beneath the gigantic summit ice mushroom. All the way up the 3,000-foot face we had been wondering about this fantastical, Gaudiesque confectionery. To engineer one's way precariously up those overhanging, whirling, rime formations, hanging stirrups from alloy snowstakes, would probably take several hours, and our only realistic hope lay in the ramp, which we hoped led out on to the ridge. Tim raced up the gangway, followed by John and then me. It did slant obligingly right underneath the immense overhang and soon I saw the other two waiting at the top of the ramp, silhouetted in a notch against the bright sky. It felt miraculous to emerge so easily from the shadowy South Face into brilliant light; even more miraculous to climb out of the notch and discover a smooth broad ridge leading straight to the top of the summit mushroom where we gathered at three o'clock in the afternoon to enjoy our moment of success.

If only Wickwire could have been with us. I wondered whether he was watching from Punta Arenas, a hundred miles away. On a clear day you could see Sarmiento from the sea port. And we had been blessed with the one totally clear day since we had left Puerto Williams three weeks earlier. Unlike my last summit on Panch Chuli V, this one could be savoured, with time and space to enjoy the luminous pattern of mountain and sea, stretching for a hundred miles in every direction.

Tim produced his summit surprise, a huge slice of the fruit cake his mother bakes for all his expeditions – the same rich recipe that had already been twice to the summit of Everest, to Annapurna II and Dunagiri, to Gasherbrum IV ... I insisted on some summit photos and another last look round, to soak up the precious moment. Tim and I looked across at the East Summit. Like the West Summit, the East had only been climbed once, in 1956. The expedition was led by a Salesian missionary called Alberto de Agostini, and it concluded a quest he had first started in 1913. As Wickwire had said, 'we're not interested in besting Italians, but it would be nice to pull off both summits in a single three-week trip.'

We gazed along the connecting mushroomed ridge. Tim reckoned that we could do it in two hours, with another hour back to the col in the middle. It would mean a bivouac at the col without sleeping bags, but perhaps we could dig a snowcave ... Before we took our dreams any further, Roskelley made it quite clear that no one was staying up for the night. Our new route up the West Peak was reward enough. Like Tilman on Nanda Devi we had to be grateful for our 'forty-five minutes into which was crowded the worth of many hours of glorious life' and return to earth before nightfall.

Roskelley set a brisk pace but, racing after the tugging rope, I tried to memorize the serene beauty of it all – the figures silhouetted against the unearthly crystalline form of the East Peak, with the Darwin range, first explored by Eric Shipton in the sixties, stretching into the distance; then the warm glow of evening sunlight as we descended the ramp to set up the first abseil beneath the great overhang of the mushroom, glinting against the orange sheen of the sea below.

The abseils went smoothly but darkness fell before we reached the foot of the face. We stopped to put on headtorches and, after some discussion, decided to put on parkas as well. Five minutes later we thanked ourselves for this precaution, when we suddenly had to pull hoods tight over our helmets. Without any warning, as if in vindication of Roskelley's decision not to linger, the wind had returned. Our benign mountain was transformed instantly into a malignant maelstrom. Within seconds, the spindrift was pouring down the face – limitless cataracts of it, falling on our heads with a relentless swishing noise, forcing its way behind glasses, plastering itself on to foreheads and freezing them to a numb ache.

Visibility was reduced to a few yards. Perched at the abseil anchors, waiting my turn to descend into the darkness, I was suddenly back on Panch Chuli, reliving the nightmare. As the waves of spindrift poured over my head, stifling my breath and freezing the exposed skin on my face, fear also seeped through my consciousness. Piercing the darkness with my headtorch beam, I stared in terror at the ice screw anchors, watched the ropes disappearing into the emptiness beneath my feet. With horrible clarity I visualized the lurching fall down the mountain, imagined the detail of each bulging ice cliff, felt the air thumped brutally from my lungs, heard the ringing explosions in my skull, calculated how far I would fall before being smashed to death and thrown, crumpled, on to the glacier.

All desire to lead and take charge drained away. I just cowered and shivered, moaning with the cold pain of it all, relieved to let

Roskelley and Tim organize the abseils. Groping though the swirling black torrent, I let them guide me into the anchors, let them navigate with masterly intuition back through the maze of ice hummocks at the bottom of the face, and just followed meekly out on to the flatter surface of the glacier.

After two hours of malevolent torment it was all over and by nine o'clock that night we were safely back in the tent, thawing out beside the roaring stove, enjoying the sweet thrill of success. In the morning we clawed our way back down to Camp One, roping up on the most easy terrain, determined not to let the wind inflict any more injuries. Two days later Wickwire, true to his word, arrived to fetch us in a chartered fishing boat; *Gondwana* was moored near Punta Arenas and Charlie was already on his way to the capital, Santiago, to see Chile's top orthopaedic surgeon.

Another fierce storm swept through from the Pacific that night, the fishermen anchoring in a sheltered cove, but by the time we continued in the morning the storm had blown over. The Magellan Strait was calm and the surrounding islands were bathed in pellucid, blue autumnal light. As we chugged north towards the South American mainland, the Tierra del Fuego archipelago dwindled on the southern horizon until all that was left was the impossibly white tower of Monte Sarmiento, its twin summits gleaming above an infinity of blue water. It was hard to equate that benign radiance with the vicious storm four days earlier when we had fought our way down through the spindrift cataract – hard to decide which image should be retained as the truer memory – the dream or the harsh reality?

During the grim descent, drowning in icy spindrift, I had kept telling myself to fix the sheer awfulness of it in my memory, so that every time in the future when I dreamed heroic dreams of tantalizing castles in the sky I would just have to click on the memory to deter myself. A nice idea, but it's never as simple as that. The memory of the suffering always fades, while the fulfilment glows brighter. Even the horror of falling through the Himalayan night had not changed that. Panch Chuli had not proved to be the Road to Damascus. It had certainly made me more nervous, more cautious, more hesitant, more aware of how much I wanted to stay alive; but it didn't make me a different, better person, striking out in a completely new direction. At best I had learned a little humility. The accumulated experience of half a lifetime wandering in mountain country was too deeply ingrained to shrug off so irrevocably. And it was not *just* wandering. I knew perfectly well that, exciting as it had been to sail through the Fuegan channels and explore the fantasy forest, the plot would have been incomplete without the final summit denouement. Just *looking*, was, sadly, not enough. That was why Jim, for all his generous congratulations and obvious pleasure in the success of the expedition, later admitted his disappointment at missing that effulgent hour on the summit.

Home was in all our thoughts. Wickwire had an important lawsuit to conclude. Roskelley was longing to get his teeth into his new career in Spokane. Tim and I both had lectures booked in four days' time, and I was now completely ready to return to the northern spring, with a whole summer stretching ahead, at home with Rosie, Ollie and Edmond. I was happy to be leaving the huge skies of southern Patagonia, but the leaving was all the sweeter for having so recently stood on that ice tower now fading on the southern horizon.

For all the richness of 'normal' everyday life, it is good sometimes to trespass high in the sky and live life with uncommon intensity, experiencing something that gets close to the sublime. I had no idea when I would next be returning to the mountains, but I knew that I had already had more than my fair share of those sublime moments. I had touched some of the most magical places on Earth – places whose beauty is inherently dangerous and where Man was never meant to go – and in the process I had seen my companions, those strangely driven oddballs and misfits who make up the mountaineering community, at their very best. Nowhere had that been truer than on Panch Chuli V, the Pandava's hearth where I so nearly left the Earth.

Appendix 1

INDO-BRITISH PANCH CHULI EXPEDITION 1992

Climbing team:

Bhupesh Ashar
Chris Bonington (co-leader)
Muslim Contractor
Monesh Devjani
Harish Kapadia (co-leader)
Vijay Kothari
Graham Little
Dick Renshaw
Victor Saunders
Stephen Sustad
Stephen Venables

Liaison Officer:

Wing-Cdr Anil Srivastava

Support team:

Pasang Bodh (sirdar)
Harsinh Balaksinh

Harsinh Mangalsinh
Khubram
Prakash Chand
Revatram (cook)
Suratram
Sundersingh
Yograj

Sponsored by:

Godrej
Kodak
The Times
Future Publishing
Air India
Mount Everest Foundation
British Mountaineering Council

Appendix 2

EXPEDITION DIARY

6 May British team (apart from Little) departs from London.

7 Arrives in Bombay.

10 Indo-British team departs from Bombay on night express.

11 Little meets rest of team in Delhi

12 Arrive a Ranikhet.

13 Arrive at Munsiary.

15 Drive to roadhead and start walk-in from Madkot.

18 Reach First Base Camp at tongue of Uttari Balati Glacier.

22 Whole team established at Glacier Camp.

23 Recce to Advance Base.

28 Bonington and Little make *first ascent of Sahadev West.* Rest of team established at Advance Base.

1 June Kapadia's team makes first recce towards Balati Plateau.

1–5 Renshaw, Saunders, Sustad and Venables traverse Menaka /Rajrambha (*First ascent of Menaka and new route on Rajrambha*).

6–7 Contractor, Devjani and Bodh make *second ascent of SW Ridge of Panch Chuli II.*

6–8 Bonington and Little make *first ascent of W Ridge of Panch Chuli II.*

8 Kothari helicoptered from Glacier Camp with sprained ankle.

11 Rest of team all back at First Base Camp.

14 Ashar and Little depart for home. Rest of team starts traverse to Pyunshani valley.

16 Second Base Camp established in Pyunshani Valley.

17–20 Renshaw, Saunders, Sustad and Venables (with Bonington climbing to final camp) make *first ascent of Panch Chuli V.*

20 Contractor, Devjani, Kapadia, Khubram and Chand make *first ascents of Draupadi and Panchali Chuli from Bainti Col.*

21 Accident on Panch Chuli V. Venables lowered to camp in high cwm.

22 Bonington and Sustad descend to Second Base Camp.

23 Bonington reaches Munsiary. Rescue operation started.

24 First helicopter recce from Bareilly.

25 Venables lifted from high camp on third attempt. Flown to Bareilly.

27 Rest of team all back in Munsiary.

29 Venables flies back to London.

1 July Rest of British team flies back to London.

Appendix 3

Approaching from west	Approaching from east
1929	Hugh Ruttledge reaches c.5700 m on Sona Glacier. He thinks that the main peak is climbable by North Arête.
1950	Bill Murray and the Scottish Himalaya Expedition get slightly higher on the Sona Glacier, but fail to reach the North Col.
1951 Heinrich Harrer and Frank Thomas pioneer the route up the Uttari Balati Glacier to the Balati Plateau and attempt West Ridge of main peak.	
1952 P. N. Nikore attempts western approach.	
D. D. Joshi leads an Indian team as far as the Balati Plateau.	
1953 P. N. Nikore claims first ascent of main peak via Uttari Balati Glacier. With no convincing evidence, his claim is rejected.	
1964 Group Captain A. K. Choudhary leads Indian Mountaineering Foundation team to Balati Plateau and attempts South-West Ridge of main peak. Mistaken claim to have climbed P.III, P.IV and P.V all in one day is not formally withdrawn until 1992.	
1970	C. K. Mitra leads team of Indian National Cadet Corp to explore Sona and Meola Glaciers.

207

1972   Hukam Singh leads India Tibet Border Police team to make first ascent of Panch Chuli I via Uttari Balati Glacier.

1973   Mahendra Singh leads another ITBP team to make first ascent of main peak (Panch Chuli II) by South-West Ridge.

1988   Aloke Surin's Bombay team attempts to reach South Col from Meola Glacier.

1991   Captain N. B. Gurung leads Indian Army Gurkha regiment to climb North-East Ridge of P.II – second ascent of main peak.

A month later (September) Colonel Siraj Bhan Dalal leads a Kumaun-Naga regiment team to climb East Face and East Ridge of P.II from Meola Glacier. Third ascent of P.II.

1992   Chris Bonington and Harish Kapadia lead Indo-British Expedition. P.II climbed by South West Ridge and West Ridge (4th and 5th ascents of main peak). First ascents of Panch Chuli V, Sahadev West, Panch Chali Chuli, Draupadi and Menaka. Also first ascent of Rajrambha from south.

1993   New Zealand team led by John Nankervis makes first ascent of Panch Chuli IV from Pyunshani valley.

1996   A team from Bombay, led by Divyesh Muni attempted Panch Chuli III from the Pyunshani Valley. The attempt was abandoned after E. Theophilus was injured in a fall, trying to reach the col between Panch III and Panch II.

A team from the Indian Mountaineering Foundation, led by S. Bhattacharya attempted Panch Chuki III from the Meola Glacier. They climbed the east ridge direct to within 80 metres of the summit.